MICHAEL SHAMIYEH ❮
and DOM Research Laboratory (Ed.)

G000113149

ORGANIZING
FOR Ǝ⅁NAHƆ\
PROFESSION Integrating architectural
thinking in other fields

Birkhäuser – Publishers for Architecture
Basel | Boston | Berlin

Editor
Michael Shamiyeh

Copy Editing
Kelly Klingler

Design
Reklamebüro Linz/Austria

A CIP catalogue record for this book is available from the
Library of Congress, Washington D.C., USA

Bibliographic information published by Die Deutsche Bibliothek Die Deutsche Bibliothek lists this publication in the
Deutsche Nationalbibliografie; Detailed bibliographic data is
available in the Internet at http://dnb.ddb.de.

© 2007 Birkhäuser – Publishers for Architecture,
P.O.Box 133, CH-4010 Basel, Switzerland
Part of Springer Science+Business Media
Printed on acid-free paper produced from
chlorine-free pulp. TCF ∞

2

Printed in Germany

ISBN-10: 3-7643-7809-3
ISBN-13: 978-3-7643-7809-7

Despite intensive research efforts it was not possible to identify the copyright
holders in all cases. Justifiable claims will be honoured within the parameters
of customary agreements.

9 8 7 6 5 4 3 2 1

BUNDESKANZLERAMT ∎ KUNST

Michael Shamiyeh

Architect in practice and head of Design-Organisation-Media
Research Laboratory. Graduated with distinction as an architect from the Technical University of Vienna and has a Master
in Architecture from Harvard University Graduate School of
Design. He has done extensive research work in Jerusalem
and Berlin. Together with the cultural theorist Thomas Duschlbauer he is co-founder of the interdisciplinary Bureau for
Architecture, Urbanism and Culture (BAU|KULTUR) that
seeks to define new relationships – as much theoretical as
practical – between a contemporary architectural production and a contemporary cultural situation. Thus, the firm is
concerned with realising projects at home and abroad, teaching, consulting and investigation of cultural phenomena.

Design Organisation Media Research Laboratory (DOM)

3

DOM is based at The University of Arts and Industrial Design
and run in close collaboration with the Ars Electronica Center, Linz. Point of departure for DOM is the assumption that
contemporary societal and technical changes have led to
new conclusions in the field of urbanism, architecture and
design. As a sort of independent Think Tank DOM attempts
to help organisations to innovate, to define early relevant
topics, to show the need for action, and to formulate a set of
future actions. For this purpose DOM closely operates with
other institutions and experts at home and abroad, and organises international conferences and workshops.
In presenting the results of investigations in a clear and understandable way DOM intends to bring in lasting impulses
and fundamentals for (public) debate.

TABLE OF CONTENTS ❮

5

ACKNOWLEDGEMENT ❮

Organizing for Change is the third book on a series of DOM conferences that began with an idea in 2002 to establish architecture as the host of a cross-cultural and multi-disciplinary discussion of architecture and contemporary culture. It was never spoken publicly but primary intention of organizing those conferences was to start a process of rethinking the legitimacy of architecture and to discover another kind of architecture. Accordingly, the objective of those conferences was a) to investigate on different levels some of the effects of Western societies and market economy on architecture and on the architects in particular, b) to question how architects justify their creative activities to society, and c) to identify possibilities to actively apply core competencies of our profession in other areas of life. In preparing the book on the subject of the 3rd Conference I got the strong conviction that we have made a substantial step in this process – a step which would not been possible without the great participation and support of a multitude of institutions, sponsors, hosts, and of course, ambitious architects, designers, theorists, historians, artists, philosophers, cultural theorists, economists and many others, who shared their work and ideas in discussions and books like this one, giving content and meaning to the project. Many thanks to all of you! Without your engagement and tireless support, neither DOM nor the conferences, and subsequently this book, would exist.

In particular I would like to mention my mentor and indefatigable rector of the University of Arts and Industrial Design, Reinhard Kannonier, who has to be thanked for his long lasting trust and support in this challenging endeavor. I also thank Gerfried Stocker, director of the collaborating Ars Electronica Center, who from the first day on helped to make DOM happen and supported it with his crew.

A great dept of gratitude I owe to my colleague and cultural theorist Thomas Duschlbauer as well as Christian Presslmayer, who – coming from the field of economics – helped me to get deeper insights on system thinking and organizational theories. Due to their commitment, intelligence and knowledge of this subject, they had a great impact on the development and success of DOM3.

The extraordinarily ambitious crew of AEC, in particular Katrin Emler, Ellen Fethke, Elisabeth Sachsenhofer, and Manuela Pfaffenberger assumed the fiscal responsibilities for the conferences and provided valuable expertise in managing them. Furthermore, I wish thank the following staff members of the University of Arts and Industrial Design Linz as well as of the AEC for their great support: Gregor Traugott for maintaining each year's website; Siglinde Lang for her support in press and communications agendas; Karl Schmidinger and Magnus Hofmüller for their technical support and last but not least Irene Roselstorfer, who assisted me in the production of this book.

Ulrike Ruh of Birkhaeuser Publishers deserves special thanks as she has helped again to bring the discussed subject to the attention of an international audience by publishing this book. Claus Zerenko, director of Reklamebüro, and his staff members successfully managed the book's layout for the third time with great conviction. Mel Greenwald, a reliable contributor to DOM since the first days, translated again most of the German written articles.

Above all, one is constantly mindful of the generous confidence displayed by the State Secretary for the Arts and Media of the Federal Chancellery of Austria and the governments of the Province of Upper Austrian and the City of Linz who, since the beginning of DOM, have provided grants to help support the conferences and subsequently this publication. Lastly, the greatest contribution, the one for which I am most grateful, is the unwavering support of all the authors whose work appears in the following pages. Without their extraordinary commitment and energy, the project would not be as exciting and interesting as it is now.

Michael Shamiyeh

FOREWORD ‹

In the '90s, it became abundantly clear that globalization was triggering substantial changes in the field of architecture too. Previous DOM conferences sought to elaborate on them on a number of levels with the aim of yielding insights applicable to architecture as practiced in this day and age. The "Organizing for Change" conference constituted an effort to come to terms with this wide-ranging transformation. After all, at this point, particularly acute powers of comprehension are hardly called for to recognize the breathtaking speed with which the framework conditions

– AND ESPECIALLY THOSE THAT IMPACT ARCHITECTURE –

9

are changing under the influence of the manic cycles of the market economy and intensifying mediatization.

The following focal-point issues were discussed in this connection:
First off, that it simply takes too long to bring an architectural project from conception to fruition. As is patently obvious, the realization process of a major piece of construction now lasts several years. In stark contrast to this, however, there are hardly any political or economic factors that, after having served as the bases of architectural decisions, have not changed – and radically so – over this same length of time. In other words, we are confronted today by the paradox that the slowness of architecture has been left in the dust by the changes that all political or economic initiatives have been undergoing. The bottom line: architecture is in a certain sense too slow to be able to effectively participate in what is going on around it.

What's more – and this is indirectly connected with the first point – it is increasingly clear that the static character of architecture is sharply at odds with rapid changes and developments in the market economy. No sooner is a building completed than it is outed as already obsolete. Thus, one can nowadays proceed under the assumption that the design of cities goes hand in hand with the design of their decay. Also (digital) media's penetration into and saturation of every aspect of our lives – together with the dissolution of physical boundaries that is associated with this phenomenon

– massively calls into question one of architecture's most elemental concepts: namely, either to bring people together physically or to physically separate them.

Isn't it typical that just as architecture's legitimation seems to be on the wane, the term "architecture" has become one of the most frequently employed metaphors for the organizational structures of all aspects of life? Consider, for example, buzzwords like systems architecture, corporate organizational architecture, etc. Whereas architects deal solely with the design of physical structures, the rest of the world speaks of architecture as if it were a medium in which the essence of all types of organizations and structures manifests itself.

Paradoxically, we architects cannot participate in this process. The reason for this is apparently simple to explain: All that we have ever learned has been to translate the organizational formulations that we have come up with – for instance, the organization of functions – into physical-material forms. This means that the most fundamentally definitive values of our discipline have made it incumbent upon us to react in the form of an architectural structure instead of inquiring into the extent to which the organizational structures that we create might also be feasible in some other form or even applicable to and utilizable in other spheres of life.

THIS SEEMS TO BE PRECISELY THE PROBLEM OF ARCHITECTURE THESE DAYS.

Therefore, it is up to us to assess the extent to which architectural thinking can also be applied to other areas in order to thereby perhaps succeed in making the transition from an architecture of form to the architecture of organization.

The following specialized fields and issues occupied the focal point of our analyses:

Business Meets Design

Stirrings of great interest in design are evident throughout the US economy at present, whereby what is at the core of this interest is not so much the realization that dawned in the 1990s that design plays not an insignificant role in net value added to the economy as a whole but rather the recognition that our world – and our business enterprises and organizations in particular – should not be regarded as something static but as a living system. The rapid transformation process that has been taking place worldwide thus necessitates that we pursue lifelong learning in order to adapt to and successfully deal with constantly emerging changes. In fact, many managers have come to regard the way that designers go about their tasks

– PROCEEDING IN A MODE THAT IS CREATIVE AND PRAGMATIC IN EQUAL MEASURE –

as a very promising approach to effectively confronting a wide variety of problems. According to this view, planning and strategic processes should be reformulated as design processes and managers converted from administrators to business designers.

Interact Or Die

The rules governing the way things work in the media nowadays and the associated intensification of the mediatization of all aspects of our lives raises the issue of how to adequately design the flows and activities of human beings and organizations. Since time immemorial, architecture – due to its material presence – has either brought elements together or separated them from each other. But now that media have fundamentally modified the very concepts of fusion and partition, the question that increasingly insinuates itself into the spotlight of our attention is whether or not architecture must, in response, revise its own core values and essential concepts. Then, the issue would no longer be the accommodation or implementation of programs and how these might be experienced, but rather the design of flexible organizations, and thus no longer design concentrating on form but the design of processes.

Designing Communication

The EU's wish to establish itself more solidly in the perception of its citizens as well as to achieve increased

visibility as the center of change and the accompanying commissioning of architect Rem Koolhaas/ AMO to design a new graphical language, a new symbolic vocabulary for the EU constitutes a striking illustration of how the architect's sphere of activity can undergo a substantial shift nowadays. For many Europeans, the EU exists solely as abstract flows of funds and streams of data, as a market and a media-based reality, which is why it is thoroughly justifiable to speak of the Union's identity problem. The vision of a future Europe that Rem Koolhaas/ AMO came up with revealed architecture's great potential in this context: the capacity to offer intelligent strategic approaches and, in doing so, to design a cultural concept.

Positions of Neo-realism

Architecture has always had to do with the design and organization of physical spaces. Even if steadfastly upholding architecture's most fundamental values prevents the discovery of another type of architecture – since, after all, if everything is architecture or architectural, then we can expand our sphere of activities without any restrictions whatsoever – erecting physical structures will nevertheless remain an essential aspect of the architectural domain. The question that then arises is, on one hand, how the architect operatively faces the problem of the metamorphosis of reality and on the other hand, how the constructed reality permits or even furthers the emergence of changes. Numerous models of operative activity are under discussion, ranging from total rejection of a particular assignment

– IN THIS MODEL, THE PROJECT REMAINS UNREALIZED BUT RE-MAINS DISCURSIVELY IN PLAY AND THEREBY LEADS TO CHANGES –

and reprogramming all the way to the organization of unsolicited interventions or "event structures" in space and time.
Considering architecture in the context of the massive changes currently taking place reveals that our profession is more reactionary and conservative than the rest of the world might suspect. Accordingly, the challenge that

architects today ought to – or perhaps even have to – face involves questioning the definitions of our profession. It is essential to ask which skills or what bodies of knowledge are – or could be – inherent to architecture; how we could go about legitimating ourselves to society on the basis of these capabilities and insights; and which possibilities exist to apply these skills and this knowledge in other areas too.

THIS BOOK REPRESENTS THE EFFORT TO CONTRIBUTE TO THIS IN A WAY THAT IS INTERESTING AND INTERDISCIPLINARY.

11 As dictated by the theme itself, this volume has been intentionally divided into two interrelated domains that deliver insightful reflections of one another. The PROFESSION section focuses on the change or even transformation of the profession into other fields; the SPACE section sheds light on operative and architectural strategies, and elaborates on concrete findings and insights that have emerged from dealing with change. Thus, depending on the reader's interest, each section constitutes a discrete entity that can be read independently of the other.

Michael Shamiyeh

SPEAKERS ❮

 Marko Ahtisaari ❮ Marko Ahtisaari is Director of Design Strategy at Nokia, a world leader in mobile communications. Prior to this role Ahtisaari worked in the Insight & Foresight, Corporate Strategy unit at Nokia where he was responsible for identifying and driving new growth opportunities based on user experience. Born in Helsinki, Finland and raised on three continents in Helsinki, Dar es Salaam and New York, Ahtisaari studied economics, philosophy and music at Columbia University in the City of New York where he went on to become a popular lecturer. Prior to joining Nokia, Ahtisaari built and lead the mobile practice at startup design consultancy Satama Interactive. He is a founder and chairman of the board of Aula, a network of technologists, designers, artists, entrepreneurs, researchers and civil society actors with the goal of creating innovations for a better mobile life. Ahtisaari is a recognized thought leader on the future of user experience and mobile culture. In the in-between moments he continues to compose ambient music for public and private spaces.

 Robert Bauer ❮ Robert M. Bauer is Associate Professor of Organizational Design at Johannes Kepler University Linz, Austria. Currently he is a Visiting Professor at the Joseph L. Rotman School of Management, University of Toronto. His research aims at a better understanding of different ways of knowing, including, but not limited to, formal and every day language statements. He explores the consequences of different epistemological modes for organizational design and behavior as well as for the philosophy of organization science. He is also a registered psychotherapist and has worked extensively as an executive coach and management consultant.

 Norbert Bolz ❮ Norbert Bolz was born in 1953 in Ludwigshafen, Germany. After graduating from the Max-Plank-Secondary School, he studied Philosophy, Religion as well as German and English language and literature studies in Mannheim, Heidelberg and Berlin. He wrote his dissertation on the aesthetics of Theodore Adorno under the religious philosopher Jacob Taubes and remained his assistant until Taubes death. He wrote his postdoctoral on „The Philosophical Extremism between the World Wars". From 1992–2002 he was University Professor for Communications Theory at the GH Essen University, Institute for Art and Design. Since 2002 Professor at the Technical University in Berlin, Institute for Language and Communication in the field of Media Science.

 Ole Bouman ❮ Ole Bouman is editor of Archis International and www.archis. org. He is event designer, writer and curator in architecture, art and design. Recent booksinclude Time Wars, 2003, a revaluation of the time dimension in our society. He was curator of Manifesta 3 in Ljubljana, 2000. He is head of the current series of "rsvp events" in collaboration with AMO, to be held in 9 global cities.

Thomas Duschlbauer ❮ Associate Member of Faculty of Goldsmith College, London; cultural theorist and lecturer at the FH Hagenberg. Graduated in Science of Communication and Politics at the University of Vienna. Several research stays in the USA (University of North Carolina at Chapel Hill and Duke University) and U.K. (University of Birmingham and Open University at Milton Keynes). Furthermore, he graduated with a Ph.D. on the socio-cultural implications of new media from the University of Vienna and as a Master in Arts in Cultural Studies at the University of London. He participated in several congresses and published in scholarly magazines. 2001 he published „Medien und Kultur im Zeitalter der X-Kommunikation" (Braumüller Vlg., Vienna). Together with Michael Shamiyeh he is co-founder of the Bureau for Architecture, Urbanism and Culture (BAU|KULTUR).

Michael Kieslinger ❮ Michael Kieslinger is founder and CEO of Fluidtime Ltd., a company focusing on the communication of dynamic time information. He was Associate Professor at the Interaction Design Institute Ivrea in Italy from 2001 until 2004 responsible for the Service Design unit. From 1995-98 he worked for a research group based at the Royal Institute of Technology in Stockholm, Sweden developing interactive music systems. He received his MA in Computer Related Design at the Royal College of Art, London, UK, 2000 and earned his first degree in Computer Music from the Academy of Music, Vienna, Austria.

Scott Lash ❮ Born in Chicago, Lash took a Bsc in psychology from the University of Michigan and MA in sociology from Northwestern University. He received his PhD from the London School of Economics (1980). Lash began his teaching career at Lancaster University. In 1998 he moved to London to take up his present position as Director for the Centre for Cultural Studies and Proffessor of Sociology at Goldsmiths College, London University. He is (co-)author of The End of Organized Capitalism, Sociologiy of postmodernism, Reflexive Modernization, Economies of Signs and Space, Another Modernity, A Different Rationality and Critique of Information. His books have been translated into 10 languages.

Peter Senge ❮ Peter M. Senge is a senior lecturer at the Massachusetts Institute of Technology. He is also founding chair of the Society for Organizational Learning (SoL), a global community of corporations, researchers, and consultants dedicated to the „interdependent development of people and their institutions." He is the author of the widely acclaimed book, The Fifth Discipline: The Art and Practice of The Learning Organization (1990) and, with colleagues Charlotte Roberts, Rick Ross, Bryan Smith and Art Kleiner, co-author of The Fifth Discipline Fieldbook: Strategies and Tools for Building a Learning Organization (1994) and a fieldbook The Dance of Change: The Challenges to Sustaining Momentum in Learning Organizations (March, 1999), also co-authored by George Roth. In September 2000, a fieldbook on education was published, the award winning Schools That Learn:

A Fifth Discipline Fieldbook for Educators, Parents, and Everyone Who Cares About Education, co-authored with Nelda Cambron-McCabe, Timothy Lucas, Bryan Smith, Janis Dutton, and Art Kleiner. The new book, Presence: Human Purpose and the Field of the Future, co-authored with Claus Otto Scharmer, Joseph Jaworski and Betty Sue Flowers, has been published by the Society for Organizational Learning in March 2004

The Fifth Discipline hit a nerve deep within the business and education community by introducing the theory of learning organizations. Since its publication, more than a million copies have been sold world-wide. In 1997, Harvard Business Review identified it as one of the seminal management books of the past 75 years.

The Journal of Business Strategy (September/October 1999) named Dr. Senge as one of the 24 people who had the greatest influence on business strategy over the last 100 years. The Financial Times (2000) named him as one of the world's "top management gurus." Business Week (October 2001) rated Peter as one of The Top (ten) Management Gurus.

Michael Shamiyeh ❮ Architect in practice and head of Design-Organisation-Media Research Laboratory. Graduated with distinction as an architect from the Technical University of Vienna and has a Master in Architecture from Harvard University Graduate School of Design. He has done extensive research work in Jerusalem and Berlin. Together with the cultural theorist Thomas Duschlbauer he is co-founder of the interdisciplinary Bureau for Architecture, Urbanism and Culture (BAU|KULTUR) that seeks to define new relationships – as much theoretical as practical – between a contemporary architectural production and a contemporary cultural situation. Thus, the firm is concerned with realising projects at home and abroad, teaching, consulting and investigation of cultural phenomena.

BUSINESS
MEETS DESIGN 〈

ROBERT BAUER ‹

We are currently witnessing a great outpouring of interest in design on the part of corporate executives. This is not simply a matter of the apparently strong increase in design's share of value added to the economy as a whole, or of predictions that careers in design will be a driving force behind future economic growth, rather this has just as much to do with designers' creative, artistic and pragmatic approaches to the world, from which managers could learn quite a lot.

IN THE FUTURE, MEN AND WOMEN RUNNING BUSINESSES WILL BE CONFRONTED WITH AN EVER WIDER RANGE OF PROBLEMS THAT WILL DEMAND INCREASINGLY RAPID SOLUTIONS. TO KEEP UP WITH SUCH DEVELOPMENTS, THEY WILL HAVE TO TURN PLANNING AND STRATEGIC PROCESSES INTO DESIGN PROCESSES.

Instead of being business administrators, managers have to become business designers. When renowned economist Alfred Chandler recommended that modern corporate executives adopt "structure follows strategy" as their guiding principle, hardly anyone was aware of its origins. In retrospect, though it could hardly have been more appropriate. After all, the motto that has been omnipresent in the field of strategic management for over 40 years paraphrases what is arguably the most important principle of design: form follows function! As we can see from the example of Canada's leading college of business administration, the University of Toronto's Rotman School of Management, prominent educational facilities are already at work building bridges between design and management. This dynamic institution – which, under the leadership of Dean Roger Martin, has vaulted from 65th to 21st place on the list of the world's best B-schools in only five years – has secured the copyright to Business DesignTM and is already collaborating with the Ontario College of Art and Design to offer the first courses in which future designers and managers are receiving joint instruction.
Top-flight design firms like IDEO in Palo Alto, California are delivering real-life examples of what managers ought to be learning from the design process.

- Designers are borrowing methods from anthropology in order to conduct "field studies" of future users and to see the world through those users' eyes.
- Designers take advantage of the possibilities of brainstorming in a team setting. During lengthy sessions, all kinds of ideas – no matter how seemingly absurd – are tossed out and kicked around. They automatically become community property that any participant is entitled to modify.
- As experts in visualization, designers place great stock in the powers of the imagination and in imagineering. And they "think with their pens," meaning that they can use drawing techniques to create images that were still inchoate concepts in their minds before they got them down on paper.
- Design processes are based on intensive prototyping – i.e. on working with initially primitive three-dimensional models that, in countless rounds of trial and error, are continuously improved in accordance with the motto "He who fails the quickest is first to succeed."

In stark contrast to these points, the processes that lead up to strategic management decisions are still extremely hierarchic: too far removed from future "users" and more strongly characterized by power and diplomacy than by the desire to jointly do creative designing. Decisions are all too often dominated by pre-determined factors. Developing conceptions of what could be usually gets short shrift. And last but not least, planning is still a too-highly-centralized affair that relies on unwieldy committees instead of one that concentrates right from the outset on pilot projects that make faster learning cycles possible. A deep philosophical crisis has been the prelude to "management as design." Scholarship on management has been oriented for far too long on a worldview engendered by the natural sciences in the 19th century, which posited an objective world that just is the way it is, a world whose eternal laws are ultimately revealed by science and can be neatly attired in mathematical formulas. But this does not resemble the real world of business executives in the least – that world is manufactured; it originates only as an outcome of action and reaction, in a dialog and it changes quickly. Managers are not independent observers rather hopefully they are right in the middle of things. What they need is a burning desire to actively shape their world and good judgment based just as much on analytical thinking as they are on the ability to empathize on aesthetic capacities.

19

**CONTEMPORARY THEORIES OF
CHANGE SEEMED, PARADOXICALLY,
NEITHER NARROW ENOUGH
NOR BROAD ENOUGH.**

The changes in which we will be called upon to participate in the
future will be both deeply personal and inherently systemic.
The deeper dimensions of transformational change represent a
largely unexplored territory both in current management research
and in our understanding of leadership in general.

There's nothing more elemental to the work of leaders than creating results. But it's no longer possible to create positive results in isolation. With organizations, economies, and entire societies increasingly interconnected, our actions affect (and are affected by) others, often literally a world away. It's impossible, in today's world, to think about how to have an impact in our workplace without also asking ourselves a deeper question: What does it means to live in a global society?

This question was brought home to me by Mieko Nishimizu, one of the most gifted executives at the World Bank. Shortly after attending the SoL Executive Champions' Workshop in August 2002, she addressed business and political leaders observing the 50th anniversary of Japan's membership in the post-World War II Bretton Woods Agreements. Speaking with candor unusual for such an affair, she described what it meant for her, after growing up with many material benefits, to come to grips with poverty. For example, she told of meeting an Indian woman who had to walk four hours each day to gather fresh water. As they walked together, the woman told her, "This is not life. This is only keeping a body alive." For Mieko, such conditions – which are a reality for an increasing number of people in most of the developing world [1] – cannot be separated from the forces shaping an increasingly global society:
The future appears alien to us. It differs from the past, most notably in that the earth itself is a relevant unit with which to frame and measure that future. Discriminating issues that shape the future are all fundamentally global. We belong to one inescapable network of mutuality – mutuality of ecosystems; mutuality of freer movement of information, ideas, people, and goods and services; and mutuality of peace and security.

WE ARE TIED, INDEED, IN A SINGLE FABRIC OF DESTINY ON PLANET EARTH.

Policies and actions that attempt to tear a nation from this cloth will inevitably fail.[2]
Few of our institutions are prepared for a truly global society. Indeed, it appears that much of the preparation nature has invested in us – our physiological, cognitive, psychological, and cultural evolution – is failing us. Our neuroanatomy is tuned to respond to sudden, dramatic changes in our environment: clap your hands loudly and watch it react. We focus on immediate needs and problems, and are trapped by the illusion that what is most tangible is most real. We've been conditioned for thousands of years to identify with our family, our tribe, and our local social structures. A future that asks us to overcome this conditioning and identify with all of humankind looks alien indeed. On the other hand, in some ways we've long understood our place in the world. Early in our history, we learned that if we depleted our topsoil or our local fishery, we paid a price. Today, we call it sustainability (see sidebar, "Improving the Triple Bottom Line"). However, we've never before lived in a world in which one's actions, through global business, can have their primary consequence on the other side of the world.

NOR HAVE WE EVER BEEN SO DEPENDENT ON THE ACTIONS OF OTHERS.

In the late 1980s a US emergency preparedness study estimated that the typical pound of food that an American consumed traveled an average of 1,500 miles, often from outside the US. In the years since, the developed economies' reliance on the developing world for essential goods and services has only increased.
The challenges of living in such an alien, interconnected world are both practical and deeply personal.
Ultimately they lead us to reflect on who we are individually, who we are in our local networks of colleagues, and what we're committed to. Such understanding is essential to being effective in our work as managers, teachers, parents, and citizens.

1 Despite pledges by the G7 nations to cut the incidence of global poverty by half, the only region to see significant decline is East Asia, with a 12-percent reduction since 1990. In Africa, South Asia, and Latin America the number of people living on less than $1 per day grew by about 80 million from 1990–1998. Worldwide, the number of people living on less than $1 per day remained static at about 2.7 billion throughout the 1990s, and the number living on less than $2 per day grew from 2.7 billion to 2.8 billion, according to Oxfam. http://www.oxfam.org/eng/pdfs/pp000721_G7_missing_the_target.pdf. **2** For the full text of Mieko Nishimizu's address, see "Looking Back, Leaping Forward," Reflections, Vol. 4, No. 4. http://www.reflections.solonline.org.

Creating Desired Results

Adam Kahane,[3] a SoL member and gifted facilitator who specializes in cross-sector dialogue and scenario building, says that three types of increasing complexity are at the root of organizations' and societies' toughest problems:

- *dynamic complexity: cause and effect distant in time and space*
- *social complexity: diverse stakeholders with different agendas and worldviews*
- *generative complexity: emergent realities wherein solutions from the past no longer fit.*

In the face of such complexity, the very concept of "problem solving" can be an impediment. It can lead us to think of fixing something that is broken. It can lead to imposing solutions from the past. And, it can lead to seeing reality as the adversary rather than the ally. But, none of these arises necessarily if we see problem solving as part of a larger process of creating what we truly want. Realizing desired results in a global society – or in any context – requires both learning and leadership, but above all it involves collective creating. In fact, I see learning, leading, and creating as three ways to talk about the same basic phenomenon. Effective leadership, for instance, draws on the belief that we have positive choices and can overcome fear to bring about a better future together. Learning – whether learning to manage a department, speak a language, or raise a child – is about creating new capacities to bring new outcomes into reality, especially outcomes we genuinely care about. That is also

22

THE ROOT DEFINITION OF "CREATE" – TO BRING INTO EXISTENCE.

Creating is not a mystical state that we simply fall into; it is a discipline that can be understood and developed. Robert Fritz,[4] a musician, filmmaker, organizational consultant (and in many ways my mentor in the study of creating as a discipline), has articulated three principles that can help leaders of all sorts more effectively create desired outcomes.

---

3 Adam Kahane's new book, The Victory of the Open Heart: Solving Tough Problems Through Talking and Listening, will be available in 2004. His work in developing capacity for groups to function in the midst of this complexity appears in "How to Change the World: Lessons for Entrepreneurs from Activists," Reflections, Vol. 2, No. 3. An earlier discussion of the first two types of complexity can be found in G. Roth and P. Senge, "From Theory to Practice: Research Territory, Processes and Structure at an Organizational Learning Center," Journal of Organizational Change Management, Vol. 9, No. 1 (1996).
4 For more on the work of Robert Fritz, see http://www.robertfritz.com. See also "A Lesson From the Arts," Reflections, Vol. 2, No. 4. http://www.reflections.solonline.org. See also Your Life As Art (Newfane, VT: Newfane Press, 2002).

Improving the Triple Bottom Line

There's little you can say with certainty about the future of the global economy. But one thing is certain: it can't continue as it is. The planet's resources, its natural systems, and at least one-third of its population, living in desperate poverty, simply won't allow it.

HOW CAN LEADERS RESPOND TO THIS REALITY?

What can we do to shift from mere regulatory compliance and incremental process improvements to real innovation – to environmentally intelligent products and services, developed and marketed in responsible ways? The SoL Sustainability Consortium, a learning community of organizations, has developed some practical answers to these [5] questions. The consortium applies the disciplines of systems thinking and organizational learning to better understand how companies can be profitable while nurturing local communities and natural systems – the so-called "triple bottom line." Early on, consortium members, including BP, Shell, Ford, Nike, United Technologies, Harley Davidson, and Visteon, decided they needed a simple, operational definition of sustainability. They came up with the following picture that distinguishes present industrial systems from natural systems.

While individual companies can reduce waste, like the Xerox copier team, modern products contain huge amounts of toxic substances that no single company can eliminate entirely. Many believe that this toxic load is the prime source of the rising incidence of cancer and other diseases in industrialized countries, as well as the destruction of ecological systems. To address these problems, environmentalists have advocated "materials pooling" – working collaboratively and systematically across complex value chains to identify and eliminate sources of waste and toxicity. [6] But actually building such cross-organizational learning communities requires trust, shared vision, and shared understanding of larger systems. This is what members of the SoL Sustainability Consortium are attempting to do today, with working groups focused on reducing and, ideally, entirely eliminating toxins and waste in a broad array of industrial and consumer products. But what they really are doing is learning to build sustainability-learning communities.[7]

A sustainable industrial system strives to transform all sources of waste and toxicity into "technical" or "biological nutrients" that can be reused indefinitely without harm to living systems.[8]

If your primary role is to fix problems rather than create something new and meaningful, it's hard to maintain a sense of purpose.   *Michael Goodman*

---

5 P. Senge and G. Carstedt. "Innovating Our Way to the Next Industrial Revolution: Building Sustainable Enterprises," Sloan Management Review, Winter 2001, Volume 42, Number 2, pp. 24–38. http://mit-smr.com/past/2001/smr4222.html. **6** Ibid.
7 For more information on the Sustainability Consortium, see http://www.solonline.org/public_pages/comm_SustainabilityConsortiumCore/
8 W. McDonough and M. Braungart. Cradle to Cradle: Remaking the Way We Make Things (New York: North Point Press, 2002).

23

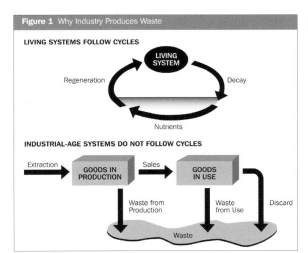

Figure 1 Why Industry Produces Waste

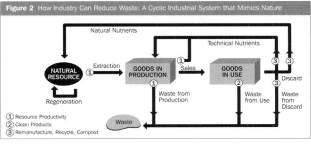

Figure 2 How Industry Can Reduce Waste: A Cyclic Industrial System that Mimics Nature

1. Creating is different from problem solving.

The fundamental difference between creating and problem solving is simple. In problem solving we seek to make something we do not like go away. In creating, we seek to make what we truly care about exist. Few distinctions are more basic. Of course, most of us, in both professional and private life, spend far more time problem solving and reacting to circumstances than focusing our energies on creating what we really value.

Indeed, we can get so caught up in reacting to problems that it is easy to forget what we actually want. Organizations must do both – resolve day-to-day problems and generate new results. But if your primary role is to fix problems, individually or collectively, rather than create something new and meaningful, it's hard to maintain a sense of purpose. And without a deep sense of purpose, it's difficult to harness the energy, passion, commitment, and perseverance needed to thrive in challenging times.

If you wonder which is primary in your work, simply ask yourself or your team, "What are we trying to accomplish today?" Usually teams will describe a set of problems they're trying to manage. Then, ask what they could accomplish by eliminating those problems. Typically, they'll describe yet another set of problems that could then be tackled – for instance, preventing a service breakdown if only they first could solve their interpersonal conflicts. What often is forgotten is the more basic question:

WHAT ARE WE TRYING TO CREATE?

Without a compelling answer to this question, it is hard to know why all the problem solving actually matters. Problem solving becomes the busywork of organizations in which people have forgotten their purpose and vision. Reconnecting with that purpose always starts with asking questions like: Why are we here? What are we trying to create that will make the world a better place? And, who would miss us if we were gone? (By the way, if you are in a business, "our investors" is never an answer to the last question – investors will always find another company where they can earn an adequate return on their capital.)

2. The creative process is animated by the gap between vision and reality.

When we picture something we want to create, we're imaging a vision of the future, which also evokes the implicit difference from what currently exists.

EVERY CREATIVE ARTIST UNDERSTANDS THIS PRINCIPLE.

Fritz calls it "structural tension," and says it can be resolved by taking action to achieve our vision. Closing the gap between vision and reality is the essence of the creative arts. Artists get no credit for brilliant ideas unless they can bring them into reality.

THIS "BRINGING OF VISION TO REALITY"

is also the essence of great social, political, or business leadership. However, because this tension between vision and reality can be uncomfortable, creative tension becomes emotional tension and we often seek ways around it. One way to lessen the emotional tension is simply to reduce our true vision, to give up our dreams and aim for only "realistic goals." While this might reduce our discomfort, it also reduces creative energy. The second way is even more troubling: we do not tell the truth about current reality. Just as the dynamics of compromise – lowering our vision – are common in human affairs, so too are the dynamics of denial. But to the extent that we misrepresent current reality, we lose the capacity to change that reality. The energy of the creative process is released not just by holding true to a vision, but also by telling the truth about what is.

3. Understanding your constraints frees you to create.

One thing that distinguishes the master from the novice is an appreciation of the constraints of his or her medium. Or, as Fritz put it, "No painter paints on an infinite canvas." John Elter, a former vice president at Xerox, used this principle to great effect. Early in a multiyear, product-development process to create the company's first fully digital copiers, Elter took his team on a two-day wilderness expedition in the New Mexico desert.[9] On the way back, they happened to walk by a dump – at the bottom of which they discovered a Xerox copier. It was a revelation. They returned to work with a new vision for the product and their entire enterprise: "Zero to landfill, for our children." Says Elter, "Most of the constraints engineering teams deal with are management claptrap. All the managers make them up: The product has got to grow revenue by this amount. It's got to achieve these cost targets." However, says Elter, after their epiphany in the desert, "We discovered our real constraint – that nothing from this product should ever go into a landfill." The product they designed was ultimately 94 percent re-manufacturable and 98 percent recyclable, and met or exceeded all its sales targets. The team created a great product – perhaps saving the company from bankruptcy or takeover – by redefining the constraints they worked against. As Elter and his team showed, as we go forward, the constraints that can enable creativity will come from appreciating the environmental and social realities of an increasingly interdependent world. Nature produces no waste. Why should business be different? But, by and large, we fail to see these constraints because we fail to see the interdependence out of which they arise.

Feeling the Heat

Researchers John Sterman and Linda Booth Sweeney wondered why, despite overwhelming scientific evidence, so many Americans are complacent about the threat of global warming. Their study points up the trouble people have seeing connections among related forces, and thus framing good solutions.[10]

Sterman and Booth Sweeney described the dynamics of global warming to MBA students at Harvard, Stanford,[11] and MIT, using data from the 2001 report of the UN's Intergovernmental Panel on Climate Change (IPCC). The findings themselves are not in dispute. As shown in Figure 1, the flow of CO emissions resulting from human activity increased steadily from 1850–1950, and precipitously since 1950. As a result, the total concentration of CO has increased some 30 percent in the last 150 years – to the highest concentrations of the last 420,000 years (see Figure 2). Average global temperatures are trending in the same direction, as shown in Figure 3. IPCC concludes that "most of the warming observed over the last 50 years is attributable to human activities."

NOT SHOWN IS THE RATE AT WHICH CO_2 IS REMOVED FROM THE ATMOSPHERE – WHICH HAPPENS, OF COURSE, WHEN GREEN PLANTS CONSUME CO_2 AND RETURN OXYGEN.

This is vital information for projecting future CO_2 levels. By best estimates today, the outflow of CO2, which has declined due to deforestation, is about one-half the emissions. Therefore, emissions would have to decline by 50 percent just to stabilize the current stock of CO_2 in the atmosphere – well beyond what the Kyoto protocols would accomplish, even if all countries of the world adopted them. So, anything less than a 50-percent decline in emissions will result in a continuing rise in CO_2 levels for many years.

Furthermore, the effects of CO_2 in the atmosphere are long lasting – temperatures would continue to rise for years even if the CO_2 concentration leveled off today. Yet, presented with two scenarios based on these data, no more than 38 percent of the students correctly predicted what would happen. The principles at work, say Sterman and Booth Sweeney, are "as simple as filling a bathtub: humanity is injecting CO_2 into the atmosphere at about twice the rate it is drained out. Stabilizing the concentration of CO_2 requires substantial cuts in emissions." The authors call for better science reporting, noting that "even the simplest systems concepts help." They conclude, "The sooner people understand these dynamics, the sooner they will call for leaders who reject do-nothing, wait-and-see policies and who will turn down the tap – before the tub overflows." This is the natural state of the human world, separation without separateness. While most Americans believe global warming is real, they feel little sense of urgency to do anything about it.

10 See Sterman, John D. and Booth Sweeney, Linda. "Cloudy Skies: Assessing Public Understanding of Global Warming," System Dynamics Review, Vol. 18, No. 2, 2002. http://web.mit.edu/jsterman/www/cloudy_skies.html. See also the presentation at SoL Research Greenhouse III in 2002, at http:// www.solonline.org/repository/download/Sterman_Greenhouse3.pdf_1.pdf?item_id=364437.
11 See http://www.ipcc.ch.

Figure 3 The CO_2 Stabilization Task

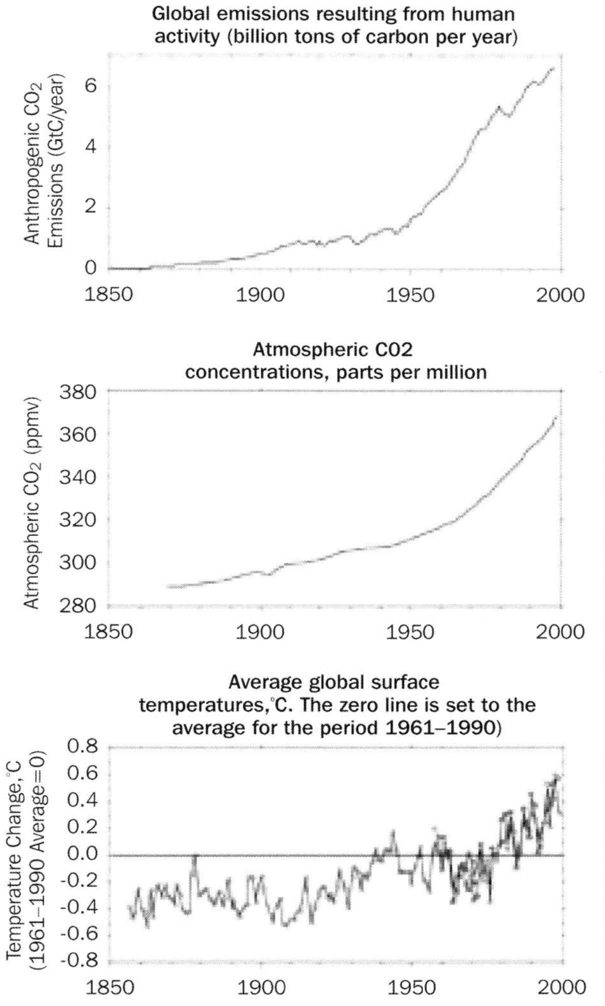
Global emissions resulting from human activity (billion tons of carbon per year)
Anthropogenic CO2 Emissions (GtC/year)
6
4
2
0
1850
1900
1950
2000
Atmospheric CO2 concentrations, parts per million
Atmospheric CO2 (ppmv)
380
360
340
320
300
280
1850
1900
1950
2000
Average global surface temperatures,°C. The zero line is set to the average for the period 1961–1990)
Temperature Change,°C (1961–1990 Average=0)
0.8
0.6
0.4
0.2
0.0
-0.2
-0.4
-0.6
-0.8
1850
1900
1950
2000

Missing the Connections

To redress the imbalances in our global society, whether of income distribution, development of civil society, or destruction of living systems, we must see the connections that permeate natural and social systems. But for most of us, the noise of modern societies obscures those connections and thus inhibits action – starting with our own thinking. For example, recent research by MIT's John Sterman shows why vague concerns about global warming don't necessarily translate into political action (see sidebar, "Feeling the Heat").

Sterman was struck by a curious disconnect in public opinion: polls show that while most Americans believe global warming is real, they feel little sense of urgency to do anything about it. To test his hypothesis that "much of this complacency arises from poor systems thinking skills," Sterman and his colleague Linda Booth Sweeney designed a thought experiment. They created two different scenarios, based on the known stock of CO_2 in the atmosphere and the flow of new CO_2 emissions, and asked graduate students from three elite universities to predict the likely outcome of each scenario.

NEARLY TWO-THIRDS OF THESE STUDENTS FAILED TO RECOGNIZE THE LOGICALLY CORRECT TREND (WHICH IS CONTINUED GLOBAL WARMING).

Their poor performance was based not on a lack of technical understanding, but on the failure to see the relationships between stocks (the current level of CO_2) and flows (the rate of new CO_2 emissions). If the rate of new CO_2 emissions is higher than the rate at which CO_2 is removed from the atmosphere, the overall level of CO_2 will continue to increase, and with it, the likelihood of global warming. If people are confused by such basic interrelationships, it is little wonder that it becomes easy for politicians and citizens alike to pretend either that such problems do not exist or that someone else will deal with them. Sterman, Booth Sweeney and a growing number of educators around the world believe these failings reflect a massive neglect of systems education.

AN INCREASINGLY INTERDEPENDENT WORLD MEANS THAT SYSTEMS THINKING MUST BECOME AN EDUCATIONAL PRIORITY.

Ted Sizer, former dean of the Harvard School of Education and founder of the Coalition of Essential Schools, writes, "It is not hyperbole to say that the growing gap between the complexities we face and our capacity to come to a shared understanding of that complexity poses an unprecedented challenge to our future…. Even older students have little… understanding of the world's undeniable complexity." [12] But the motivation for radical innovation in education will remain limited so long as the urgency of issues like global warming remains limited or absent. We are stuck in a "Catch 22": systemic imbalances fail to compel our attention because we simply do not see them in the same way we see more immediate and local problems. And, we fail to see the systemic issues because we define urgency by what is immediate. We are victims of a self-reinforcing crisis of perception – a crisis of our own making. If it persists, we doom ourselves to continued passivity. Only catastrophe will compel action, which, given the growing social divide that distributes problems like global warming unevenly between rich and poor, is likely to manifest as social and political disruption – not unlike what we are already seeing around the world. My view is that nothing short of a profound shift in the Western, materialistic worldview is likely to dislodge this crisis of perception. How can diverse people from around the world come to a fuller sense of the whole – that is, the social, economic, and ecological systems we share? Perhaps that will begin when, together, we start to appreciate the exquisite web of interconnectedness that enables life in the universe, wherever we stand, and the role of our own consciousness in that web.

[12] T. Sizer, P. Senge, and L. Booth Sweeney. "Systems Schooling for School Systems," working paper, Harvard Graduate School of Education, 2003. See also, P. Senge, et al. Schools That Learn: A Fifth Discipline Fieldbook for Educators, Parents, and Everyone Who Cares About Education (New York: Doubleday/Currency, 2001).

Of Parts and Wholes

Our normal way of thinking cheats us. It leads us to think of wholes as made up of many parts, the way a car is made up of wheels, a chassis, and a drive train. In this way of thinking, the whole is assembled from the parts and depends upon them to work effectively. If a part is broken, it must be repaired or replaced. This is a very logical way of thinking about machines. But living systems are different. Unlike machines, living systems, such as your body or a tree, create themselves. They are not mere assemblages of their parts but are continually growing and changing along with their elements. Almost 200 years ago, Goethe, the German writer and scientist, argued that this meant we had to think very differently about wholes and parts. For Goethe, the whole was something dynamic and living that continually comes into being "in concrete manifestations."[i] A part, in turn, was a manifestation of the whole, rather than just a component of it. Neither exists without the other. The whole exists through continually manifesting in the parts, and the parts exist as embodiments of the whole.

THE INVENTOR BUCKMINSTER FULLER WAS FOND OF HOLDING UP HIS HAND AND ASKING PEOPLE, "WHAT IS THIS?" INVARIABLY, THEY WOULD RESPOND, "IT'S A HAND." HE WOULD THEN POINT OUT THAT THE CELLS THAT MADE UP THAT HAND WERE CONTINUALLY DYING AND REGENERATING THEMSELVES.

What seems tangible is continually changing: in fact, a hand is completely re-created within a year or so. So when we see a hand – or an entire body or any living system – as a static "thing," we are mistaken.

"What you see is not a hand," Fuller would say. "It's a 'pattern integrity', the universe's capability to create hands."[ii] For Fuller, this "pattern integrity" was the whole of which each particular hand is a "concrete manifestation."

[i] According to physicist and philosopher of science Henri Bortoft, The Wholeness of Nature: Goethe's Way Towards a Science of Conscious Participation in Nature (Hudson, NY: Lindisfarne Press, 1996. [ii] Amy Edmondson, A Fuller Explanation, 56-59 (Birkhaeuser, Boston, 1987) and Buckminster Fuller, Synergetics: the Geometry of Thinking (NY: Macmillan, 1976).

Making the Connections

In recent years, thought leaders from many scientific disciplines have begun to construct a picture of an interdependent universe far richer than almost any of us might imagine, catalyzed initially by findings in quantum physics. In his 1951 book, Quantum Theory, physicist David Bohm proposed a hypothesis based on the mathematics of quantum theory: if you separate an atomic particle and the two elements of the particle go to opposite ends of the universe, then altering the spin of one element will change instantaneously the spin of the other. Bohm posed this conceptual challenge because he believed that quantum theory revealed the "unbroken wholeness of the universe," contradicting our culture's dominant Newtonian view of separation and causality arising from one thing acting on another. Bohm's supposition was later taken up by physicist J. S. Bell.

BELL FURTHER DEVELOPED THE THEORY AND DEMONSTRATED EMPIRICALLY THAT BOHM WAS RIGHT:

a change in spin of a single particle could be observed immediately, across a very large distance, in a separate particle previously connected to the first. Physicists call it "Bell's Theorem" or the "Principle of Non-Locality," and its repeated empirical corroboration has been called "one of the most shocking events in twentieth-century science." [13] Physicists are quick to caution that, while non-locality operates at the subatomic scale, whether such interdependence exists at more "macro" scales remains to be demonstrated – leaving many questions regarding the relevance of this phenomenon for humans and the social world. An astonishing recent project, in a different context, suggests that new answers may be coming.

A team of engineers, physicists, and psychologists has been studying the output of 37 random-number generators in 17 countries, to see whether there is a level of connectedness operating at the human level, and not just at the subatomic level of Bohm's prediction. These machines, used for scientific research, are isolated from every known form of human or natural interference, such as electromagnetic or telecommunications waves. Yet, on the morning of September 11, 2001 the random-number generators behaved in very nonrandom ways, inexplicably showing the influence of some non-ordinary disturbance, presumably human in origin (see sidebar, "A Non-Random Occurrence"). Interestingly, pioneers like Bohm and Albert Einstein never had much doubt that the implications of quantum theory extended into the domain of human awareness and social harmony. "The most important thing going forward," said Bohm in 1980, "is to break the boundaries between people

so we can operate as a single intelligence. Bell's theorem implies that this is the natural state of the human world, separation without separateness.
The task is to find ways to break these boundaries, so we can be in our natural state." [14] Einstein, Bohm's colleague at Princeton, spoke of a similar aspiration:

"The human being experiences himself, his thoughts and feelings as something separate from the rest. A kind of optical delusion of our consciousness. This delusion is a kind of prison for us, restricting us to our personal desires, and to our affection for a few persons nearest to us. Our task must be to free ourselves from this prison by widening our circle of compassion to embrace all living creatures and the whole of nature in its beauty."

What does this mean practically? For Bohm, it meant dedicating much of the last 10 years of his life to understanding the potential of dialogue to foster deep personal and collective awareness of connectedness. Sadly, he did not live to see the growing evidence of its application. Kahane talks about one such application in South Africa in the early 1990s. With the apartheid regime coming to an end, people who had been killing one another were struggling to form a democratic government. Says Kahane, "A popular joke at the time said that, faced with the country's daunting challenges, South Africans had two options: a practical option and a miraculous option." The practical option was that everyone would "go down on their knees and pray for a band of angels to come down from heaven and fix things for us." The miraculous option was that people would "talk with one another until we found a way forward together." [15] Fortunately, South Africans opted for the miraculous option – talking with one another and discovering their interconnectedness to their common homeland, to their future, and to one another.

MANY BUSINESSES ARE RECOGNIZING THAT TRADITIONAL, TOP-DOWN CONTROL BECOMES LESS VIABLE AS INTERDEPENDENCE GROWS.

[13] D. Radin. The Conscious Universe (San Francisco: Harper, 1997): 278.
[14] J. Jaworski. Personal communication, 1980. See also J. Jaworski. Synchronicity: The Inner Path of Leadership (San Francisco: Berrett-Koehler Publishers, 1996).
[15] A. Kahane. The Victory of the Open Heart: Solving Tough Problems Through Talking and Listening (San Francisco, Forthcoming 2004).
[16] Radin, D. "Global Consciousness Project Analysis for September 11, 2001," at http://noosphere.princeton.edu.
[17] R.D. Nelson, D. Radin, R. Shoup, and P.A. Bancel. "Correlations of Continuous Random Data with Major World Events," p. 10, article (currently in review) available at http://noosphere.princeton.edu.

A Non-Random Occurrence

Random-number generators – devices used to generate sequences of random numbers used in scientific and industrial research – must be insu-lated from external forces, such as electromagnetic radiation, telecommunication signals, and every known form of human or physical inter-ference, or they cannot perform their function.

Since 1998, within the Global Consciousness Project (a social version of J. S. Bell's quantum physics experiment), an interdisciplinary team of scientists has been monitoring more than three dozen random-number generators around the world to track possible effects from unexpected sources.[16] What they found on September 11, 2001 was unexpected indeed.

Something went amiss with the random-number generators in the world, individually and collectively, at exactly the time of the terrorist attacks. Beginning a few hours before and continuing for two days after the attack, the data showed unexpected deviations in the output of individual devices, and an unprecedented correlation among different devices across the network. The researchers estimate the probability of what was observed at less than one in one thousand. They conclude that "it is unlikely that (known) environmental factors could cause the correlations we observe...." Barring demonstration to the contrary, "we are obliged to confront the possibility that the measured correlations may be directly associated with some (as yet poorly understood) aspect of consciousness attendant to global events." [17]

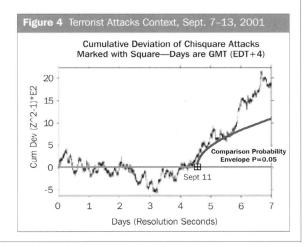

Figure 4 Terrorist Attacks Context, Sept. 7–13, 2001

Cumulative Deviation of Chisquare Attacks
Marked with Square—Days are GMT (EDT+4)

Applying Wisdom of the Past

The challenges we face can seem overwhelming. But humans have innate capacities, beyond our social conditioning, to develop a more holistic awareness of our relationship to the world. The connection between human consciousness and the material world has been a foundational idea in many of the oldest societies in history. It is now reentering the mainstream of Western culture due, in part, to new scientific theories that are more holistic.

AFTER ALL, SCIENCE IS THE RELIGION OF THIS AGE, AND THE SOURCE TO WHICH WE LOOK FOR THE MOST AUTHORITATIVE INTERPRETATIONS OF REALITY.

Business leaders, teachers, and other professionals also are drawing from the wisdom of the past, and from their own experience, to create more inclusive and integrated ways of living and working. This encompasses diverse global movements, from holistic health, to restorative justice, to learner-centered learning in schools.

Many businesses are recognizing that traditional, top-down control becomes less viable as interdependence grows. Increasingly, businesses are striving for fewer layers of management and encouraging more "self-organizing" – operating with minimum imposition from the top, and continually bringing change from the periphery to the center.

BUT WE ARE AT THE VERY OUTSET OF THIS JOURNEY,

and the immense stresses on traditional institutions of all sorts are causing some institutions to become more hierarchical and rigid. While it is fashionable to claim the spread of democracy around the world as a victory of Western ideals, in fact, many experience the opposite: the imposition of a new world order, driven predominantly by authoritarian institutions unresponsive to broad constituencies whose lives they are altering. Yet, older notions of self-organizing and self-governing exist throughout the world – in native and indigenous cultures, for example – wherever human beings have tried to understand nature deeply enough to live according to its guidelines. Perhaps the scientific era is about to move to another phase – and the democratic era, as well. I suggest that we don't understand democracy well. Like Western reductionistic science, the present "Washington consensus" view of democracy is but one prototype, with great strengths but also great limitations.
Most people in the US think of democracy as a kind of bequest, like an old suit of clothes.

But what if it is actually something we're still learning and creating? What if, to create a more desirable global future, we must rediscover and more effectively apply the lessons we claim to know so well? In his 1871 essay "Democratic Vistas," Walt Whitman wrote:

We have frequently printed the word democracy. Yet I cannot too often repeat that this is a word the real gist of which still sleeps quite un-awakened....
It is a great word whose history, I suppose, remains unwritten because that history has yet to be enacted. It is, in some sort, younger brother of another great, and often used word, "nature," whose history also waits unwritten.

Were he alive today, I believe Whitman would be writing not about American democracy, but about global society, and its as-yet-unwritten links to nature. When executives in global companies talk candidly, their real concern usually is not the cost of capital or return on sales; it is the social and political stability of the world they will leave behind. [18] They, too, see the future as an alien place. If it is to become more hospitable, it is up to us to create it so.

[18] SoL provides opportunities for executives to engage in this type of frank conversation. As a specific illustration, please refer to an invitation from a group of SoL executive members to the larger community called "the Marblehead letter." For the full text of "the Marblehead letter," see http://www.solonline.org/repository/item?item_id=163561. The initial economic sponsors of the global SoL network met in June 2001 to review the results of the first three years of organizing work and to provide input on SoL's potential contribution to issues of importance for firms and societies. The group, meeting in Marblehead, Massachusetts, identified a small set of issues fundamental to creating positive futures in an interdependent world, and invites the SoL community into ongoing dialogue on these topics:
The social divide: the ever-widening gap between those who participate in the increasingly interdependent global economy and those who do not.
- Redefining growth: economic growth based on ever-increasing material use and discard is inconsistent with a finite world.
- Variety and inclusiveness: developing inclusion as a core competence in increasingly multicultural organizations.
- Attracting talented people and realizing their potential: developing commitment in a world of "free agents" and "volunteer" talent.
- The role of the corporation: extending the traditional role of the corporation, especially the global corporation, to be more commensurate with its impact.
- The system seeing itself: the challenges of coordination and coherence in social systems.

Instrumental rationality, the defining element of economic action, dominates economic and, more specifically, managerial reasoning.

YET, INSTRUMENTAL RATIONALITY ALONE CAN NEITHER EXPLAIN NOR INFORM ECONOMIC PRACTICE.

Instead, it needs to be complemented – i.e. supported and challenged – by other ways of knowing such as aesthetic judgement. Indeed an aesthetic dimension is inherent in managerial practice and, therefore, leadership and organizational design rely on aesthetic judgement.

As used here, the (technical) term 'aesthetic' has three integral aspects: sensing, evaluation and principles. Consistent with its original meaning – Greek 'aisthesis' means sensory perception – 'aesthetic' refers to a specific epistemological mode employing visual, tactual, auditory, olfactory and proprioceptive experience. Unlike in the vernacular, 'aesthetic' in aesthetic theory refers to both positive and negative evaluations: the sensory information can be perceived as exciting, pleasing, beautiful, harmonious, amusing, or as boring, disgusting, ugly, disharmonious, disturbing and so on.

ALL OF THESE ARE AESTHETIC CATEGORIES.

In addition, aesthetic judgement is governed by a specific type of rules, by principles rather than laws (of nature). First, these rules cannot be fully denoted (i.e., explicitly spelt out); hence, they require additional exemplification (i.e., demonstration through samples).[14] Second, these rules are applied rather than obeyed. Aesthetic creation relies on a critical balance between conventional rule-following and exceptional rule-breaking.

I first encountered the aesthetic approach to management – long before I would be able to name it in a lecture on incentive systems, which I attended as a student of business administration. In the midst of elaborating on piece-work systems, the professor suddenly paused and then asked the class: How do you decide if the number of pieces required is set rightly? The professor was an authority in this field, frequently called as an expert witness when courts had to settle labor disputes, in particular when deciding if a certain piece-work system was exploitative or fair. In addition, we perceived him as quite intimidating. He had a reputation as an authoritarian character with debatable interpersonal skills, yet possessed the most brilliant intellect to which we had been exposed. It took a while until the first student dared to propose an answer, and the professor didn't even bother to point out why it was wrong. He just demanded that someone else answered the question: How do you decide if the number of pieces a worker (or group) is required to produce is just? We tried various approaches, including considerations of

labor-market efficiency, benchmarking, cultural norms for standards of living, philosophical considerations of justice, and analyses of data on workers' health. Nothing, however, satisfied our professor. He just continued demanding that someone give the correct answer. Eventually, we were relieved from our misery. "The rhythm, gentlemen!" he declared (although one third of the class were women), "The rhythm! Watch an experienced workman producing the required number of pieces per hour. If the movement is flowing smoothly and economically, the required number is fine. However, if the movement is hasty and jagged, or on the contrary sluggish, unnecessarily complicated or pausing, then the number needs to be adjusted."

His answer left me baffled and dazzled. The famous business professor had just shared his believe that making quick and informed judgements about critical, controversial managerial issues requires an aesthetic view. He had learnt to look at the world of factory workers through the eyes of dancers and choreographers. None of us students, on the other hand, would have dared to even imagine this approach. We were deeply entrenched in thinking about business and management in terms of numbers, markets and some abstract political principles of justice.

1. The nature of organizational design: shaping human experience

Instrumental rationality is central to the economic paradigm that currently dominates organization studies. This market-centered perspective the firm views as a nexus of contracts through which economic actors trade more or less specific goods and services, thereby maximizing their wealth. In order to unveil the aesthetic dimension of organizations and managerial practice I will propose an alternative view, namely organizations as orientation systems.

This perspective views organizations as structural arrangements comprising elements as different as incentive systems, chains of command, corporate strategies and visions, job profiles, report systems and control devices, formal and informal codes of conduct, technical equipment, facilities and so forth. The orientation systems perspective perceives these various elements as woven together

– thereby establishing the organization – for the purpose of guiding the perceptions and actions of the individuals working 'in' the organization. Organizations shape what individuals pay attention to or ignore, what they care about, desire, despise, or fear, what they fight for or let go of. Organizations are epistemological devices guiding individual perception, sensemaking, valuing and, most of all, choice and action.

THEY PROVIDE ORIENTATION FOR HOW INDIVIDUALS EXPERIENCE LIFE AT WORK.

As a result of this orientation, individuals' knowing and doing become interlinked and converge into larger patterns. Through the orientation provided by the organization, innumerable individual acts of perception and judgement jointly give rise to a (more or less) coherent stream of activity. It is this pattern that provides the grounds for referring to an organization as an agent doing something (e.g., embarking on a certain strategy, exploiting workers, taking over a competitor etc.).

For example, consider the epistemological effects of functional division of labor. Organization theory has known since the late 1950s that functional departments (e.g., procurement, production, marketing, sales, human resources, or accounting) develop different epistemological habits.[2] 'Sales', for instance, typically focuses on the organization's environment, on customers and competitors, at the expense of 'internal affairs'.

It is primarily future oriented, and speed is critical, though precision might get compromised ('Quick and dirty' is a viable option in 'sales' and a struck deal involving compromise is usually favored over a potential perfect one). 'Accounting', on the other hand, is typically governed by contrasting epistemological habits.

---

[1] Goodman (1976).
[2] E.g. Lawrence and Lorsch (1967), Dearborne and Simon (1958), Quinn and Rohrbaugh (1981).

It focuses on the company, as opposed to its environment, and primarily pays attention to what has already happened (in the past). If necessary, speed gets compromised to achieve the expected flawless precision. Functional departments evolve as cultural microcosms differing with regard to rules, values, behaviors, and personal experience. Consciously or not, through daily interaction individuals in each department reassure each other of the rightness of their respective worldview, which in turn tends to become reified and taken for granted – no longer perceived as a worldview, but as the world.

ORGANIZATIONS AS EPISTEMOLOGICAL TOOLS EXERCISE SIGNIFICANT POWER OVER INDIVIDUAL AND COLLECTIVE EXPERIENCE.

Each functional department deeply entrenches itself in its own specific epistemology, which has proven successful in dealing with the group's immediate task. In consequence, interdepartmental coordination may only be achieved at the cost of involving third parties: that is, departments with 'intermediate' epistemological habits that understand both sides and are perceived as taking a balanced stance.[3<]
To hint at another example, the working of organizations as orientation systems is particularly manifest in performance measurement and incentive systems. Far from being unobtrusive, performance measures do not just reflect reality but instead intervene in it powerfully by signaling what is important and what is not. Employees, in turn, tend to produce what is measured and rewarded, and sacrifice the rest. ("Beware of your wishes; they might come true.") Performance measures do not primarily communicate – bottom-up – truth about performance; much rather they communicate – top-down – what has been chosen as a priority. Designing performance-measurement systems means designing orientation systems – intervening into human experience and shaping what people think, feel, and do, by influencing what matters and what does not, what is experienced as important and what is not.
Although organizations guide the senses, feelings, thoughts, intuitions, and most notably actions of humans in powerful and often unconscious ways, we must not see

humans as mere passive victims subjected to organizational designs that imprinting experience and actions on them. On the contrary, organizations provide hints and clues, pointers and landmarks that trigger and inform the member's creation of their personal experience, which is a highly active process with far more degrees of freedom than conventional wisdom would assume.

In this respect, organizations function like artistic artifacts. For instance, watching a well-made movie strongly affects what one senses, feels and thinks; at its best, it can be an experience so enriching that one feels no longer quite the same person as before. However, although it can powerfully intervene into one's experience, a movie is by no means a remote control determining the viewer's sensations, emotions and thoughts. On the contrary, a director's mastery lies in the ability to draw the audience into co creating the experience. A viewer 'agrees' to fill in massive gaps between scenes, to imagine what is not shown but hinted at, and, at best, to transcend the movie by experiencing oneself creating the experience. An artifact is a piece of art if and only if it succeeds in involving the observer into a process of sense-making that simultaneously creates and reveals the artistic nature of the artifact – a principle exemplified, for instance, by Malewitsch's legendary 'Black Square', a black square on white square ground.[4]

2. The essence of organizational design: from the edge of chaos to the principles of consonance

The challenge in organizational design – how to design organizations that effectively shape personal experience – is twofold: namely, how to trigger and fuel the creation of experience, and how to lead this process of creation into certain directions. The particular problem for organizational designers lies in the antagonistic relationship of these two challenges.

Over-directive organizational designs specify with low ambiguity and in great detail what to focus on, how to make sense of events and which action to take. They provide strong guidance but little stimulation and drive. They are boring, thus leading to physical and mental absence rather than commitment and effort. Early assembly lines and large administrative bureaucracies provide examples of over-directive organizational designs that guide too closely and therefore sedate rather than activate individuals. Even worse, they may lead individuals to turn their creativity and energy against the organization (e.g., sabotage). Under-directive organizational designs, however, leave the organization's members with many open questions.

TO A CERTAIN EXTENT, MISSING, AMBIVALENT OR CONTRADICTORY INSTRUCTIONS CAN TRIGGER DESIRABLE PROBLEM-SOLVING AND SEARCH BEHAVIORS.

The organization becomes somewhat uncomfortable, but highly activating and energizing. Although they usually stimulate high levels of individual activity, under-directive organizational designs commonly fail to integrate the individuals' efforts into a consistent patterned activity set. In other words, lack of orientation makes the organization probably ineffective, despite everyone being indeed busy. In addition, extreme organizational under-direction can cause such uncertainty and chaos that it no longer increases activation but leads into paralysis instead.

To summarize, masterful organizational design triggers and guides individual sense-making and action through maintaining a critical balance between the presence and absence of instructive constraints, between providing meaning and exposing to noise, between determinacy and openness, between order and chaos.

This kind of dynamic equilibrium has been studied most thoroughly in complexity science. Through computer simulations, complexity theorists, most notably at the Santa Fe Institute, have shown that complex systems rely on a critical balance between mutual dependence and autonomy of their components and display behaviors that lie at the intersection of order and disorder. Complexity emerges at the edge of chaos.[5]

3[Lawrence and Lorsch (1967).
4['Black Square' (1915), oil on canvas, 79,5 x 79,5 cm.
5[Kauffman (1993), Langton (1990).

The computer program is the most unambiguous (i.e. explicit) form of knowledge making computer simulation the approach par excellence to complexity science. Yet, for the same reason computer simulation is also a simplistic approach to the complex; it depicts only the orderable aspects of the balance of order and chaos.

Within organization science, consistency theory is the branch that has most clearly addressed the critical balance underlying organizational design. Consistency theorists maintain that an organization cannot provide orientation unless its various elements are aligned.[6] Without consistency among its design parameters an organization sends contradictory messages to its members and fails to integrate their decisions and actions into a coherent pattern. However, a totally streamlined company, where everything and everybody is perfectly aligned, would be a poor alternative. In such an organization, devoid of conflict and disagreement, members do not confront or challenge each other from alternative perspectives. In addition, provided with next to complete, unambiguous information about what to focus on, how to make sense of events and which action to take, individuals tend to adopt mechanical rule-following behavior rather than paying attention to specifics and discrepancies. Though some individuals may feel comfortable about total guidance, others find it confining and eventually dehumanizing. From a consistency perspective, good organizational design involves finding a middle ground between a lack of consistency and an overdose thereof. The latter can be highly successful initially, but its success is short-lived because over-aligned companies suffer an inability to learn.[7] In essence, maintaining this critical balance – between consistency, consensus, clarity, guidance and constraints on the one hand and inconsistency, disagreement, ambiguity, openness and freedom – is to balance order and chaos.

CONSISTENCY THEORY HAS ATTEMPTED TO CAPTURE THIS CRITICAL BALANCE IN TWO DIFFERENT WAYS: TYPOLOGIES AND TAXONOMIES.

Typologies describe and prescribe archetypical organizational forms that sufficiently balance various organizational aspects of order and chaos.[8] Typologies succeed in offering design principles: however, they fail to address the diversity of organizational forms.[9] Taxonomies, by contrast, present empirically derived types of organizations by showing that certain organizational-design features tend to coincide (i.e., form statistical clusters).[10] Taxonomies, however, have failed to explain why most organizations rely on certain combinations of design features. Consistency theory is thus left struggling with the gap between empirical findings and relevant concepts. Addressing this gap, consistency theorists have hinted

at aesthetics as the missing link that could join everyday practice with design principles such as, most prominently, the critical balance between order and chaos. Consistency theorists' descriptions of their findings and reasoning suggest that understanding organizational design requires both analytical thinking and aesthetic judgement. They have characterized organizations as both 'logical configurations'[11] and 'Gestalts'[12] (a term from the psychology of sensory and, in particular, visual perception).[13] Organizational consistency has been defined as "the degree to which an organization's elements are orchestrated and connected by a single theme".[14] The formation of configuration, the actual task of organizational design, is seen as both "strongly underpinned by provinces of meaning and interpretive schemes"[15] and governed by "principles of consonance".[16] These terms emphasize two epistemological modes involved in organizational design: first, the intellectual mode of logic and argument that dominates current organization theory; and second, the aesthetic mode of sensory perception that, until recently, has received insufficient attention in organization theory.[17]

THE REFERRAL TO SENSORY PERCEPTION AND TO VARIOUS FORMS OF ARTISTIC CREATION IS NOT MERELY A LOOSE METAPHOR.

By contrast, the twofold problem of organizational design is most accurately and beautifully captured in Miller's notion of orchestrating and connecting through a (dominant) theme – a term referring to the topic and content of written or spoken language as well as to a melody or, more specifically, the 'Leitmotiv' in musical works.

For instance, the rules of harmony, the basic tool for composers, are not concerned with maximizing consonance (which could simply be achieved by, say, everybody in an orchestra playing the same note). Instead, they inform the creation of a critical balance between consonance and dissonance, between musical order and chaos. Composers guide the listeners' attention and shape the listeners' experience. They get listeners to form expectations, which they subsequently meet or frustrate by creating a critical balance in the listeners providing them with enough orientation for 'getting a sense' of what is going on, yet also surprising them. The rules of harmony help composers to stimulate and guide individual sense-making without losing their audience to boredom stemming from simplicity or to overload resulting from chaos.

This collinearity between organizational design and aesthetic/artistic creation – how both aim at shaping human experience – also sheds light on why it has been difficult for organization science to grasp the problem of organizational design. Like the rules of harmony, rules in organizational design fall under the reign of plausibility rather than (absolute) truth. They are powerful guidelines, yet different from Newtonian laws of nature, which can be refuted, in principle, by a single disconfirming incident. By contrast, the rules of harmony and of organizational design are meant to be applied by composers and managers, respectively. More specifically, in aligning form and matter, they call for a critical balance between generally following and occasionally breaking the rules.[18] Because specifying rules for breaking the rules leads into infinite regress,[19] the rules underlying aesthetics necessarily remain partly implicit; they can only be expressed through (explicitly) denoting and (implicitly) exemplifying.

FOR THE SAME REASON THEY CAN NEVER BE COMPLETE, BUT INSTEAD REMAIN IN PROGRESSION.

Art works and organizations are embedded in social contexts and, therefore, evolve as society evolves. The rules of harmony, for instance, are context dependent in the sense that they vary between (regional) cultures and historical periods (of 'the same culture'). In Baroque music, for example, dissonant chords were forbidden, with the exception only of the dominant seventh chord if immediately followed by the chord that sets the key of the piece (e.g., the C major chord in a piece written in C major). Hence, Baroque rules of harmony allow just one possibility for some dissonance and that experience of dissonance had to be 'cured' immediately by the greatest amount of consonance possible. Over the course of musical history, however, dissonance has gained territory. For instance, in the late nineteenth century Richard Wagner exposed his audience to sequences of dissonant chords.

41

6[E.g. Burns and Stalker (1961), Khandwalla (1973), Miller and Friesen (1977, 1984), Miles and Snow (1978), Mintzberg (1979), Greenwood and Hinings (1993). 7[Miller (1993), Miller and Cheng (1996). 8[E.g. Burns and Stalker (1961), Miles and Snow (1978), Mintzberg (1979). 9[Typologies that distinguish more than basically two generic organizational forms do not pass empirical tests. Doty, Glick and Huber (1993), for instance, find empirical support for the typology proposed by Miles and Snow (1978), which is a variation of the distinction between organic and mechanistic organizations (Burns and Stalker 1961). However, they find no support for Mintzberg's typology (1979) that distinguishes between five archetypical forms. 10[E.g. Miller and Friesen (1977, 1984). 11[Mintzberg (1979). 12[Miller (1981). 13[Ehrenfels (1890), Wertheimer (1912, 1923). 14[Miller (1996). 15[Hinings and Greenwood (1988). See Gadamer (1960) for a treatise on the intimate link between interpretive reasoning and aesthetic judgement. 16[SIAR (1973). 17[Bauer (2003). 18[For an extensive analysis of the mutual dependency of rule following and rule violation in organizations see Ortmann (2003). 19[Gödel (1931), Turing (1936).

But what Wagner aficionados experience as a climax of Occidental culture would have been pure cacophony to Händel's contemporaries: in turn, some Wagnerians would not hesitate to apply the some judgement to the even more dissonant works of twentieth-century Avantgarde music. But this irreversible progression of art forms is not expected to culminate in an ultimate work of art. Similarly, the rules governing organizational design can be expected to progress over time without ever leading to an ultimate organizational form. Aesthetics is central to the organizations-as-orientation-systems perspective, from which I shall now briefly recount current developments in organizational design and speculate about what might be seen in the near and not so near future.

3. Contemporary organizational design: from disaggregating structures to synchronizing rhythms

In the early 1990s, the world of modern organizations had a deja vu. Once again, car manufacturers, competing in the market for the single most expensive item in private consumption, were in turmoil. One particular company had deployed a superior production system that eventually would revolutionize not only the automotive industry, but also all industrial production of goods and services. Like Ford in the early 1900s, Toyota in the 1990s had made a quantum leap forward:

CUSTOMERS RECEIVED HIGHER QUALITY AT LOWER PRICES AND WERE OFFERED A GREATER VARIETY OF MODELS TO CHOOSE FROM WHILE PROFIT MARGINS WENT UP.

In the case of both Ford and Toyota, the major productivity gains were derived from a strong will to improve every detail rather than from a single ingenious idea. Yet, the innumerable minor innovations that together resulted in enormous improvement were connected in each case by a main theme: 'standardization' at Ford, 'inter-organizational networks' at Toyota.

Toyota pioneered the disaggregation of the global firm or, in other words, the decay of the vertically integrated enterprise. As a consequence, the automotive industry was radically transformed. The number of Original Equipment Manufacturers (OEM) went down rapidly; suppliers gained importance taking over increasing shares of developing and manufacturing cars, while OEM's focused more on marketing and distribution. In two decades, Toyota evolved from a small firm producing technically inferior copies of Western cars to the second largest, and by far the most profitable, car manufacturer. Large integrated firms became extinct in the automotive industry and cars, initially produced by a single company, became the product of an inter-organizational network comprised of hundreds of intimately linked firms. Other industries – computers, consumer electronics, apparel, and food processing being the early ones – followed. Although each industry has its own specifics, it is probably fair to say that the inter-organizational network has emerged as the dominant organizational form for producing complex goods and delivering complex services.

From an organizations-as-orientation-systems perspective, the replacement of large integrated corporations by assemblies of smaller organizations comes as no surprise.

LARGE INTEGRATED ORGANIZATIONS ARE IN AN INFERIOR POSITION REGARDING THE AESTHETIC CHALLENGES OF ORGANIZATIONAL DESIGN.

True, size results in market power and puts large firms at an advantage, but size also tends to coincide with heterogeneity of activity sets. A firm pursuing diverse activities lacks a coherent task. It faces a problem similar to that of a film-maker aiming to make one movie catering to several different audiences: an acceptable solution may be possible, but most likely compromises on many audience-specific criteria for quality and probably cannot arrive at a distinct artistic language. By contrast, small organizations must be highly selective about what they do and, consequently, can be specific about how they do it. An organization focusing on a single coherent activity set can deploy all the elements of organizational design in such a fashion that they jointly provide optimal stimulation and guidance for the individual workers. Coherent activity sets provide the basis for consistent organizational designs and consequently for motivating, meaningful work experiences. However, a large firm pursuing incoherent activity sets faces two unfavorable alternatives: either providing as many specific organizational designs as there are distinct tasks, thereby rendering the organization as a whole incomprehensible and unmanageable; or imposing an overall, unspecific design on everyone, thereby imposing compromised working conditions on most if not all of its members.

From a work-centered perspective – organizations seen as epistemological devices that shape work experience – the disaggregation of the global corporation is an important step forward in organizational design. Large integrated organizations as orientation systems are prone to mediocrity, lack distinct activity profiles and thus fail to necessitate and facilitate their members' co-creation of specific, captivating work experiences. For the most part, they are being replaced by numerous, generally smaller firms that manage to develop a pronounced style of what and how they do. These firms reflect an 'aesthetic' approach

to (re-) focusing domains and outsourcing non-core activities as an alternative to merely reducing (fixed) costs, which often deprives firms of necessary slack and erodes core capabilities. Instead, (re-) focusing and outsourcing are used to create clearly focused work-centered organizations – devoted to productivity and creativity in work processes and to significance work experience. The proposition that firms pursuing clearly focused activity sets more probably maintain distinctive organizational designs that function as powerful orientation systems,[20] can be read as an instantiation of Leopold Kohr's famous formula

'SMALL IS BEAUTIFUL'.

However 'small' here refers to clarity of focus rather than just size, and 'beautiful' rather than merely indicating sensory pleasure denotes – pars pro toto – aesthetic capability, which is the power to shape experience. The literature commonly attributes the disaggregation of the global corporation to two main causes. First, improved infrastructures for transporting physical entities and symbols (i.e. telecommunications) have helped overcoming spatial barriers. Second, efficiency gains in financial markets mean that corporate owners can manage their risk better by holding portfolios of equity shares in several companies than by diversifying whatever company they own. However, the organizations-as-orientation-systems perspective suggests that the aesthetic dimension of organizational design is driving the disaggregation. As geographical barriers are losing their power and owners protect their interests through markets (rather than organizational forms) organizational design becomes less constrained. Consequently, the 'logic of work' – the technical requirements of work processes and the aesthetic principles of work experience – becomes more prominent in contemporary organizational design.

ENHANCED FIRM-SPECIFICITY IS COMPLEMENTED BY A TREND TOWARDS MORE SPECIFIC LINKS BETWEEN FIRMS.

These linked trends have pushed the division of labor to a new level: the joint creation of integrated and often complex products or services by sets of highly specialized and specifically connected organizations. Admittedly, specialized firms with specific organizational designs predate the disaggregation of the global corporation; however, those firms catered to others through arms-length

---

20[For a detailed analysis see Bauer (2003).

market transactions. Markets, highly unspecific interfaces, work best for non-specific transactions between many anonymous trade partners (exchanging standardized information). Hence, next-to-perfect markets are mirror images of large integrated corporations.

THEY ALLOW FOR SPECIALIZED FIRMS WITH CONSISTENT ORGANIZATIONAL DESIGN, BUT REQUIRE GENERIC OUTPUT THAT CAN BE TRADED EFFICIENTLY.

Big hierarchies, on the other hand, can require their subsystems (subsidiaries, departments etc.) to produce specific output, but are limited as to how specifically they can organize each activity. By contrast, the new organizational forms pioneered in automotive industries are specific in the senses of both products and services customized for certain partners and of organizational designs specifically complementing activity sets. The disaggregation of the global corporation is still under way, gaining momentum from a massive wave of global (out)sourcing triggered by China and India joining the world economy. In addition, it is fueled by a trend towards self-employment intimately tied to growing individualism and, more critically viewed, eroding social bonds in Western societies. As a result of this change in labor relationships, the disaggregation of the large integrated firm reaches its ultimate limit – the firm comprised of one individual. While there is much debate about the extent to which people choose to become free agents [21] or are forced into self-employment,[22] there is growing evidence that firms, particularly the small and smallest ones, are employed 'like artists'. Temporary engagements ('projects'), permanent pressure for high technical quality and distinctively innovative performance, and an uneven distribution of income leaving the majority with very little to live off – the usual situation of actors, musicians, writers, filmmakers etc. – are becoming standard working conditions for increasingly more businesses.[23] Although the two realms significantly differ, creating works of art and producing industrial goods and services converge remarkably. As public funding declines, artists are increasingly required to participate in market contests.

In addition, artists, like scientists, are no longer expected to be geniuses, but instead to function as professionals – 'creative workers', like 'knowledge workers'.[24] As a result, art is losing much of its sacred aura. Firms, on the other hand, are concerned with problems that lie at the core of artistic success. They need to develop a distinct style – a specific approach to what they do and how they do it (and communicate it) – and retain creativity – the ability to permanently reinvent in order to escape obsolescence and commoditization.

The disaggregation of the global firm underscores both the aesthetic dimension and the plurality inherent in organizational design. Companies of various shapes and sizes, each with its own rather distinct style, are linked into fine-grained networks spanning the globe. These networks are enabled by specific bilateral links between firms – links that emerge from combinations of coordinating mechanisms [25] and allow firms to collectively transcend the limitations to which they individually subscribe to by restricting themselves to coherent activity sets.

THE DEPTH AND PRECISION THAT FIRMS GAIN FROM ENHANCED SPECIFICITY COME AT THE COST OF SIMPLIFICATION DUE TO MORE HOMOGENOUS ACTIVITY SETS.

By connecting with each other, these firms establish inter-organizational networks that enable them to overcome firm-level simplification and to create highly complex and neatly integrated goods and services. Like postmodern art at its best, these sets of specifically-linked specific firms deliver coherent creations emerging from combination, hybridization and occasional amalgamation of various distinct styles.

Finally, this trend in organizational design, which first received attention under the 'just-in-time' label, has implications for processes within and across firm boundaries. In automotive industries, for instance, it has become common for suppliers to share the same plant and engage in a joint process of car assembly, instead of merely delivering auto parts 'in time'. Rapidly innovating firms in high-velocity industries rely on projects to an extent that renders the concept of departments virtually insignificant.

What distinguishes successful project based firms from their less successful competitors is the ability to develop an 'internal clock' through synchronizing and overlapping projects.[26] They succeed in creating a continuous flow of knowledge and people across projects, thereby lowering employee uncertainty and enhancing utilization of capacity. In short, these firms are integrated through rhythm rather than through structure; by finding their own rhythm they occupy a middle ground between (reactive, external) adaptability and (proactive, internal) initiative.[27] Similarly, firms around the globe can be expected to relate to one another by intensifying existing inter-organizational activity patterns and by developing new ones.

THESE PATTERNS REFLECT DYNAMICS OF DEMAND AND SUPPLY AS WELL AS RHYTHMS OF NATURE AND WORK.

(E.g., operations in time zones separated by eight hours of time difference make it possible to shift (digital) work around the globe in three day shifts per day.) The disaggregation of the global firm will result not only in firms with distinct organizational designs dispersed around the globe but also, eventually, in rhythms pulsating through a global mosaic of organizational designs – global pulse(s) underneath layers of differentiated local 'beats' elaborating on the basic metre. Organizational design, as stated at the outset, is intimately tied to the rhythm of work. This rhythm is becoming increasingly global and demands that contemporary organizational design enables firms to resonate with the global pulse, yet maintain their own momentum.

21[E.g. Florida 2002, Pink 2001. **22**[E.g. Sennett 1998. **23**[E.g. Rothauer 2005. **24**[Brodbeck (1999), McRobbie (2002, 2004). **25**[In particular, these inter-organizational network ties combine universal standards (e.g., market price), local standardization (e.g., industry standards and bilaterally agreed custom definitions) and unique agreements (e.g., ad-hoc inter-organizational coordination primarily relying on oral cross-organizational and cross-disciplinary communication). For further details Bauer (2003). **26**[Brown and Eisenhardt (1998). **27**[In large software firms it is considered normal that up to 30% of potential members of project teams are 'between' projects (Jittandra 19xx).

Coda

Despite growing attention, the study of organizational and managerial aesthetics is still in its infancy. The twentieth century was the century of language, of propositional knowledge captured in natural and formal language, of thinking and of thinking about thinking. Only recently have alternative ways of knowing, most prominently sensing and feeling, become the focus of significant, growing research efforts. The collinearity between artistic creation, and leadership and organizational design now provides a foundation for aesthetic analyses of organizations. It has also given rise to a renaissance of the artist as a role model for managers and self-employed agents of various kinds. However, the proliferation of the 'artist' model for economic actors has its problems.

FIRST, THE NATURE OF ARTISTIC WORK APPEARS IN FLUX.

Some artists see art as a profession and, accordingly, define themselves as 'creative workers'; others see it primarily as an intrinsically driven process, more pronounced, as a 'way to survive'. Hence, it is not clear as to what extent professions with disruptive workflow and high pressure for innovation can accurately be described and explained as artistic or quasi-artistic, and to what extent the 'artist' metaphor euphemistically disguises the ugly face of unemployment and forced self-employment.[28]

Second, to keep organization and management theory from reverting to naive conceptions of agency it is critical to emphasize that artists do not create ex nihilo. They require an audience co-creating the artistic experience and therefore rely on criteria underlying aesthetic judgement that are beyond their control. As Kant showed, these criteria are essentially collective, reflecting epistemological habits shared within the community. The role of artists as a vanguard of society is less to actively shape the epistemological habits – i.e. the cultural identity – of the community than to heighten awareness of epistemological changes as society evolves. Accordingly, artists describe the process of creation as equally relying on receptive capabilities and on the will to shape. Hence, an aesthetic perspective should not provide grounds for simplistic conceptions of agency, such as great-man theories of leadership and organizational design.

Finally, the aesthetic realm is shaped by fundamental tensions such as 'innovative versus conservative' or 'pluralistic versus totalistic'. As for the first, psychological studies show beauty as a proxy for memory, in the sense that what is familiar – even if there is no conscious recognition – is more likely to be found beautiful.[29] Recognizing this conservative tendency in aesthetic judgement is particularly important because many existing accounts of the relevance of aesthetics for management emphasize innovation. As for the second, aesthetics is a realm of genuine plurality, because aesthetic judgement varies substantially between (sub-) cultures in the sense both of historical periods and of geographical regions.

However, these differences do not account for 'better' or 'worse' on any general scale beyond culture. Devotion to a particular style can easily turn into disregard of any other style; the prevalent idea of 'perfection', which presupposes and embraces one specific, partial ideal is inherently totalistic. Given the tension between the plural and the total in aesthetics, condemning managerial aesthetics as a potentially fascist instrument of totalitarian domination, as Critical theory tends to, falls as short as welcoming managerial aesthetics in a Postmodernist fashion as a natural remedy for intolerance.[30]

AESTHETIC JUDGEMENT CAN NEITHER SUBSTITUTE FOR ANALYTICAL THINKING NOR FOR ETHICAL DELIBERATION.

It has a potential to correct shortcomings of intellectual and emotional knowledge and, in turn, needs to be complemented by other ways of knowing. Aesthetic accounts of management and organization, as advocated in this article, represent a step towards 'epistemological pluralism' – a meta-theoretical stance, according to which human knowledge relies on various mutually irreducible epistemological modes that inform each other.

References

Bauer, Robert (2003): Effizienz und Effektivität in Netzwerk-Organisationen: unterwegs zu einer epistemologischen Theorie der Organisation; in: Weiskopf 2003, pp. 227-257.

Brodbeck, Karl-Heinz (1999): Entscheidung zur Kreativität; Darmstadt: Primus.

Brown, Shona and Kathleen M. Eisenhardt (1998): Competing on the Edge; Boston, Mass.: Harvard Business School Press.

Burns, Tom and George M. Stalker (1961): The Management of Innovation; London: Tarvistock.

Dearborne, DeWitt C. and Herbert A. Simon (1958): Selective Perception: A Note on the Departmental Identification of Executives; Sociometry, 21, pp. 140-144.

Doty, Harold D., William H. Glick and George P. Huber (1993): Fit, Equifinality and Organizational Effective¬ness: A Test of Two Configurational Theories; Academy of Management Journal, 36, pp. 1196-1250.

Ehrenfels, Christian von (1890): Über „Gestaltqualitäten"; Vierteljahresschrift für wissenschaftliche Philosophie, 14/3, pp. 249-292.

Florida, Richard (2002): The Rise of the Creative Class; New York: Basic.

Gadamer, Hans-Georg (1960): Wahrheit und Methode; Tübingen: Mohr, 2 Bände; hier: 6. Auflage 1990.

Gödel, Kurt (1931): Über formal unentscheidbare Sätze der Principia Mathematica und verwandter Systeme, I; Monatshefte für Mathematik und Physik, 38, pp. 173-198.

Goodman, Nelson (1976): Languages of Art; Indianapolis: Hackett.

Greenwood, Roystone and C.R. Hinings (1993): Understanding Strategic Change: The Contribution of Archetyps; Academy of Management Journal, 36/5, pp. 1052-1081.

Hinings, C.R. (Bob) and Royston Greenwood (1988): The Dynamics of Strategic Change; Oxford: Basil Blackwell.

Huber, J., Eds. (2002): Singularitäten - Allianzen; Wien - New York: Springer.

Kauffman, Stewart A. (1993): The Origins of Order; New York: Oxford.

Khandwalla, Pradip N. (1973): Viable and Effective Organizational Designs of Firms; Academy of Management Journal, 16/3, pp. 1278-1313.

Kunstverein München, Eds. (2004): Atelier Europa; München.

Kunst-Wilson, William Raft and Robert B. Zajonc (1980): Affective Discrimination of Stimuli that Cannot Be Recognised; Science, 207, pp. 557-558.

Langton, Christoper G. (1990): Computation at the Edge of Chaos: Phase Transitions and Emergent Computation; Physica D, 42, pp. 12-37.

Lawrence, Paul R. and Jay W. Lorsch (1967): Organization and Environment: Managing Differentiation and Integration; Boston: Graduate School of Business Administration Harvard University.

Leadbeater, Charles and Kate Oakley (1999): The Independents. Britains New Cultural Entrepreneurs; London: Demos.

Magris, C. / W. Kaempfer, Eds. (1981): Problemi del nichilismo; Roma: Shakespeare.

McRobbie, Angela:
(2002): Jeder ist kreativ. Künstler als Pioniere der New Economy?; in: Huber 2002, pp. 37-60.
(2004): Kreatives London – kreatives Berlin. Anmerkungen zum Erwerb des Lebensunterhalts in der neuen kulturellen Ökonomie; in: Kunstverein München, München 2004, pp. 22-33.

Miles, Raymond E. and Charles C. Snow (1978): Organizational Strategy, Structure and Process; New York - Tokyo - Hamburg: McGraw-Hill.

Miller, Danny:
(1981): Toward a new contingency approach: The search for gestalts; Journal of Management Studies, 18, pp. 1-26.
(1993): The Architecture of Simplicity; Academy of Management Review, 18/1, pp. 116-138.
(1996): Configurations Revisited; Strategic Management Journal, 17/7, pp. 505-512.

Miller, Danny and Ming-Jer Chen (1996): The simplicity of competitive repertoires: An empirical analysis; Strategic Management Journal, 17, pp. 419-439.

Miller, Danny and Peter Friesen (1977): Strategy Making in Context: Ten Empirical Archtypes; Journal of Management Studies, 14, pp. 259-280.
(1984): Organizations - A Quantum View; Englewood Cliffs: Prentice-Hall.

Mintzberg, Henry (1979): The Structuring of Organizations; Englewood Cliffs: Prentice-Hall.

Ortmann, Günther (2003): Regel und Ausnahme; Frankfurt a.M.: Suhrkamp.

Pink, Daniel (2001): Free Agent Nation; New York: Time Warner.

Quinn, Robert E. and John Rohrbaugh (1981): A Competing Values Approach to Organizational Effectiveness; Productivity Review, 5, pp. 122-140.

Rothauer, Doris (2005): Kunst und Kapital; Wien: WUV.

Sennett, Richard (1998): The Corrosion of Character: The Personal Consequences of Work in the New Capitalism; New York: Norton.

SIAR, Scandinavian Instituts for Adminstrative Research Group of Sweden (1973): Management Survey of UNICEF; Report, Stockholm.

Turing, Allen M. (1936): On Computable Numbers, with an Application to the Entscheidungsproblem; Proceedings of the London Mathematical Society, 2/42, pp. 230-265.

Vattimo, Gianni:
(1981): Apologia de nichilismo; in: Magris / Kaempfer 1981.
(1985): La fine della modernita; Milano: Garzanti.
(1989): La società transparente; Mailand: Garzanti.
(1998): Die Grenzen der Wirklichkeitsauflösung; in: Vattimo / Welsch 1998, pp. 15-26.

Vattimo, G. / W. Welsch, Eds. (1998): Medien-Welten Wirklichkeiten; München: Fink.

Weiskopf, R., Eds. (2003): Menschenregierungskünste; Wiesbaden: Westdeutscher Verlag.

Wertheimer, Max:
(1912): Experimentelle Studien über das Sehen von Bewegung; Zeitschrift für Psychologie, 61, pp. 161-265.
(1923): Untersuchungen zur Lehre von der Gestalt; Psychologische Forschung, 4, pp. 301-350.

INTERACT OR DIE ❮

Interaction Ivrea is Olivetti's latest answer to the information society. Where typewriters were once fabricated, they now do research into communication processes. The discipline of architecture could learn something from this example of a strategic shift of focus. One cannot mention Ivrea but in the same breath as Olivetti. Lying in the Aosta valley not far from Turin, the town was once the capital of one of those industrial empires that typified the era of the typewriter.

THANKS TO OLIVETTI, IVREA BECAME A SOCIAL EXPERIMENT IN WHICH CITY, CULTURE AND INDUSTRY WENT HAND IN HAND.

Countless architects erected elegant modern buildings over the years, buildings which were notable for their blend of functionality and landscape-awareness. One of the most familiar names was that of Adriano Olivetti, who founded a centre for social sciences with a brief to study a post-war form of corporatism in Ivrea.

The enlightened Olivetti corporation stood symbol for an aspiration to couple rapid industrial progress with social improvement. Then one day the knowledge economy, the digital economy, the New Economy arrived. It proved disastrous for Olivetti. The story is soon told. Olivetti went on making typewriters while the rest of the world migrated en masse to word processors. Their stalwart attempts to turn the tide were all too little and too late. If you care to press your nose to the window of one of the run-down, dusty warehouses that dots the industrial zone of Ivrea, you stand a good chance of spotting a teetering stack of unsold typewriters. A blanket of dejection drapes over this former industrial paradise, where company pride and labour productivity once shared a happy home. And had Olivetti not formed suitable alliances - just in time - the family name would have been consigned to the realm of cultural heritage long ago. What was wrong with Olivetti that almost put it out of business? Suppose you make machines. As long as there is a demand for those machines, you can sell them. You build up an enlightened company culture around this activity, complete with a modern housing policy, a research programme and a company social scheme. Once demand for the machines slides, however, prosperity flies out of

the window. The usual mistake is that after a century of company growth you tend to identify with the product instead of with the demand. Good intentions founded on the economic laws of the market. The lesson is that rather than building a company that makes machines, you ought to build one that generates knowledge about the social situations in which a need for that hardware arises. You can't just carry on being a box shifter, because your company has to instigate and manage 'consumption paths'. It's not enough to understand the nature of the demand, but you must identify where desires are born. Economy is tantamount to knowledge and a capacity to innovate. The error was nearly fatal for Olivetti, but there are countless other areas of society in which exactly the same kind of thing is ongoing without the reckoning being finally settled yet. The sciences, professional disciplines, political parties, artistic movements, shops, educational institutes: they are all prone to founder in the belief that their own existence is a fact of life; that they exist because they exist. Meanwhile, insurgent tendencies could take an axe to the roots of all these institutions. Much of their adaptive capacity, in as far as it still exists, is then directed at a last-hour attempt to incorporate the 'new facts'. An ancillary discipline emerges, for example, or a political renewal committee is set up, a product range is expanded somewhat or an additional professor is appointed. But there is seldom any ability to turn the insurgent forces to advantage, and to start again from scratch. That can only happen once the pressure has become so great that a choice is unavoidable; for example when a company like Olivetti is on the verge of collapsing.

WHAT DOES A COMPANY LIKE OLIVETTI DO WHEN THINGS HAVE REACHED THAT POINT?

Why, it sets up a new research institute for interaction design, of course. It no longer develops products, but situations, interfaces and possibilities for communication. When products cannot withstand the Zeitgeist, you had better change the conditions for the Zeitgeist. Together with Telecom Italia, Olivetti put up 40 million Euros to found an independent centre that would apply itself exclusively to devising and testing theories about how people

relate to digital technology and how they organize their communication. The institute's education and research aims at understanding how communication takes place and how communication processes renew themselves - instead of at the technology to achieve it. Technology and cultural production are treated as one. Heavily sponsored as it is by business, the institute will naturally also consider the business models implicit in this new outlook. The bulk of the programme, headed by the former Professor of Computer Related Design at the Royal College of Art, Gilian Crampton Smith, will consist of areas like wearable computing, smart urbanism and hybrid knowledge environments on the cutting edge of physical and virtual reality. The starting capital, the founding principle, the lecturing staff, the curriculum, the technical equipment, the international network: all these things have been brought jointly to bear on the central issue of interaction as part of the design task. Ivrea resurgent! It is striking that at least two of the research themes relate to architecture. While it is growingly obvious that no early breakthrough in 'smart spaces' is to be expected from the architectural design discipline, and that interesting developments in this area are more likely to come from services technology or interior design, the institute's programme continues to nurture the architectural and urban design component. The issue is not what the discipline is doing now, but what its future tasks will include. This means Interaction Ivrea is important to architecture for an even deeper reason: taking the discipline's task as primary instead of its achievements, is bound to bring it to the same crossroads as Olivetti. Architecture, too, is often little more than 'box shifting', the disposition and marking of building volumes in which to accommodate programmed functions.

IT IS INCREASINGLY CLEAR HOWEVER THAT THE ISSUE IS MOVING FROM ACCOMMODATION TO THE PROGRAMME AND HOW IT IS EXPERIENCED,

from an unequivocal style to flexible organization, from form-centred design to a psychology-driven process. That too is 'space' and 'context', of course, but no longer in a physical sense. The architecture associated with this is not concerned with the demarcation of space but with the 'in between', the transitional zones, the facilitation of physical and programmatic mobility. The practice of architectural design which is in touch with this tendency, which does not focus on enclosure but on the moments of interaction between people, goods and information, holds the future. This is where the crux lies.

IT IS PRECISELY THE DECISION TO GET IMMEDIATELY INTO INTERACTION DESIGN AND POSTPONE THE QUESTION OF ITS MATERIAL EMBODIMENT THAT GIVES ARCHITECTURE THE SCOPE TO FULFIL ITS NEW MANDATE.

If it sticks with box shifting (or arranging, trimming, stretching, slicing, tilting or any other kind of volume-related action), architecture could easily - like Olivetti - find itself lost for answers in the face of its new task. With this in mind, the location chosen for the new institute is surprising. The Interaction Ivrea institute chose to settle into one of the finest industrial buildings on the Olivetti campus - Edoardo Vittorio's 1950s Blue House, which owes its name to the ceramic tiles adorning its exterior. The architecture does not give even the least hint that the building contains an ultramodern design institute. On the contrary, the renovation by Marco Zanini of Sottsass Associati makes it into more of a building than it already was: interface design housed within a bastion of architecture. This does not of course imply the impossibility of results.The specification is full of testing rooms, lounges, studios, research labs and so on. The vicissitudes of the institute and its network may be followed on www.interaction-ivrea.it.

SCOTT LASH ❮ Paris/Shanghai

TRANSACTIONS BETWEEN THE CITIES OF A GIVEN COUNTRY ARE THESE DAYS LESS IMPORTANT THAN THE TRANSACTIONS – CULTURAL, ECONOMIC, TECHNOLOGICAL, HUMAN – BETWEEN LINKS OF THE CHAIN OF GLOBAL CITIES.

At perhaps opposite ends of the continuum of that chain stand, on the one hand *Paris* and on the other, *Shanghai*. Paris, as Walter Benjamin observed, was the capital of the nineteenth century. It was also, we might add – though Berlin was the strongest competitor-, the capital of the first half of the twentieth century. Shanghai in contrast is well on its way to being capital of the twenty-first century.

DESCARTES MADE A FAMOUS DISTINCTION BETWEEN RES EXTENSA, AND RES COGITANS.

Res extensa is the Cartesian body. *Res cogitans* is Cartesian mind. Res extensa is volumetric; it is composed of solids, it is governed by cause and effect; it follows clock time; it works like a Newtonian mechanism. Res cogitans is immaterial, timeless, self-causing and somehow vital. These days, with the distribution of mind - and more generally the sensorium - onto the networks, flows and fluxes of information and communication of the global village, res cogitans becomes *res intensiva*. In this sense, midway through the first decade of the twenty-first century, Paris is the world's prototypical *extensive city* and Shanghai the world's paradigmatic *intensive city*.

PARIS AS EXTENSIVE CITY IS ALL STRUCTURE, SHANGHAI AS INTENSIVE CITY IS A COMBINATOIRE OF FLOWS.

In Paris you know what can happen. In Shanghai anything can happen. Extensive Paris is Baron Haussmann's planned city, caused as it were externally from the outside. In intensive Shanghai planning never works: its unintended consequences are a wonderful out-of-controlness and on good days self-organisation, mutation, creative evolution. Baron Haussmann's nineteenth-century extensive and planned city destroyed the alleyways and labyrinths of the faubourgs, where the working class could barricade themselves in for revolution. In their place came the boulevards, along which troops from Bretange could be brought in by railway to Gare du Nord, Gare de Lyon, Gare de Montparnasse and could march the boulevards to quell the uprisings. Shanghai's post-revolutionary intensive

city in 2004 is also post-colonial: the French and English Concessions described in J.G. Ballard's and Steven Spielberg's *Empire of the Sun* displaced by – Nanjing Road and Huaihai Road - never-ending boulevards for walking. Paris as extensive city is a closed system: immigration is less than a third of say London or Los Angeles; finance markets are controlled and closed; the bourse is ineffective; labour markets are at their most rigid. Shanghai is an open system. It is a system that is indeed doubly open: first, as self-organizing and second, in being chronically traumatized from the outside. Immigration in Shanghai from Sizchuan and elsewhere in western China is swelling the population to some 20 million by 2005. Indeed in China there will be a migration of yet another 100 million to the cities from the countryside in the next fifteen years. This makes the quickest previously expanding western city, Berlin from 1890-1914 look like child's play. Finance markets in for example Pudong Shanghai's Special Economic Zone are nearly unmatched. Shanghai is the home to the world's highest levels of foreign direct investment and amazingly high levels of portfolio investment. London has its Pudong in Canary Wharf and the City. Paris does not. In intensive Shanghai and urban China in general, CDMA phones are everywhere and ADSL television is widespread. In extensive Paris, they are still waiting for roll out. Thus when Shanghai and Paris were in head-to-head competition for the 2010 World Expo, it was no contest. Shanghai won, hands down. Paris was all extensivity – nineteenth century, national, planning and industrial, closed and blocked off. Shanghai all intensivity: twenty-first century, global, mutating, informational and open.
The World's Fair is at the heart of all this.

BECAUSE IT IS AT THE EXPOSITION UNIVERSELLE IN PARIS IN 1855 THAT THE INTENSIVE CITY WAS BORN, WHOSE CHRONICLERS WERE CHARLES BAUDELAIRE AND BENJAMIN.

Amidst and among the overbearing extensivity of bureaucratic Paris of Haussmann and the boulevards – in the nooks and crannies that were the World's Fairs, the arcades, the haunts of the poètes maudits

— the intensive city was born. If the extensive city was described by the materiality and homogeneity of the *commodity*, intensivity was born in the immateriality, the difference, of the *commodity* fetish. The mechanism and instrumental rationality of the *commodity* is displaces by the phantasmagoria, the dream-like nature of the commodity-*fetish*. And it was the commodity-fetish that figured Baudelaire's and Benjamin's poems and epigrams. The commodity with its homogenous material mechanism was based in a logic of the Cartesian atom. The commodity fetish — which is heterogenous, immaterial and vital - found its logic, as Benjamin noted, in Leibniz's *monad*. Both the atom and the monad are simple substance. But the atom is simple substance as *identity*. Whereas in the monad simple substance is *difference*.

ALL ATOMS LIKE ALL COMMODITIES ARE THE SAME AS ONE ANOTHER.

All monads like all fetishes are different from one another. The commodity has to do with cognition of extensivity. The fetish is the imagination: it is intensivity. The atom (commodity) is the materiality of manufacturing production: the fetish the immateriality of information and communication. In the extensivity of the atom and the commodity the city dies. The intensivity of monad and fetish brings the city to life. Walter Benjamin saw Paris as the city of memory in which the ancient persists in the modern. Shanghai instead is conceived in a flux of impermanence, much as the built structures of the Chinese Empires were ephemeral, in the flow of continuity of language and being-Chinese. Baron Haussmann never expected his structures to last forever. Yet in Paris, all is protected. You cannot build. At the very centre of Paris is the disaster of Les Halles, under whose ground urban Paris yields to the hyper-extensity of suburbanization by the Reseau Express Régional. Yet plans to counteract this disaster are limited to changing a few ornaments in the garden on the surface. In contrast, Shanghai, and especially Pudong is a maze of building sites: chantiers of builders going 24/7: architects queuing for the main chance. Intensive Shanghai is of course a space of markets. But it is also a space of fantasy where anything is possible.

Thus Paris/Shanghai. Thus the Expositions Universelles in 1855 (Palais Industriel) and 1889 (Eiffel Tower) Paris, in the world headquarters of the extensive accumulation of capital.

AND THUS WORLD EXPO 2010 IN SHANGHAI, THE TWENTY-FIRST CENTURY WORLD HEADQUARTERS OF CAPITAL'S INTENSIVE ACCUMULATION.

If turn-of-the-20th-century capital accumulation was of factories, material goods and heavy-industrial means of production, then twenty-first century and Shanghai's intensive accumulation is of flows: of finance, communications, information and technology. Of fantasy and imagination.

This article aims to address some issues relevant to the design of time based flows and activities of people and organisations. Similar to buildings, that shaping the movement of people, the design of communication services influences the interaction between people and organisations.

The first part of this text sketches a historical perspective, outlining the cultural developments in the context of time and coordination.

The second part lists three parameters relevant in the design of flexible social interactions: time personalities, hierarchies and coordination models.

The third part outlines the conceptual frameworks that emerged out of a research project called Fluidtime, which will be described with an example.

The Fluidtime project, which recently turned into a commercial company, aims at contributing to developments in mobile and flexible time management.

WE ARE WORKING ON ENGAGING, CONVENIENT AND EFFECTIVE MEANS TO VIEW AND INTERACT WITH REAL-TIME INFORMATION IN A CONTINUOUS AND AMBIENT WAY, SOLVING THE PROBLEMS DISCOVERED IN CURRENT SYSTEMS.

Pre-Clock Era

Before the clock was invented, people were living close to
nature and oriented themselves by means of the cyclical
time flow given by nature. Nobody would have thought
about asking for the time. Work did not last for eight hours
but until either the fieldwork was finished or the sun set.
This was the era of event time. People started and ended
events when the time was right. Without the structure of
the clock, it was difficult to coordinate activities. There
were basically two times of reference: sunrise and dawn.
(Levine, 1997)

People's concept of time had a cyclical structure. Time was
organised in a rhythmical way that did not know progress
and repeated itself. The term „progress" was not used
until the beginning of industrialisation. (Geissler, 1999). The
conceptual understanding of future was of further significance for this era.

THE WORD „FUTURE" AS WELL AS THE WORD „PROGRESS" BECAME PART OF HUMAN LANGUAGE IN THE 18TH CENTURY.

This understanding of time can be imagined best as an
ascending line (Geissler, 1999)

Clock Era

In Europe, the transition from the pre-clock to the clock era occurred at the end of the Middle Ages. Monks first invented clocks in order to structure prayer times. (Levine, 1997). Tradesmen and mechanics adopted the clock and brought it into the cities. In the beginning each city ran on an independent clock and as a result had its „own time". With the introduction of train travel in the 19th Century, it became important to standardise schedules and a unified chronology was adopted. (Levine, 1997)

The use of clocks has interfered with our relationship to event time and new time patterns have emerged. No longer relying on nature or our own biological clock to decide when to begin and end activities we have become less attuned to both the outside world and our own bodies.

Artificial light also plays a large role in the modern use of time. The inventions of gas and electric lighting have significantly changed our relationship with time.

People have become able to pursue activities during the evening and night hours that once could only be carried out during daylight.

Post-clock Era

Today, we are facing a transition from the clock to the post-clock awareness of time. The Victorian principle of home, family and work being separate is changing. The fact that clocks are disappearing from public places is evidence that clockwork mechanisms are becoming metaphors or symbols of the past. They are no longer the only instrument for time orientation. We learn to understand that time does not mean just watches, clocks, or the oscillations of caesium atoms. Time is more than being exact. We are more and more experiencing that the clock separates people from the actual experience of time.

THE CENTRAL CLOCK TIME THAT HAS BEEN THE ORGANISING PRINCIPLE FOR MANY CENTURIES IS BEING REPLACED BY A MULTITUDE OF TIMES IN OUR NETWORKED SOCIETY AND BY INCREASED FLEXIBILITY.

As a result of this flexibility, everyone has a better possibility to live by his own time. For example, taking breaks when feeling tired and working when being productive. Traditional boundaries between work and home, between night and day, weekday and weekend are dissolving. The internet allows us to go shopping any time, even to consult doctors 24 hours a day. Technology has also made work portable, allowing it to merge with our personal lives.

Time Personalities - the Opportunist and the Squanderer

The case study of Noel Perlas (Philippines) above demonstrates how new communication technology changes the coordination behaviour of our lives. The two friends sent thirteen messages within a timeframe of two hours in order to arrange a meeting.

DEALING WITH TIME IS A HABIT THAT DEVELOPS THROUGHOUT A LIFE.

Therefore, many time habits depend on individual psychological structures. The less rigid the social demand for punctuality, the more space there is for different time personalities. The more flexible a society deals with time, the more people need to manage their own time and that of others if they want to coordinate it.

On the one side, Noel tries to locate different opportunities in time for a meeting with Tony. On the other side, Tony regularly reschedules the appointment and increases complexity by giving unclear predictions.

Obviously it can't be guaranteed that a design is only used in the way it is planned for. Opening up the time dimension as a space for design, we will need to respect the psychological dimension of its users.

SMS Conversation between Tony and Noel:

[TONY] Hey Noel, I need you to give something for chris, tell me when you are free.

[NOEL] Hey Tony. Ok. Will TXT u when

[NOEL] Hey Tony. I'm in the mall right now meeting friends for dinner wanna meet after that?

[TONY] Ok. I will be in that same mall for dinner. Great.

[NOEL] R U in the mall now? maybe we can meet before dinner instead. I have some time.

[TONY] Guess what, my dinner there didn't push through. I will meet you after dinner anyway. :)

[NOEL] Ok. See U then.

[NOEL] where r u?

[TONY] sorry traffic jam

[NOEL] where r u now?

[TONY] almost there, maybe 10 mins

[NOEL] it's been 10 mins, where are you? Should I order dessert for you?

[TONY] 5 mins, parking. :)

Time Coordination - from Fixed to Progressive

The clock and the calendar are the main tools for time-based coordination in our society. These "artifacts of temporality" (Palen 1999) are needed to schedule appointments on a fixed grid divided into months, days, hours and minutes. However, according to Kretzman, the increased in-ter-connectivity of ubiquitous communication transforms our life and activities into a constant flow rather than a succession of fixed points. (Kreitzmann, 1999)

The case study has demonstrated that within a networked culture friends do not make appointments by the minute when going out in the evening but agree to talk to or text each other and slowly tune into each other's flow of time and space, until they meet. The use of mobile phones for example, allows people to modulate the fixed coordinating grid of calendars and fosters connectedness and flexibility. As the networked coordination becomes more omnipresent we also adopt habits of progressive coordination.

The left part of the diagram above visualises what happens in a fixed coordination. People agree on a fixed time and everyone tries to meet that goal and comes at that time. If anyone is delayed, this point moves to a later stage.

The right part of the diagram shows what happens if we do not define a fixed time point in the future but a time frame. In the beginning this frame has a wider span; the closer an appointment comes, the narrower the frame gets and finally it turns into a point – the point of the meeting. This progressive process is only possible through constant communication.

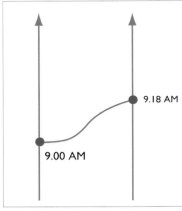

fixed coordination

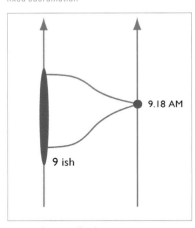

progressive coordination

Time Hierarchies - Pace Setter and Pace Taker

In a 24/7 society, anything can happen anytime, anywhere. There is an opportunity to give personal time to individuals, allowing them to decide when to do things. If things can happen all the time, people have the power to decide at what time they happen. (Kreitzmann, 1999) Nevertheless, many day-to-day interactions are bound to physical space and contact. In this con-text, a second important parameter comes into play: time-based relationships, which form a web of hierarchies between different actors.

WAITING INVOLVES A TEMPORARY RE-DEFINITION OF POWER. THE PERSON WAITING – THE PACE TAKER – IS LESS POWERFUL THEN THE ONE WHO MAKES HIM/HER WAIT – THE PACE SETTER.

When people wait, time becomes a resource, and the ones waiting have no control over it. The clash between personal time flow (e.g. getting food, going home) and the public time flow (e.g.standing in a queue) is experienced as disturbing. People always have to adjust their personal time to the public time. Public time flows are based on other people, services, or processes that have their own timing. In the context of hospitals and medical examinations, temporal coordination between doctors and patients is usually based on standard scheduling tools without any connection between the doctors' and the patients' flows of time. If any changes happen and are not communicated, time based con-flicts occur. The hospital waiting room is the buffer zone between the pace setters and the pace takers, allowing time based synchronisation.

Bridging Flows of Time

The framework above describes the stages that lead to the consumption of a service in the context of travel. The first stage of this model is about planning and informing. The customer requests and receives information from the service organisation in order to make travelling choices based on information. This planning activity can either happen by phone, via the web, or through a printed schedule. If necessary, in the second stage, the traveller interacts with the organisation in order to book a seat on a particular bus or train and buy the ticket. In the third stage, the traveller has made all the necessary arrangements and is looking forward to the trip.

THE TRIP MIGHT STILL BE DAYS AWAY AND THE SERVICE ORGANISATION COULD UPDATE THE CUSTOMER ON ANY IMPORTANT CHANGES.

The day before the travel, the company might remind the customer of the upcoming trip. In the fourth stage, now being only hours or minutes away from the actual consumption of the service, the traveller leaves home, the office or another location to go to the bus stop or train station. At this point, the service organisation updates its customers on any delays or provides other temporal information. Once the traveller arrives at the location of the service interaction, s/he will orientate himself/herself, for example, by finding the platform, etc. The sixth stage covers the activity of waiting for the bus or train to arrive.
The vertical arrows show the points where communication service can bridge the gap between the personal time flow of the customer and the public one of the service company.

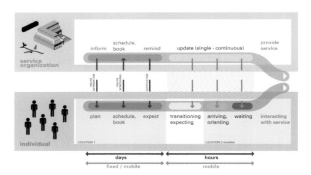

66

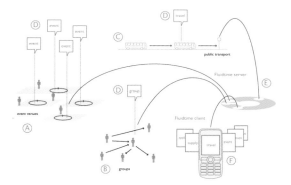

Time Windows

The concept of time windows has emerged out of the need to build a communication service that is able to flexibly combine various context sources into a homogenous service environment with high usability and effective deployment. A time window is a mental model that can assign any type of information about an ongoing event, a public transport vehicle or a service delivery status in the hospital.

A), B), and C) show three contexts where flexible coordination takes place: events, group gatherings and travel. Each of these environments implies a dynamic process. In the group context, for example, people are moving around in order to meet up and in the travel context, public transport vehicles are driving along predefined routes.

D) Each time window is a live presentation of one of these specific contexts, for instance a certain bus stop, describing when the next bus is scheduled to arrive and when it actually will arrive.

E) A server is the communication node for the various time windows. It aggregates content, divides it into small units, and organises the user requests.

F) The concept of the time window is pursued from its creation to the user interface.

Fluidtime Service Interfaces

A public transport service in Turin, Italy, was the first project that was realised using the concepts described above. It was chosen since it is the domain where most technological development is happening at the moment and where constantly updating travellers with real-time arrival information is highly welcome. The service covered the stages of expecting, transiting, arriving, and waiting, since these activities are the stages where the dynamic changes are most prominent and re-scheduling of timetables more frequent; they take place during the time scale of hours and minutes.

Interfaces:
Perspective visualisation: The interface shows how far a certain preselected bus is away from the chosen stop. The application permanently updates the visualisation with data originating from the Turin transport authorities.
Iconic representation of time: An icon on the upper part of the screen indicates the state, in which the user should be, in order to catch the next bus.

IF THE ICON REPRESENTS A TRANQUIL CHARACTER, THE USER CAN BE RELAXED. IF IT IS A RUNNING FIGURE, THE USER KNOWS THAT THE BUS IS DUE TO ARRIVE.

Fluidtime gives people the opportunity to know and decide about the time they have. It gives them the chance to decide about their waiting or idle time and to make their personal time flow.

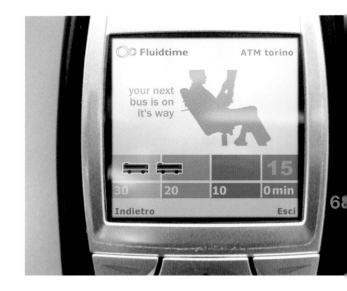

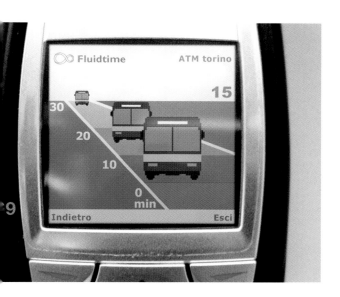

References:
Geissler K. A., Vom Tempo der Welt, Freiburg, Herder, 1999
Kreitzman L., The 24 Hour Society, London, Profile Books,
1999, Levine R., A Geography of Time, New York, Basic
Books, 1997, Palen, L., Individual & Technological Issues for
Groupware Calendar Systems. In Proceedings of the ACM
Conference on Human Factors in Computing Systems (CHI
99), Pittsburgh, pp. 17-24, 1999

**THE LOGIC OF THE MEDIA IS TAKING OVER
MORE AND MORE AREAS OF LIFE, AND
INDEED OF INORGANIC MATTER TOO.**

In this paper I want to argue that there are two modernities and that the second modernity is one of generalised mediatization. The second modernity is one in which the media spread like a disease. The first modernity describes a process of rationalization. And the second modernity describes one of mediatization. This paper partly grows out of a debate in the sociology of the media or cultural studies of the media. Here there is a debate between those who say that media are texts that are encoded by their producers decoded by the media audience. This media audience is socially located. And how they will decode the media texts is connected to their social location. Another position associated with writers like Baudrillard and Castells - who sees a move from a logic of structure to a logic of flows, - will presume that we as social beings are not outside of the media. On this view we live in a very important sense in a mediascape. It is that with the spread of more interactive platforms – the new media of satellite and now interactive television, consumer brand environments, mobile phones, 8MB internet, digital cameras and video and ubiquitous iPods – that we live in mediascape. You will see over the course of this paper that by media, I mean something that is the equivalent of digital media. This is partly because just about all our media now are becoming digital media. Digital media or its equivalent is becoming paradigmatic for media per se. This is an expanded definition of media. Or could it be, as this paper argues, that the media themselves have been expanding?

IN THE SECOND MODERNITY THE LOGIC OF MEDIATIZATION EXPANDS FROM THE CLASSIC MEDIA TO THE OBJECTS OF CONSUMER CULTURE. IT PERVADES, INDEED INVADES, NATURE AND THE BODY ITSELF.

It invades and reconstitutes the social. I am not arguing like Marshall McLuhan that we are increasingly prosthetic beings: that the media are extensions of man, though this is happening too. I am arguing that the logic of the media is taking over more and more areas of life, and indeed of inorganic matter too.
Just what main features of media will emerge over the

course of the paper. I need to make a few preliminary points though.
I think that both rationalization and mediatization are equally structured by reason. Mediatization we will see has to do with reflexivity, which is not a post-modern irrationality, but the form that reason takes in the second modernity. Rationalization and mediatization both have, at their core, a paradigm of rules. These rules are also a pivotal locus of reason. Thus mediatization in the second modernity or post-modernity is not anti-rule, or anarchistic, it just operated with different kinds of rules. Here is where the likeness ends. The rules of first modernity rationalization are regulative rules. In them reason as rules operates from the outside. In the first-modernity thus universals subsume particulars. Causes as rule-boundedness operate from the outside. Social actors confront rules as regulative norms. In second-modernity mediatization, rules – and reason - are not regulative. They are also not primarily constitutive. They are instead generative. Rules and reason are generative. They are informational. More precisely they work like algorithms. As sets of instructions. Algorithms are rules.[1]

They are rational in that they are sets of instructions. As in computer programming, these rules are instructions that generate difference. They generate different outcomes under different conditions. These rules, these generative rules that generate difference are not external to things as in rationalization, but compressed at the very core of the media themselves. As reflexive subjects - engaging with a mediascape that generates difference out of its own self-causation - we self-cause in a similar sort of way.

FROM A CONSTELLATIONS OF GENERATIVE RULES WE IN THE SECOND MODERNITY SELF-LEGISLATE.

Moreover the result of first modernity rationalization is more or less reproduction and equilibrium. In second modernity mediatization the result is chronic disequilibrium or at least far from equilibrium outcomes. Enough said for the moment by way of introduction. Let us trace this generalized mediatization.

THIS PAPER WILL TRY TO ARGUE HOW A LOGIC NOT JUST OF FLOW (THOUGH ALSO OF FLOW) BUT OF THE MEDIA, OF MEDIATIZATION IS ATTAINING UBIQUITY. IT WILL DO SO IN REGARD TO 1) NATURE 2) THE COMMODITY 3) CULTURE AND 4) SOCIETY, OR THE SOCIAL.

1❮ 'Algorithm' comes from the name of the Baghdad based Persian mathematician, Muhammed Al-Khwarizmi (c. 790-840). Al-Khwarizmi's book on computation published in 830 was origins of the term 'algebra'. Later the word 'algorism' referred to performing arithmetic using Arabic numerals. From the 18th century the word 'algorithm,' was in use, already meaning a set of well-defined procedures. A computer programme is an algorithm. Arguably the first written was in the mid-19th century by Ada Byron for Charles Babbage's never completed 'analytic engine'. Alan Turing in his abstract model of the computer put mathematical rigour into the algorithm: its formal criteria being a procedure that can be implemented on a completely specified Turing machine. Turing demonstrated that every method yet found for describing well-defined procedures could be emulated on a Turing machine. An algorithm is a finite set of well-defined instructions for accomplishing a task or solving a problem. This task, given an initial state, will terminate in a recognisable end state. Algorithms have been compared to recipes, especially in that the steps must precisely be followed in their order. In the US some algorithms can be patented, but only if a physical embodiment is possible in for example the arithmetical unit of a microprocessor.

Nature

Nature came first to rationalization, and maybe last to mediatization. But a new generation of writers such as Thacker (2004) and Parisi (2004) born in the early 1970s are producing books about biomedia. Rationalization of nature arises with Galileo's physics, is extended quickly to politics by Hobbes, and then is systematised in Descartes, Newton and Kant's epistemology. Here nature is conceived as mechanism. Nature is mechanism and observed by a reason that is external to it. This mechanism is a bit like a clockwork.

CAUSE IS EXTERNAL TO EFFECT.

This is already quite a move from pre-modern doctrines of creation. In Christian creationism, God is the prime mover. God in Genesis is the creator. Reason resides supremely in God. In the move from creation to rationalization, God's reason is displaced onto man. Man does not create here. He observes and finds. God's power is displaces onto the causes and effects of bodies on bodies in physics. The assumptions of rationalized nature are atomistic: of identical parts making up wholes. These atoms that are involved indeed in what Galileo called exchanges. In which, one can take the place of the other without any change. Nature here becomes objective. Reason is not in nature. Reason takes nature for its object. Reason is outside of nature. Its relation to nature is epistemological. This is what Kant called the understanding. This is Max Weber's famous Entzauberung. De-magicification. Nature loses agency. Life is drained from nature.

Think of how we discuss the media and especially digital media in terms of 'machines', 'codes', 'translation', 'transcription', 'information', 'instructions'. Now look at the most hit-upon website for genetic nucleotides. University of Utah. It says the structure of the double helix holds the genetic material. The gene is the genetic unit of 'information': the 'byte' of information.

THE DNA (DEOXYRIBOSE NUCLEIC ACID) CONTAINS GENETIC 'INSTRUCTIONS'.

Instructions and this is the language of computer science, are information that is 'communicated' to explain how a task is conducted. We already have the algorithm. Now let me say at once that media are only complete for me with digital media: that is with computing. Media are only completely media with Alan Turing. This was always there in the germ. What is the task to be conducted with genetic media? It is very centrally the constitution of proteins. The musculature, ligaments, skin and hair of the body are largely comprised of protein. The DNA, the 'genetic material' contains

information. But this information is not yet the byte of information. It is not yet the gene: the difference that makes the difference. But who decides what the gene is? The cell does. The DNA lies in the nucleus of the cell. The DNA comprises sequences of paired – hence a double helix – bases of the four nucleotides: A (adenine), C, (cytosine) G (guanine), T (thymine). Nucleotides are small molecules – monomers – that, in their chaining, form polymers or the macromolecules that are DNA and RNA. It is the cell, the unit of life, which 'transcribes' the DNA into RNA. Media, says Friedrich Kittler, are 'transcription systems' (Aufschreibsysteme). It transcribes by copying the DNA into messenger RNA. This is all inside the cell nucleus. Then the messenger RNA travels out of the nucleus into the cytoplasm where the ribosome (the protein-making 'machinery') 'reads' the sequence. In this 'reading' the ribosome translates. It reads three nucleotides at a time. Each group of three specifies a particular amino acid. Protein molecules themselves are strings of such amino acids. These are the building blocks of tissue.

THE 'UNIVERSAL GENETIC CODE' THUS IS THE CODE OF TRANSLATION.

It translates RNA 3-nucleotide segments ('codons') in the cytoplasm into amino acids. The twenty common amino acids make up chains of different sequences which themselves are protein molecules. The ribosome reads the three-nucleotide chain as an amino acid and arranges them in chains as proteins. But information is always a difference that makes a difference. The question is for whom. And here it is for the cell. The cell is the unit of life. Its machinery does the transcribing that is copying and translating. A particular DNA sequence – often more than 40 bases long becomes information, becomes the gene for the cell that transcribes and translates it thus that the organism can live. The cell does the selecting. As in computing and media the issues of 'storage' and 'transport' are important. The DNA stores generic information. The RNA transports it. Media always, we will see below, involve not just structural or algorithmic generation, but also selection through structural coupling with the environment. And such selection modifies the structure itself.

Matter - like genetic matter - that reads and stores and transports is intelligent. Reason enters matter, as it is mediatised. Now reason is no longer just outside of matter. Intelligence is no longer just outside. Intelligence is distributed. Media presume distributed intelligence. Media presume a certain dying of the author. Rationality or reason, once it is distributed, becomes reflexivity. Thus nature becomes intelligent, becomes pervaded by reason as it is mediatized. The same can be said for the smart atoms of inorganic matter in nanotechnology.

At the same time that nature becomes intelligent it becomes technological. Thus the rise of the human genome project (i.e. the project to sequence the human genome) is connected to the rise of biotechnology as an industry. The Project was to identify the 25,000 genes in every cell nucleus, each with its characteristic sequences. Science is different than technology. Science finds and discovers. Science, at least classically, presumes reason is outside of nature. When science is outside nature, it asks 'what' questions. When reason is inside nature it asks 'how' questions. How questions are like instructions. This is a technological intelligence. In an age of generalised mediatization there is a certain convergence of science and technology. Kant's Critique of Pure Reason, divided reason into two realms – one the Verstand or understanding was epistemological: the other, Vernunft, about the being of things-themselves was ontological. With mediatization, the understanding becomes ontological.

But in biology nature is generated through code, or at least partly. Mediaitization always as we shall see involves technologization. Molecular biology often slides into biotechnology and physics slides into nanotechnology. What abut mathematics? Computer Science develops from mathematics. Computer science is a certain technologization of mathematics. In each case we have a partial transformation of science into engineering. Science is not technological. It is, as we said, about the 'what'. It is about finding the 'what'. Technology is about the 'how'. It is about not so much finding as making. Engineering is about making. It is often about locating new materials, new structures with what we might call 'load-bearing' capabilities. Thus the engineer used steel in bridges and buildings that had load-bearing possibilities that were unimaginable with the stonemason.

THERE IS A VERY STRONG ENGINEERING PRINCIPLE OR LOGIC IN MEDIATIZATION.[2] SCIENCE AND ART, WHICH IN THE FIRST MODERNITY TOOK THEIR DISTANCE FROM ENGINEERING, NOW FIND THEMSELVES PERVADED BY IT.

Research, which is finding becomes R&D, which is making. Papers become prototypes. The difference in contemporary engineering, be it biotech or nanotech or computer science is that materials becomes intelligent.

---

2 Of course software engineering is very widespread today.

The Commodity

First modernity rationalization took the form of the mechanization of nature. It leads at the same time to the commoditisation of goods. The commodity is in many senses very much the instrumentalization of mechanism as discussed above. Abstract homogenous, atomized nature becomes Marx's exchange-value (or commodity) comprised of abstract homogenous labour. The commodity or commoditised economic goods presume that we have a distance from them that we can deal with them objectively in terms of utility and exchange. This is true in Marxist economics and neo-classical economics.

7

THERE ARE IN EACH ASSUMPTIONS OF EQUILIBRIUM, OF THE CAUSES OF GOODS AS COMING FROM THE OUTSIDE.

How then is the commodity mediatized? Well first the production process in the economy comes to resemble that in the media. With demands of consumers growing for ever new and different products, production has had to move towards the relatively smaller batch production of more and more different and specialised products. With smaller product runs, more and more work is carried out in the design of new products, and less proportionally is carried out in making more and more copies of the same product. Thus there is a growth of people employed in the design process and a relative shrinkage of the workforce employed in the labour process. But this pattern had been established in the media industries a half-century ago. So much more work is done in the studio in film production than in the mere printing of copies of the same film. And so much more work is involved the commissioning, recording and design of a record-album than in the stamping of CDs in a CD plant.

With so many new products there will be a shift in property regimes of law towards one of intellectual property. These new products will often need to be copyrighted or patented. What is copyrighted or patented can be new designs but also new applications and say operating systems. In these cases it is code or algorithms that are patented. These can even be platforms or standards, i.e. the sort of things you need in order to be able to gain entry to informational practices. These too are codes or constellations of algorithms. They can be single-authored or as is perhaps increasingly the case come from the distributed intelligence of teams, of project-networks, non and anti-bureaucratic, heterarchic organization either within or between firms (Grabher, Powell, Stark). Platforms give you access to flows – even to transportation flows – in the mediatised society. Take a platform or to be open standard like MPEG7 that is being developed by a forty-nation team of computer scientists. This MPEG distributed intelligence is so distributed that to copyright it is impossible, indeed unwanted. MPEG will be an 'open source'. And distributed intelligence in the mediatised modernity can be more or less open-source intelligence' (Speaks 2005)

Increasingly though in terms of intellectual-property court decisions, it is not so much patent or copyright, but trademarks that are in dispute. You can be sued for infringement of trademark law, if you publicly connect to your product a set of marks or properties – and these can be also colour or smell or a phrase lie 'to infinity and beyond' – that are already associated with another product from another company. These must be associated by the public, in the public domain (Lury), like for example the Buzz Lightyear character in Toy Story. Or Nike's Swoosh. Or Sony's logo. It is not the author or inventor that decides who trademarks belong to, but the public. That is, trademarks as Klein has argued have to do not with the author but with the 'social imaginary'.

THE IMAGINATION FOR KANT, WHAT IS NOWADAYS THE IMAGINARY COMES INTO PLAY IN ART, RELIGION AND POPULAR CULTURE.

For Kant, in art, it along with reason came into play in experience. This is an even more radically distributed intelligence. That intelligence is distributed beyond the project-networks of production to the consumers themselves. Though it is the imaginary that is at stake it is still intelligence that is distributed. The imaginary (imagination), though not reason itself, does mediate

between reason on the one hand and intuition or perception on the other. The social imaginary of the consumer is thus at stake in the mediatization of the commodity.

AND WHEREAS THE ECONOMIC GOOD IN FIRST-MODERNITY CAPITALISM WHICH IS THE COMMODITY,

is experienced objectively through the instrumental reason of agents on markets and comes under regimes of property law, the economic good in today's mediatized capitalism is experienced more 'subjectively' through the social imaginary of agents often in brand environments and comes under regimes of intellectual property law. And what the instrumental reason of individual agents encounters as abstract homogeneity (Simmel), the imaginary of social agents encounter as difference. Now a branded product also in a sense operates algorithmically.

A brand will generate a range of products, but these products must be consistent with the structure at the heart of that brand. This structure is inter alia, a constellation of trademarks. These are compressed and abstract. They are intensive and noon-metric. But they generate as if they are a set of instructions, a constellation of algorithms, the range of products in the brand. Yet these products need to interface with the social imaginary of consumers. And this social imaginary is particular in terms of determining the type of information it will experience and take from the product and brand. At stake is what Maturana, Varela and Luhmann call 'structural coupling'. The consumers, in a sense as a reflexive community, couple with the product and brand. Structurally. The collective social imaginary of the consumer is a deep structure. It is based on social memory, fantasy, reason and a number of dimensions. And this structure couples with the deep structure of the meditated product. That is with the virtual core of the brand. This coupling can produce change in both deep structures: in both the social imaginary of the consumer, which is itself a history of previous couplings, and in the algorithmic structure at the heart of the branded product. Thus the economic product, once a commodity, is meditatised in the second modernity.

Culture

In nature, in the first modernity rationalization was a
question of reason's objective understanding of the
phenomenon. In economic life, and it was reason's
instrumental use of the phenomenon in the commodity.
But culture and art have always formed against and in the
interstices of this rationalization and bureaucratisation.
This is true not just of avant gardes but of the original
critique of such instrumental rationality in romanticism. And
it was romanticism that gave us not only a body of poetry
but also the novel (le roman). If first-modernity science
and the economy gave us the phenomenon, art gave us the
noumenon.

AND HERE SIMMEL'S NOW TRANSLATED ESSAY ON GOETHE AND KANT ON THE MODERN WELTANSCHAUUNG IS MOST LUCID.

First modernity science and the economy were always
about the thing-for-us i.e. the phenomenon. This is the
thing for us to know or to instrumentally use. Art was
always about the thing-in-itself. Art in first modernity
thus transcended the phenomenon to the noumenon. In
this sense art does displace religion. The creation of God
is displaced to that of the artists, the play of reason and
imaginary (and think of the illiterate Mediaeval peasants
who got their religion through the imaginary, through the
murals of figures on the stained glass windows of churches)
is at stake in religion and art, whereas science and
philosophy are much more about reason than the imaginary.
This is what Simmel understands as the other side of
modernity's Weltanschauung.
Simmel was contrasting Kant's epistemology with Goethe's
ontology. In Kant's epistemology nature is experienced
objectively, it is a means or an instrument. In Goethe - and
of course in Kant's third, 'aesthetic' critique of judgement
– nature is a finality (Zweckmäßigkeit). A finality is an end
in itself, not an instrument. It is not a means to an end.
When the object is an instrument – as in the economy – it
is a means. When the object is a finality – as it is in art
– it is, not a means, but a medium. That is instrumental

rationality's means is transmuted into art's 'substantive
rationality' of the medium. Early modernity gives you culture
in terms of the medium: whether this is the lyric poem, the
sculpture, the painting, the musical composition or fictional
narrative. This medium is a form. Beauty and the sublime in
Kant's first-modernity aesthetics are about form. Through
the form of the medium, we are to experience as if through a
glass darkly the noumenon, the thing-in-itself.
This classical medium as form becomes transmuted
in second-modernity mediatization. Contemporary
mediatization – mediatization as instantiated with the
media as instantiated in television, the internet, mobile
phones, games, the iPod and branded products (because,
as we saw above, they too are media) explodes classical
form into fragments and recombines it as technological and
informational content. Adorno said that culture industry
had captured not just industry's phenomenon, but culture's
thing-in-itself. So what happens to noumenal form – in
architecture, painting, poetry, sculpture, and music as form,
as medium, as medium in the classical and early-modern
sense.

WHAT HAPPENS THEN WITH THE LATE MODERN MEDIA?

Two things: form becomes molecularized, becomes
informationalized. The media and not the medium are
informational. The form becomes decorative, becomes a
surface, an interface. As we encounter in Robert Venturi's
'decorated shed', or the ephemerality of change in fashion
or brand environments. In art we speak of judgement, in
design we speak of taste. Art – which deals with form - is
subjective and transcendental: design – in which form
becomes decoration - is subjective and empirical. Pierre
Bourdieu had this right in Distinction, whose English
language edition subtitle is The Social Judgement of Taste.
Bourdieu empiricized Kantian judgement into the taste of
consumer culture.

But contemporary installation art and the heirs of Pop
Art – and there are many – as well as the populist shift
in conceptual art – have given us an art that is largely
decorative. Indeed all this had as their precursor Matisse's
use of textile and the decoration of fabric in his break with

the figure. The point is that a mediatized art has emerged that is decorative at the same time as it is art. This is in a sense no longer purely noumenal, nor is it just phenomenal as is design. It is in an important sense halfway between noumenon and phenomenon. It is where judgement becomes taste. It is a halfway transcendental.

We saw above how science becomes (partly) technologized in the second modernity. At stake here is technologization of art.

FORM BECOMES MEDIATIC AS IT IS TECHNOLOGIZED.

Technology in early modernity is phenomenal. Art is noumenal. Art must become technological to become mediatized. It is the technologization of the early-modern medium that makes it media.

Science and the understanding deals in concepts, the imaginary in images, which can of course be say poetic images in poetry and the novel. So narrative - which connects to the roman and the romantic - is not experienced primarily through the understanding but the imaginary. In this sense it very much takes place where we have respite from the clockwork of the state bureaucracy and economy. It takes place outside of the public, in the private. It is the locus also of religion – or where religion was until the Enlightenment. These liminal spaces are those of avant gardes and the bohemia.

BUT THEY ARE ALSO THE PRIVATE SPACES OF MOTHERS READING STORIES TO CHILDREN AND THE PASSING ON OF CORE VALUES.

Now we can in given culture speak of a 'social imaginary' that is comprised of a constellation of narratives, images. Maybe largely based on the novel, the story and narrative cinema. Now narratives, whether in stories, or the novel or cinema are a very important first-modernity forms. They are not contemporary media (in that they are not technological, informational). These narratives – along with religion – provide a deep structure to the first-modernity social imaginary. But now in the second modernity this social imaginary comes under the logic of meditatization. The social imaginary is just as structured by the non-narrative and 'play' images of gaming, football, Manga, baseball, and is also technological in the sense of operationality and play is as much a question of operationality as of meaning.

THERE IS A GENERATIVE ALGORITHMIC AND TECHNOLOGICAL OPERATIONALITY IN THE MOVE FROM NARRATIVE.

There is also a move to the surface, to the decorative surface of art and culture. A shift from noumenal form, to on the one hand the even greater depth of algorithmic generation and on the other to the surface of the interface. Perhaps play and digital gaming sets the paradigm for this mediatised modernity.

The Social

First-modernity rationalization of nature is mechanization; rationalization of goods is commoditization; rationalization of forms of relations between human beings it is societalization. Emile Durkheim gave us an idea of the social fact and by implication the social as 'sui generis'. Durkheim's social is not to be explained by the psychological factors or even necessarily climatic or other factors.

SOCIAL FACTS ARE NOT THE EXPLANANDA OF PSYCHOLOGICAL FACTS.

The first modernity social as sui generis, that is as its own genre, not the resultant of another genre. This is the social as a sort of being. Now when the social is mediatized in the second modernity, it becomes not so much sui generis and sui-generating or self-causing. Society becomes thus autopoetic, in the age of generalized mediatization, the social is no longer a being but a becoming. Society itself becomes less a question – as in for example Parsons and Bourdieu and indeed the late Marx - a matter of reproduction or being, but instead it emerges as an entity in chronic production, and often self-production. Society is now less a being than a becoming.

What about the technologization of sociology? Well it might be argued that media studies or cultural studies are a technologization of sociology. It is concerned with the 'how' as well as the 'what'. It is concerned with the production of prototypes. It incorporates lots of Literary studies, sociology and computer science. It wants to make not just scholarly articles but prototypes.
But there is a further way in which mediatization makes society technological. Let us consider code and message. What is code? In classical media and cultural studies, there is a message. The message is generated by code. Encoding is how a medium generates a message. We encounter the message and we decode it. We decode it according most likely to a different code than it was encoded with. But in each case there is code and message, langue and parole, competence and performance for Chomsky.

8

There is, on the one hand, structure and, on the other, speech-act or even agency more generally. This structure for example for Max Weber and many sociologists is a question of rules. These rules are social norms. We follow social norms or need to sufficiently in order that there be a reasonable amount of social cohesion, so that society can more or less reproduce. But media do not act according to such regulative rules. They follow a different logic. First-modernity regulative rules address us with a set of general norms; that is they are a set of 'sames'. Like rationalization's commodity, regulative rules are abstract and homogenous. They address us as if we were all the same: as if we were atoms. This is how law and on another level (that of the imaginary?) convention works. We are aware of these rules and stay within them. Social rules are regulative, and this of course is the first modernity, the one of the social, of generalized societalization.

Media rules are no less derived from reason, or pervaded with reason than are the regulative rules of the classical social. But media rules are not regulative. Nor are they, as in Quine's two types of rules, even constitutive. Media rules are neither regulative nor constitutive, but instead generative. And they are generative of a series of differences. It is largely these differences that are encountered in experience in our mediatized modernity. In Kantian epistemology, experience is Erfahrung. This is the

experience of regularities in nature. It is the experience
of abstract homogenous rules. To Kantian and positivistic
'Erfahrung', Goethe and indeed Dilthey's hermeneutics
and proto-phenomenology contrasted Erlebnis. 'Erlebnis'
extends to aesthetic experience that is also of noumena. It
is the experience not of abstract homogenous regularities,
but of the singular, of the one-off, as in the experience of art.

THIS IS THE SINGULAR, THE AUTHENTIC THAT HAS VERY LONG DURATION, OF EVEN CENTURIES.

But experience in the information order is also Erlebnis in
that it is experience, not of, homogenities or abstract rules,
but of differences. Yet it is experience not of long duration,
but of contimius change, of one Erebnis after another. Not
of the ever-lasting work of art, but of ciamnstenm change as
a series of shocks. Hence Benjamin called it Shockerlebnis.
This is our experience is a mediatized modernity. No longer
of regulative rules but of a series of differences generated
by the rules of the media.

We experience this as suggested above in our structural
coupling with the media. Luhmann has understood such
structural coupling, in taking his brief from Husserl. For
Husserl consciousness is intentional in it no longer stands
outside of its environment, but instead couples with objects
and with experiences in its environment. Husserl calls these
experiences not Erfahrung but Erlebnisse.

WHAT MAKES AN ERLEBNIS AN ERLEBNIS IS THAT IT IS DIFFERENT FROM THE PREVIOUS ONE.

No difference, no experience. Luhmann's systems
structurally couple with their environment. Here they take
in not Erlebnisse, but information. This too is difference. No
difference, no information. This encountering of mediatised
difference - rather than regulative rules – would seem to
be our paradigmatic mode of experience in what Gerhard
Schulze has called the Erlebnisgesellschaft.
Back to the rules of the media. These generative rules that
start from the compressed – fractals, vectors, differentials,
the non-metric, the molecular – take the form not of norms

but of algorithms. For computer scientist's algorithms are rules. More precisely they are instructions. This is what is at the bottom of code now. When programmers code, they write sets of instructions. This is code not as structure but as sequence. Genetic coding works similarly. It is sequence ATGC, endless permutations of ATGC, digital perhaps but not binary, that folds into structure: fold into protein structure. This is like a set of instructions written by a programmer. Programmers are called 'coders' in industry. They work with designers, who are experts of the look of the decorative surface. Rules in he second modernity become algorithmic. The rules that generate difference are like a set of algorithms.

LATE OR REFLEXIVE MODERNITY IS OF THE MOST AMAZING NON-METRIC COMPRESSION AS WELL AS THE MOST EXPLOSIVE DISTANCIATION.

Beyond the nation-state. We are not just speaking of the intensivity of Giddens's intimacy, but compression to the patterns of nerve cell firing in the brain, to the atom in nanotechnology, the DNA sequence in biology. This is at the same time a distanciation, or even distension to the decorative surface: a distension that at points explodes the decorative surface as it does the norms and forms of the nation-state. The social itself is becoming molecular and algorithmic at the same time that it globalizes. In both cases it disrupts the regulative norms of the nation-state. The social becomes less a body a la Hobbes that has functions and reproduces via norms. It becomes instead a molecular body without organs. It becomes a machine, like Turing's universal machine.

As social norms, i.e. regulative rules, weaken, we must increasingly become, in Ulrich Beck's sense, reflexive. We must become as if algorithmic. We must find our own rules and use them generatively.That is we must give the rule to ourselves. We are less rule followers than rule finders. Kant gave us two types of judgement: determinate judgement in which the rule is given to us, and reflective (reflexive) judgement in which we must find the rule. As rule-followers we are heteropoetic. As rule finders and rule givers to ourselves we are increasingly autopoetic.

WE ARE REFLEXIVE AND AUTOPOETIC INDIVIDUALS, YET AT THE SAME TIME EMBEDDED IN A COLLECTIVE AND SOCIAL IMAGINARY THAT IS ITSELF AUTOPOETIC AS IT COUPLES WITH THE MEDIA ENVIRONMENT.

I SIT HERE CONNECTED, FLYING SOMEWHERE OVER LAS VEGAS.

Wireless networks and satellite links combine to draw me online. Right now, finally always on, seems a fitting time to reflect on how we got here and where we should go next.

Introduction: Scale

Next year there will be more than 2 billion mobile phone users in the world. Over the last fifteen years the mobile industry has seen amazing growth. Much of this growth has been in the developed economies but increasingly the value is created in emerging markets.Just as it is difficult to perceive the speed of an airplane from within - blogging over Las Vegas - it is hard to fathom the scale of adoption of mobile technologies.

WE ARE NUMB TO IT.

How will we explain to our children that before, when you wanted to call someone, you needed to stand against a wall? Mobile phones today have become ubiquitous, embedded into the fabric of everyday life. They have become a mobile essential. If someone owns a mobile phone today it is likely to be one of the three things that she always carries with her, the other two being keys and some form of payment. What made this growth possible? Where did this massive scale come from? What was the structure of the mobile industry that made reaching this two billion mark possible? Three features stand out:

1. An object with a social function tied to a service. The primary human benefit driving the growth of the mobile industry was that of social interaction, people connecting with each other. Initially this meant calling people - a familiar activity at the time - but with a new twist: the cord had been cut. Over time this began to also mean sending short text messages.

2. Service providers - mobile operators - subsidizing price. To compete for customers those providing voice and messaging services subsidized - in markets where this was legally possibly - the price of the mobile devices in exchange for a longer term customer relationship. As a result, end customers rarely saw the full price of the device and the infrastructure combining both devices and networks was rolled out at unprecedented speed.

3. The shift from a familiar collective object to a personal object.

The last, and often overlooked, feature of the mobile industry is that it was based on a shift from a familiar collective object - the family phone - to a personal object, the mobile phone. The idea of a personal phone simply did not exist in the popular consciousness 20 years ago.

With this growth, this bigness, came a new communications mass market, some of the most valued brands in the world, and massive economies of scale. And with it came perhaps the strongest example of a hybrid consumer product. The mobile platform - because of it's scale and it's focus on the big human fundamental of social interaction - is a center of gravity for other familiar benefits and functionalities. Think of the clock. Imagine how many people wake up to a phone each morning, how many have stopped using a wristwatch. Or, to take a more recent example, the camera is now moving onto the mobile platform.
Against this background of scale I'll outline seven challenges to our shared mobile future.

1. Reach

The first challenge has to do with increasing access to mobile technologies. How will mobile technologies reach the next 2 billion people? One can raise legitimate concerns about this goal as an end in itself. At the very least enabling people to connect in affordable ways leads predictably to economic growth. Recent research has established that...

mobile phones raise long-term economic growth rates, that their impact is twice as big in developing nations as in developed ones, and that an extra ten phones per 100 people in a typical developing country increased GDP growth by 0.6 percentage points…[So] the digital divide that really matters is between those with access to a mobile network and those without. The UN has set a goal of 50% access by 2015 but a new report from the World Bank notes that 77% of the world's population already lives within range of a mobile network. (The Economist March 2005).

Surely economic growth alone does not define or guarantee human development, but it remains a critical component in increasing quality of life. The challenge here is how to bring access to the next 2 billion in an economically viable way.

How can we viably scale down the cost of appliances, use and infrastructures to increase reach?

2. Sometimess Off vs. Always On

Time is the ultimate scarce resource in the information age. It is the subject of endless pop song wish lists ranging from turnin' it back to makin' it (or dis moment) last forever. The desire to stop time has always been with us and the conveyor belt lyrics of today have a deep ancestry. Witness the recently deceased Pakistani master singer Nusrat Fateh Ali Khan:

THROW OUT THE CLOCKS, MY LOVER COMES HOME, LET THERE BE REVELRY.

My lover comes home, Let there be revelry.
In this excerpt from a characteristically moving qawwali „Mera Pia Ghar Aaya" ("My Lover Comes Home") Nusrat interprets the same theme. As is often the case in sufi qawwali the object of love remains ambiguous between the divine and the human. Either way, we'd like the clocks thrown out.
The same could be said of the ubiquitous mobile devices that connect us. In Finland the everyday word for mobile phone is kännykkä meaning "extension-of-the-hand."
"Because we carry our always-on cellular prostheses," Derrick de Kerckhove notes, "it is the world itself that has become always on." These technologies have become so embedded, they are invisible. Almost. These technologies still interrupt us. They make us, in principle, always available. In the rush to connect we have not designed what it means to disconnect, to tune out.

The challenge: How do we design to be sometimes off in a world that is itself always on?

3. Hackability

Brian Eno summarizes well the essence of hackability: "An important aspect of design is the degree to which the object involves you in its own completion." Some complain about the lack of „hackability" of mobile appliances. But the mobile phone if anything is a hackable platform. Think of all the examples of physical personalization that people engage in around the world e.g. changable covers and straps and self-made accessories. Physical personalization is fast extending into software. Indeed the definition of the word hack as "a way found by devious users to get inside software or hardware and make it do things the designers did not intend" may be too narrow. It hides from view the wealth of everyday hacking behavior that far exceeds the imagination and industry of semipro technologists. This trend of customizing the generic will no doubt continue. Perhaps it has not yet even begun.

Playing to this trend raises the question: How do we design for everyday hackability? How can mass economies of scale be combined with the flexibility and costs involved in enabling users to complete products?

4. Social Primitives

The big human fundamental needs and capacities on which the growth of the mobile industry was built are social. Social interaction has arguably been the driving force of adoption of both the Internet and mobile communications. Starting with voice call with the widest reach to SMS text messaging, e-mail, instant messaging, down to tens of millions of people reading and writing weblogs and sharing of photos with a close group.

HOW MANY OF THESE HAVE BEEN EXPLICITLY DESIGNED BY ANYONE?

The ones that have succeeded have been simple open ended functionalities (e.g. SMS is 160 characters of text), based on the primitives of social interaction that leave room for human interpretation and invention. Consider the big human fundamental of gift giving. Has the universal human practice of gift-giving face-to-face really gone digital yet? Could it? Should it?

The challenge has to do with the next wave of the social: What are some of the forms of social interaction existing (online and off) that could slip onto the mobile platform? What are some of the patterns of sharing that could be better designed? What could these social primitives be?

5. Openness

The renewed cycles of external innovation and internal assimilation that renew an industry often rely on open standards and interfaces, which set a playing field for competition. How the balance is struck between open standards and closed proprietary advantage is one of the key questions on the future of communications. It is not a balance easily struck. The most widespread social applications on the Internet have been based on open standards, or more accurately, the versions of these applications that have won in the end have been based on open standards.

For anyone designing the next wave functionalities and connectivity the challenge is: Where is the architecture open and where is it closed? How and when do we transition between open and closed architectures?

6. Simplicity

In an era of increasing complexity and product development driven ever more by technology and feature-creep human beings are seeking the opposite. The desire is for the simple and sensorial. The interaction design challenge of hiding this complexity – covering the deep dark plumbing of interactive objects – is perhaps the design challenge of our time. In the words of bassist Charles Mingus:

"Making the simple complicated is commonplace, making the complicated simple, awesomely simple, that's creativity."

The challenge remains: How do we hide the (irrelevant) complexity of objects from human beings while maintaining flexibility? How do we keep designing simply beautiful objects that simply work?

7. Justice

Like the first challenge, the last focuses on the normative. Clay Shirky has recently written on the networked world of blogging: "The interesting and hard question is 'Since there is to be inequality, how shall it be arranged?' I think we are going to see an explosion in work designed to alter the construction and effects of this inevitable inequality… and I am optimistic about this change, as I believe the concentration of real thought and energy on what is actually possible, as opposed to cycles wasted on utopian declarations, will be tremendously productive." I can only agree and I too am optimistic.

AS WE GO FORWARD WE NEED TO THINK NOT ONLY ABOUT THE DISTRIBUTIONAL EFFECTS OF DIFFERENT ARCHITECTURES AND TOOLS, ABOUT THE ROLES OF DIFFERENT AMPLIFICATION MECHANISMS TO USE JOI ITO'S PHRASE.

We need to also focus on the hard normative questions: What arrangements of inequality are preferable over others from the point of view of justice? How do we justify to each other the rules, architectures and tools we adopt in a world of freely forming networks?

Derek Parfit writes towards the end of his ambitious book Reasons and Persons (1984):

"[Our many false beliefs about justice and ethics] did not matter in the small communities in which, for most of history, most people lived. In these communities, we harm others only if there are people whom each of us significantly harms. Most of us now live in large communities. The bad effects of our acts can now be dispersed over thousands or even millions of people. Our false beliefs are now serious mistakes."

These mistakes are ever more serious today. In addressing these issues we can look back to understand the present. John Rawls put the task description well: "The task is to articulate a public conception of justice that all can live with, who regard their person and relation to society in a certain way. And though doing this may involve settling theoretical difficulties, the practical social task is primary." A public conception of justice for freely forming networks. That could be our shared goal.

Acknowledgements:

"Blogging over Las Vegas" is a revised version of a talk given at the Organizing for Change (DOM3) Conference at the invitation of Michael Shamiyeh and the Ars Electronica 2005 Symposium "Hybrid" at the invitation of Derrick de Kerckhove. Many thanks to Michael, Derrick and the participants at these events for their comments.
I am grateful to numerous people for discussions on these topics over the past years. I'd like to single out Joichi Ito, Matt Jones, Aditya dev Sood, Jyri Engeström, Ole Bouman and Clay Shirky for special thanks. The title is a nod of respect to Stefano Marzano's earlier essay of nearly the same name. I was reminded of the essay during a conversation with Xeni Jardin.
Despite the title, the essay was not written literally flying over Las Vegas. Many parts of it were however written in flight, with critical bits on an online leg between Frankfurt and Delhi. I have here built on several past writings and lectures. In particular I'm thankful to John Thackara of Doors of Perception and Chris Anderson of TED for the opportunity to discuss these ideas with audiences in Delhi and Oxford earlier this year.

This essay can be found at:
http://ahtisaari.typepad.com

DON'T ASK WHAT ARCHITECTURE CAN BUILD
FOR YOU, ASK WHAT IT CAN DO FOR YOU.
DON'T ASK WHERE YOU CAN FIND A
CLIENT. ASK WHERE ARE YOU NEEDED.

Architecture as harmless practice or as a real need

Recently, on my way to the United States, I was interviewed by an airport security officer. She asked me not just the usual questions about my luggage, but also about some stamps in my passport. Stamps from dangerous countries. Upon my explanation the purpose of these visits had to do with lecturing about architecture, she instantly dismissed me as being a completely innocent fellow. "Have a pleasant trip, Sir".
Besides the apparent harmlessness of architecture as rationale for travelling, her reaction shows another interesting concept for this discipline: Architecture is no longer primarily a glorification of a place, but can be as easily conceived as a justification of mobility. And this is not just related to reasons for travelling. It has to do with the mobility of the discipline itself.

ARCHITECTURE HAS BECOME AN UNIVERSAL ACCESS CODE; A MOTHER KEY THAT MAY OPEN COUNTLESS DOORS IN CULTURE AND IN SOCIETY. ARCHITECTURE MIGHT BE SEEN AS A POWERFUL KIND OF STRATEGIC INTELLIGENCE, AS A MEDIUM TO DEVELOP CULTURAL CONCEPTS, AS A MODE OF THINKING, AS TACTICS FOR SOCIAL INTERVENTION, AS A SUPPLY SYSTEM FOR PROMOTIONAL IMAGES, AS A UNIQUE VEHICLE TO APPROACH THINGS LATERALLY, AS A STRATEGY TO MITIGATE CONFLICT, AS A WEAPON TO FIGHT A BATTLE, AS A METAPHOR FOR THE REST OF THE WORLD.

Practicing architecture may become developing the skills to preside over this metaphor cleverly. This way it also can become attractive again to real intelligence. Architecture as a key to open many doors. The only problem is that most people behind the doors and most people holding the key, don't acknowledge this capacity or are utterly unable to act upon that capacity. Equally, the doors sometimes don't know as yet that they are doors that might be opened by architecture. There is an urgent need to find the doors, to engage the people who live behind them, and to convince the people who have these keys to use them properly and courageously.

A New Brief for Architecture

ARCHITECTURE HOLDS PEOPLE TOGETHER OR IT SEPARATES THEM. SO IT WAS, AND SO IT IS. BUT SINCE THE CONCEPTS OF HOLDING TOGETHER AND SEPARATING ARE CHANGING, ARCHITECTURE SHOULD TOO.

It is a very simple message, but as it turns out very hard to learn. Because with it, there comes a change in the self conception of schools, practitioners and media to an eventual degree of unrecognizability. It is extremely difficult to learn a lesson if it transforms you into someone else. Especially if that goes slow enough to make staying put in your position a short-term rewarding thing. Let's focus here on the necessary courage to face the reality of change. Architecture for a long time considered itself as a discipline between three entities: schools, offices and media. Schools produced architects. Architects produced architecture.

AND MEDIA PRODUCED ITS CULTURAL RELEVANCE, WHICH IN THE END ATTRACTED NEW GENERATIONS TO GO TO ARCHITECTURE SCHOOLS AGAIN.

This clear division of roles is no longer. Schools are engaged in producing architecture as well, and offering dialogical platforms to create relevance too. Meanwhile they deliver easily professionals who start careers well beyond traditional architecture.
Offices that are ambitious and comprehensive are often also powerhouses of new talents, laboratories for experiments and as such, act similarly as schools. They

may also start publicity campaigns that organize 'relevance'
in its own right. Perhaps the architectural media are the
slowest in adopting new roles for themselves, creating
situations that are similar to schools, and engaging
themselves with creative practical projects. But there is
no principle reason why they shouldn't. On the contrary,
in the longer term they even have to, in order to remain
relevant themselves. If an architectural medium wants to
be a place where ideas reside, it has to be open to the way
ideas organize themselves today. To achieve that openness,
it must go beyond itself.

For a long time relevance has been produced by just
following the rules of the game: some magazines were
updating you with professional information about what
happened in architecture. New buildings. New theories.
Some magazines were updating you with the ways how
these things happened. The technologies, the procedures.
The methodologies. And some magazines informed you
about who did it, the personalities. But not much was done
about the question why it happened. The only question
that can get you beyond yourself. And because of that
omission, it has taken quite some time to figure out that
many magazines were about to produce more and more
irrelevance.

ACTUALLY, THIS IS STILL THE CASE.

A massive amount of irrelevance is under construction at
this very moment. And another amount tomorrow, and the
day after...

For some time Archis has tried to do something about
this. By asking architecture "why?" all the time. And why
architecture? By showing architecture differently. By
writing about its cultural preconditions. By violating the
very concept of architectural journalism, which is most of
the time a matter of checking your mailbox or answering
device, and responding to designers who in turn have
responded to their clients. Checking what's going on and
acting upon it. An extremely reactive profession, a scripted
regime for a very reactive mindset. Besides asking "why?",
Archis also tried to activate the very format of magazine
making. To violate the reader's expectations and his
passivity to the third degree. We invited readers to invade

the magazine. And we devised tools to let the magazine invade your life with its activist strategy.

Now, recently we violate even a bit more. We moved to a degree that it doesn't even look like a magazine. I can assure you, it is still debate, it is still dialogue. It is still reflection.

SO, WHETHER YOU LIKE IT OR NOT, IT IS INTENSE MEDIATION AND SO A RIGHTFUL HEIR TO A LONG TRADITION.

Call it, a life magazine. But it might also be school. It might also be practice. Call it dialogue on site; reflection on the spot. And indeed, a way to organise encounters as schools and architectural projects can do.

But there is more to do than setting a debate.

CAN A MAGAZINE CHANGE THINGS, RATHER THAN JUST OBSERVE THEM? CAN A MEDIUM DISCOVER AND RECOVER REALITIES, RATHER THAN JUST COVER THEM. CAN IT HELP FINDING SITUATIONS WHERE ARCHITECTURAL INTELLIGENCE IS URGENTLY NEEDED, WITHOUT A BRIEF JUSTIFICATION AN INTERVENTION OR WITHOUT PEOPLE EVEN KNOWING IT. CAN IT DEVELOP A PRACTICE OF DETECTING OPPORTUNITIES?

As for instance in Ramallah, where we found a 'spatially challenging' situation of extreme proportions, a problem that raises global interest in solutions, a very specific condition to challenge by design and ideas. This was the place to debate the role of design to envision a way to deal with the daily and dramatic time loss of thousands of people. Here we situated journalism as the groundbreaker of spatial intervention. Now, you may ask if this isn't just a unique situation. But the world is full of examples of expanding mandates and finding opportunities. We only need the forensic mentality to find them. To find the traces of the future; not to suppress them, but to cultivate them.

A culture of cross selling everything

It is one thing to develop an avant-garde rhetoric about the conquest of a new mandate by architecture. To define architecture as an unsolicited cultural force, a pre-emptive strategy to anticipate opportunities where nobody has thought of architecture as protagonist. It is a completely different thing to position this ambition within certain market dynamics that have nothing to do with avant-garde, but with architecture as a business, or as a very mundane power play. But both things are perfectly arguable.

Since the beginning of this year, a new era in global politics has begun. As George Bush has announced in his inauguration speech for his second term, America is no longer a territory that has to be defended. America has become an idea that should be pursued anywhere, anytime and anyway. Although the election of the President of the United States is highly a matter of the overwhelmingly suburban population in the blue states, the power of this President is becoming virtually universal, deciding not just over the interest of the nation's state, but over the concepts, mindsets and cultural trajectories of mankind. It won't take long before he may start talking about the American gene. With the historical failure to find weapons of mass destruction to justify the invasion of Iraq post factum, this time something has been invented that can justify anything: the threat to freedom. This year marks the beginning of a world order that is just a matter of words and the power to define their meaning. America, as the self-proclaimed metonym for liberty, is entitled to pursue its realization wherever it wants by whatever means, for the sake of liberty. So, 'liberty' and 'freedom' were mentioned more than 30 times in a speech of only a few minutes. America has detached itself from its reality base. America, in the name of a concept and for the sake of a concept, can invade anything. A perfect storm of absolute power.

AT FIRST SIGHT THIS OBSERVATION SOUNDS LIKE A POLITICAL STATEMENT.

It is not. It is an anthropological statement. What counts to America, can be applied to our entire contemporary global culture. Not just America, many entities now try to occupy and control other entities, to find new markets, to cross sell themselves. Microsoft, once a producer of digital protocols, has begun to capitalize its near-monopolies to control and monitor many cultural processes, transforming from facilitator into producer, broker or creator. BP, used to be known as an oil company, is shifting into an energy giant calling itself Beyond Petroleum. Rituals, a company for beauty and home products, sells itself as the "re-discoverer of daily life", creating life styles you want to belong to. Media companies are using their powers to transcend their role as transmitters, and become allied to specific interest groups. Search engines become gateways to commerce. Transport nodes are becoming shopping malls. Politicians are becoming frequently asked talk show guests or filmmakers. The porn industry starts to organize erotic fairs, parties and festivals for general public. Marihuana is given as a free gift with a magazine. Philosophers are becoming consultants in high demand. Everything tries to cross sell itself. Everything invades everything. Sticking to

your subject, discipline, expertise, background or identity is suicidal.

SO WHY THE HELL WOULD ARCHITECTURE REMAIN ARCHITECTURE?

Its magazines remain magazines and its schools remain schools? Why would they stick to a literally corrupt world, if not because of their laziness and backwardness? One reason might be that if the whole world is messed up, it is always nice to fall back upon architecture to deny that. But hey, talent, are you an architect for that reason? So, what could happen if architecture becomes part of the same cultural dynamics and really starts to reinvent itself beyond its natural limits? What is architecture if it cross sells itself? What if building will develop from the destiny of architecture into one of its options? One of its many modalities? One of its offered interfaces?

Architectural intelligence

As said before, a country may change its character from occupying a certain territory, into representing a certain value. This value can be propagated as being universal. But as a value it might also be defended universally. Then offence is the best defence. One step further, a good defence becomes a matter of good offence. Are you offended? I'm just defending myself!

This sequel is not just a matter of new geo-politics. It accounts for many parts of our culture. For a long time for instance, people believed that a product was a thing. That materials were always material. Philosophically, for a long time people thought that to distinguish certain entities from other entities, one needs to find its exclusive attribute. For architecture it meant the identification with buildings. But not just that! For architecture one also needed a client. A site. A budget. In sum, for architecture one needed a project. As such, architecture always was conceived as a response to a given situation, according to certain given trajectories. But suppose architecture can no longer just respond to what is given? Suppose it would no longer react, but detect its challenges. That it would not just resolve issues by spatial accommodation, but pose issues by spatial intervention? Suppose an architect would not just do the job, but create a job.

FOR ALL THIS TO HAPPEN ONE THING NEEDS TO BE DONE FIRST: THE REDEFINITION OF ARCHITECTURE, SHIFTING IT FROM 'BUILT FORM' INTO 'APPLIED ARCHITECTURAL INTELLIGENCE'. A TRULY LIBERATING ACT.

Call it a new frontier, a new endeavour, a new mandate, a new market, whatever. But at least call it necessary. Two angles are important to consider. First it should become acceptable to disentangle architectural intelligence from the objects to which it seemed to be bound for ever, as in a symbiotic relationship. It accounts to a conceptual (and emotional!) detachment of architecture from its attribute: the building.

Secondly, there must be a reason to believe that this detachment is a creative and productive act, and that the result of the exercise would be something that could be in high demand. Enlarging the definition of architecture will not inevitably apply to new tasks for architecture. For that, one also needs a strong conviction, a rhetorical power, good examples and most of all good propositions tot look at architecture for issues that, until recently, were never associated with architecture. And here we find the logic to a converging practice of architectural practice, architectural education and architectural journalism: these convictions, examples, rhetoric and associations can only be found in a joint venture of the classical roles within architectural production.

So, what is architectural intelligence, after all? It has to do with a certain awareness of spatial orders, of organisation, of the production of meaning, of establishing social relations, either by connecting or by disconnecting. It also may have to do with creating a maximum off spin of this knowledge. Intelligence, as all cognitive psychologists know, has to do with perceiving common denominators between seemingly disparate items. This is what intelligence agencies do; this is what individuals do if they try to understand the world. To see patterns, to establish relations, literally making sense. What is urgently needed is a practice that understands what it is affected by daily; that architecture much more happens than it is built. Construction may distract from becoming. If only a little part of all architectural energy would be used to examine these patterns and do something with it, it would get a completely different outlook. As a creative practice that emerges where it can, and submerges where it must. A craft that derives it self esteem from affecting reality instead of concealing and solidifying it.

Architecture curbed by building

For a very long time the power of architecture to express, mediate and impose the essential features of our civilization by way of elevating buildings and buildings only, remained unquestioned. And because of the symbiotic relationship between producing cultural meaning by built form and constructing objects, the definition of architecture as the art of building remained basically unquestioned. Today, we face the question if this is still the case. If you lose control, you can try to cover it up. You can also try

to find new frontiers for your intelligence. Where once we saw architecture = building + intelligence, we might enter a stage in architectural history on which building = architecture – intelligence.

Architecture is no longer a artful and thoughtful extension of straight-forward building, but becomes an alternative to it. It may start to find new trajectories to come into existence. Perhaps today one can even say provocatively that the power of architecture is not facilitated by building, but even curbed by it. We need new frontiers for architectural intelligence. Not secretly, as an escape in case of professional failure, but as a conscious endeavour to accommodate our creativity in a productive and powerful fashion. Let's face it, if architecture step by step has been excommunicated from the building process, being seen in contempt by its very engineers, being forced to emphasize its greatness on more an more irrelevant grounds, time may be near architecture either dies or resurrects as something else. If meaning has been exiled to the decoration, then why not detach yourself altogether from building? Forget about "fuck context". The next big thing is "fuck building". Fuck any physical carrier that framed architecture and meanwhile, ridiculed its forlorn cultural glory.

BUT THE FIRST STEP TO EXAMINE THE TRUTH IN SUCH A NASTY PROPOSITION IS TO FIND OUT IF ARCHITECTURAL INTELLIGENCE HAS RELEVANCE ON ITS OWN.

What other areas for application of this intelligence are thinkable? Can architecture really live without its parasitic life at the drip of a building process? Can it really do without the motherboard of the building?
Well, of course it can: As analytical capacity for all kinds of spatial issues. Architects can think in terms of relations and organize them, temporize them, dramatize them, celebrate them, smoothen them, mitigate them, restrain them, change them, prohibit them, and so on. It may facilitate the new loyalties in a network society, but also accommodate the fears that come with it. It can hold people together or separate them, as it always did, but this time by other means. Architecture beyond brick and mortar is the insurgence of a discipline after centuries of successful marginalization. Architecture might start a life of its own, denying the building industry its costume of respectability.

Embedded architectural journalism

One can paint a very silly picture of the architectural journalism, not just anyone of its practitioners, but of almost anyone of them. He or she is the second degree of reactive mindlessness. Where the architect had to wait until he has been asked to do something for a client, the critic has to wait until the architect has done something in reaction to that client. At the end of the communication chain there is a reader who, at best, will react to this reaction. Here we have the carrousel of emptiness. No wonder architectural journalism belongs to the least respected forms of cultural mediation. It is very instructive to compare this role play with the practice of embedded journalism as we know it since the Iraq War in 2003. Highly graphical pictures were brought to us right from the battle field. But these pictures were screened. They never really showed the grim side of the story. They were reminding more of a war film, than of capturing the reality of that war. Getting glitzy pictures and paying the prize of becoming a puppet of a fabricated reality. Very much visibility, very little understanding. The embeddee infiltrates his subject, but the subject very much infiltrates the embeddee so secure 'operational security'. It is hardly exaggerated to take this description of embedded journalism as being particularly apt to the practice of architectural journalism today. The most respected magazines and most authoritarian critics are often acting as shameless ghost writers, dividing their time between laudation's and boring introductions to architect's monographies. Moreover, more often than not

THEY BASE WHOLE CAREERS ON THE ONES OF DESIGN CELEBRITIES, RATHER THAN SEARCHING THE WORLD FOR ARCHITECTURAL THEMES BIGGER THAN ARCHITECTURE.

Is there an escape from this deliberate slavery? Perhaps it can be found in the very embeddedness of architecture itself.

NO DISCIPLINE NEEDS MORE CONTEXT THAN ARCHITECTURE.

Money, adjacent environment, clients caprices, philosophies, new technologies, you name it.
If that's all very obvious, why not using this embedding to say a lot more about the bedding. He who would produce unsolicited architecture from the ivory tower, would be quickly be considered as lunatic. She, who does it from an integral expertise as generalist, will soon become a supreme voice of authority.

MICHAEL SHAMIYEH
THOMAS DUSCHLBAUER ❮ AMO Experience

THE PROCESS OF SOCIAL TRANSFORMATION HAS CERTAINLY NOT STOPPED SHORT OF THE ARCHITECTURAL PROFESSION, AND FIRMS CARRYING ON AN ARCHITECTURAL PRACTICE TODAY HAVE RESPONDED TO CHANGE BY EXPANDING THEIR RANGE OF SKILLS, AUTHORITY AND RESPONSIBILITY.

Nevertheless, a perceived concentration on architectural planning still dominates the general public's image of architects. It is precisely the initial phase of this planning process however, that calls for the application of strategic knowledge as a means of assuring long-term success in realizing a project.

A frank assessment of the strategic goals of the client commissioning the project can occasionally even lead the architect to conclude that other forms of intervention would be significantly more effective than planning a new construction project. In this regard,

THE ASPECT OF CHANGE WITH RESPECT TO ARCHITECTURE HAS LESS TO DO WITH CREATING ARCHITECTURE THAT IS AS FLEXIBLE AS POSSIBLE THAN IT DOES WITH COMPREHENDING ARCHITECTURE AS THE MEDIUM OF A COHERENT POSITIONING.

Accordingly, architects are also called upon to take leave of their one-sided role as planners and to take the liberty of analyzing and drawing their own conclusions to achieve strategic positioning. Such independent findings lead to independent solutions like for instance, those that can be recognized in the way OMA/AMO works and the projects these organizations have completed.

AMO, a think tank set up by Rem Koolhaas that is managed as a brand in its own right, has come to occupy the focal point of attention and the growing interest of the international architectural scene on account of the innovative design work OMA/AMO did for Prada Stores, a project conceived as a way of anchoring a global brand

– AND THUS SOMETHING THAT IS, BY ITS VERY NATURE, VIRTUAL –

in a real, local context. Whereas OMA continues to concentrate on carrying out construction projects and implementing urban planning concepts, AMO focuses on realms outside of the physical domain such as sociology, technology, media and politics, whereby its primary interest is in the analysis of inter-relationships among human behavior, architectural constructions and the virtual networks of commerce and culture.

The approach represented by this research and development agenda is nothing new for Rem Koolhaas, whose retroactive manifesto and analysis of New York's "culture of congestion" clearly constituted a preview of the mode of operation that AMO is pursuing today, in that he broke out of a pattern of linear thinking restricted to the level of planning and structural design in a way that reflected the overall context of a highly multifarious and drastically changing society. The needs and desires of the working class were the decisive factors for the development of Coney Island, whereas Koolhaas identified in Manhattan's skyscrapers an incubator for a wide variety of lifestyles. The Downtown Athletic Club, for example, represented the perfect machine for the urban bachelor.

THIS APPROACH TO REALITY, THIS URGENT STRIVING TO REGISTER REAL, PREVAILING CULTURAL CONDITIONS AND TO CREATE ARCHITECTURE THAT MANIFESTS A CORRELATION

to them runs through Koolhaas' oeuvre like a continuous thread that can be traced all the way back to the "Berlin Wall Project," his AA London degree dissertation. What has, perhaps, shifted as an upshot of the globalization process and numerous commissions for OMA in the global ¥€$ is the focus, as Rem Koolhaas himself made clear in a speech at the Harvard University Graduate School of Design in connection with the "Project on the City". One of the least recognized consequences of globalization, according to Koolhaas, is that architects increasingly work in contexts that are completely foreign to them. Whereas in former times they might have spent their entire professional lives dedicated to a particular culture and the effort to understand and enrich it.[1] At Harvard, he encounters that constellation of highly qualified students from all over the world that enables him not only to learn from their culture-specific insights and experiences (as opposed to imparting a body of knowledge per se to them), but also to pursue his own personal interests as the chief executive of an enterprise configured as a think tank by recruiting them to go to work for him after they graduate. Here, it should be noted that, in the Anglo-Saxon system, students accepted for enrollment in a masters program in architecture did not necessarily have to major in architecture as undergraduates. Many of them previously earned bachelors degrees in other disciplines and then switched to architecture. This is standard practice, especially at Harvard. Therefore, completing this masters program that lasts about two years does not guarantee that graduates have acquired those skills required to be productive staff members in an architectural practice. What they do possess though, is precisely that potential that Rem Koolhaas necessarily seeks for his interdisciplinary research – to wit, persons who bring with them an inquiring interest in architecture from the perspective of another discipline. Thus, considered from this point of view, AMO is nothing new, rather it is merely an institutionalized and globally active facility for the implementation of the most elemental points on Koolhaas' agenda.

Architecture and Globalization

Needless to say, AMO is much more than that. A central and recurring theme in Koolhaas' work and today, above all, one of the key justifications for AMO's activities is the search for instruments and methods that enable the profession to involve itself in what goes on in the world in an intelligent and appropriate manner.

THE IMAGE OF A PROFESSION THAT HAS BECOME "INCOMPETENT" AND IRRELEVANT, ONE THAT IS SOLELY CONCERNED WITH ITSELF AND DESIGN, AND HAS LOST TOUCH WITH REALITY IS LATENTLY OMNIPRESENT IN HIS PUBLIC STANCE.

In his elaborations of it, Koolhaas states that it is precisely the discipline's innermost values that constitute the impediment to the emergence of a different type of architectural practice.

1◀ Speech by Rem Koolhaas at the Harvard Graduate School of Design on April 16, 2002.

In particular, the rigidity of architecture is said by Koolhaas to contradict the informal structure of social processes, a position he expressed in his essay "Imagining the Nothingness" and most emphatically, in "What Ever Happened to Urbanism?". For Koolhaas, the seductive thing about architecture is its exactitude, since it by nature defines, excludes, delineates, sets off from the "rest" and in doing so exhausts precisely those possibilities that only Urbanism is capable of bringing out. Namely, furnishing staging areas for the unfolding of processes that actively resist assuming a final form. The reason why New York City, as the sum of autonomous "monuments," was so interesting for him was because as a result of the constructed environment being vertically cut up into independent strata freed of any and all specificity and individuality and of the independence of the facade, it offered freedom in its programmatic determination and utilization.

But it is not the static character of architecture alone in which Koolhaas identifies a conflict, but also the slow pace of its implementation. As he himself stresses, it takes five years nowadays to erect a building of even the slightest public importance.

NEITHER POLITICAL CONFIGURATIONS NOR ECONOMIC DECISIONS CAN REMAIN STABLE OVER THIS PERIOD OF TIME DUE TO THE MANIC CYCLES OF THE GLOBAL ECONOMY.

In other words, the slowness of architecture is thus being overtaken by the speed of all other processes and initiatives. Accordingly, the obvious solution would be to seek instruments that can be quickly implemented and no longer result in fixed, permanent structures and the establishment of boundaries. As Koolhaas explains in connection with the planning of Universal's headquarters in Los Angeles, half a century ago it was still possible to proceed under the assumption that an enterprise for example, the Seagram Company, which employed Mies Van der Rohe to work on its headquarters would retain its unity and identity beyond the five years time it took to construct its facility.[2<] Approximately 50 years later, during the period 1995-99 when Universal's new headquarters was in the making, OMA was confronted by a difficult situation in which it was commissioned to give an architectural/material form to a hybrid company organization consisting of beverage, film, publishing and music divisions whose internal structure, due to a series of mergers and acquisitions was in constant transition and ultimately as an upshot of the merger of Time Warner and AOL, suffered such a severe diminishment of its market position that the decision was made to completely refrain from even embodying it in the form of architecture.[3]

Independent of the facts of this single case, in this day and age it is obvious that a broad spectrum of media and global networks offer a much wider variety of possibilities for a company to communicate its corporate identity and to design its products and services and this in turn is an incentive for companies to prioritize organization instead of concrete structures. Take for example the Apple Company, a computer manufacturer that with the establishment of its iTunes virtual music network, very adroitly catapulted itself into the consciousness of Western consumers without – as far as we know – having pursued any significant strategy to construct a corporate headquarters or even offline Apple Stores. The same goes for San Diego-based Hewlett Packard. Despite being one of the major players in the IT industry, it does without a significant headquarters building or any sort of global chain of representative shops sporting an international cookie-cutter look. For years, HP has instead been concentrating its efforts on holding regular, temporary events like "Hype" that are designed to create a virtual association with the company.[4]

Thus, what Koolhaas certainly recognized is the fact that constructed architecture "poured into concrete," the solution architects are used to providing, is not necessarily the right answer to the particular problem. It is therefore an understandable step to strategically orient AMO on the search for instruments that are not to be found in the immediate purview of the construction industry but are instead located in the domains of media, technology, politics or finance and that do not include fixed, permanent structures or strictly demarcated boundaries among their consequences. This decision is based on the insight that even though an architect has valuable and marketable skills in analyzing organizational interrelationships, the results of this analysis do not necessarily have to be physically implemented nor, as in the case of Universal's headquarters, can they always be.

Economic Aspects

By founding AMO and setting it up as independent enterprise, Rem Koolhaas has succeeded in contributing another strategic element to the modernization and reinvention of the profession. Lately, he has been writing and speaking about the regrettable situation whereby architects remain arrested in the logic of the medieval guilds. They erect icons like Gehry did in Bilbao but derive no advantage from this.[5] A diagram comparing the earnings of celebrities such as movie stars, athletes and pop musicians with the income of the superstars of architecture makes it clear that, due to the limited possibilities of reproducing a work of architecture as is done with a blockbuster movie or a literary bestseller, the architect can hardly make a case for receiving royalties or contingent fees.[6] As we know, the architect's remuneration is usually a percentage of the cost of constructing the building he designed.

SERVICES SUCH AS CREATING CONCEPTS OR PERFORMING ANALYSES ARE NOT EVEN MENTIONED IN FEE GUIDELINES,

[2] Rem Koolhaas, Content, Cologne: Taschen: 122 [3] Ibid. 125 [4] See, for example, The Guardian: "How artwork promotes Hewlett-Packard" at http://media.guardian.co.uk/mediaguardian/story/0,7558,1143731,00.html or HP Brand campaign: http://www.hp.com/hpinfo/newsroom/hpads/demandmore/ [5] Address by Rem Koolhaas at Cornell University's Kennedy Hall on April 15, 2005. [6] Rem Koolhaas, "Beyond the Office," in VOLUME. Nr. 1. (Archis no. 20): 21.

and are compensated only indirectly in the fee for planning the whole job. An architect's earnings are thus oriented not on the know-how he produces which, in the case of OMA, took shape over several months spent analyzing Universal's organization but rather on the production cost of the physical structure. In numerous projects, Rem Koolhaas has repeatedly demonstrated how he successively reduces a given program to its core theme and in doing so achieves utmost clarity about organizational inter-relationships, which can then, in turn, contribute to solving problems. Jeff Kipnis once summed this up quite aptly by pointing out that for Rem, a library (Jussieu) is nothing but a surface with bookshelves and computers as well as a path that the public takes to get to it and an opera house (Cardiff) is nothing but a facility for the production of performances and a place for the public to gather to watch them. [7] This reduction to the essential core of the problem – instead of taking the whole problem apart piece by piece, level by level – is not unlike the procedure that corporate consultants such as McKinsey call "finding the key drivers" and practice successfully in the business world. [8] As OMA partner Dan Woods reported in connection with the Universal headquarters' project presentation, representatives of the commissioning client, in going through OMA's numerous documents, were able to rediscover some of their very own thoughts about the future of the company and recognize that the building had the potential to correct a few of these problems. [9] Thus, in addition to its planning activities, OMA was even more importantly doing consulting work too.

WHAT THE AMO THINK TANK CONSTITUTES – THE MOVE TO CORPORATE CONSULTANCY INDEPENDENT OF AN ARCHITECTURAL PRACTICE –

is not just an obvious next step; it also makes it possible for Rem Koolhaas to accomplish two things. First, to repeatedly reapply the accumulated know-how in areas far removed from the givens of a particular project (architecture, location, political decision-makers, client, etc.) and second, to institute a new and much more lucrative mode of remuneration. If we compare McKinsey's compensation model to that of architecture, we have an extremely high

consultants' fee computed per day or per month plus overhead and with no guarantee of a successful outcome on one hand and on the other, a more or less contingent fee based on a minimal percentage of the building's total construction costs. As we all realize and this is an essential difference to corporate consultancy – the more hours committed to the job, the lower the architect's effective hourly compensation.

Surplus Value of AMO

Accordingly, the setup of the AMO think tank yields four benefits: 1) AMO generates revenue on the basis of concepts instead of construction, 2) it provides its clients with solutions that correspond to their time horizon and the urgency of their needs, 3) it offers a very astutely formulated remedy to Koolhaas' fear of "junkspace" [10] and, last but not least, 4) it delivers the necessary know-how that gives OMA the "assurance" of being able to share in current developments in an intelligent and appropriate way in its work in the global ¥€$.

The alliance between Koolhaas and Prada, the objective of which was to enable a (virtual) brand with a global presence to link up with concrete local retail outlets, proved to be an ideal area of application in which to explore AMO's strategy. Hardly any of OMA's previous projects had had as a prerequisite such a profound understanding of culture and commerce or had brought with it such manifold potential for getting involved in a variety of new domains far removed from the physical sphere. Therefore, we regard it as unavoidable to shed some light on a few key concepts of branding in the context of AMO's work.

Brands and Brand Alliances

The difference between brand-name and no-name products is not only that the former bear the names of their manufacturers and are therefore perceived as more authentic and more emotionalizing but also that we make a connection that proceeds in the other direction in that we identify ourselves with a brand, consciously reflect its philosophy and deal with its message. Thus, products as well as buildings display not only a materiality but also a mentality with which they establish access to our thoughts and our habits and communicate with us. If this communication on which more money is often spent than on development and production of the goods themselves is successful, then we become enthusiastically brand-conscious, we anticipate the brand's message and we think "in" the brand.

Moreover, a strong brand communicates a promise that leads consumers to anticipate certain desirable qualities. Thus, the brand promise of BMW is "Sheer Driving Pleasure" whereas VWs are being produced of late in Europe "Out of Love for the Automobile." The expectations associated with the promise can be heightened and even exponentially intensified when brands form an alliance and promote one another. Such "mutual admiration societies" are extremely widespread today – for instance, when Calgonit laundry detergent is recommended by a leading washing machine manufacturer, quizmaster Günther Jauch does a testimonial while sipping a tall cool Krombacher and celebrity host Thomas Gottschalk gobbles Haribo jellybeans during his show. [11] The art scene too has developed a liking for alliances – for example, the Guggenheim Foundation's exhibition of BMW motorcycles and Armani fashions drew record-breaking crowds in New York.

SUCH ALLIANCES BLEND TOGETHER TWO IDENTITIES INTO A NEW CONCEPTUAL PAIR THAT IDEALLY BRINGS BOTH MEMBERS GREATER POPULARITY AND IMAGE ENHANCEMENT

(and, in the case of a museum, increased attendance). The ones who are profiting from these synergies are not only the star entertainers and professional athletes paid to endorse all sorts of consumer products, but also some creatives who

[7] Jeff Kipnis, "Recent Koolhaas," in ElCroquis No. 79: 29f. [8] Ethan M. Rasiel, The McKinsey Way: Using the Techniques of the World's Top Strategic Consultants to Help You and Your Business, McGraw-Hill, 1999: 33; or Ethan M. Rasiel, The McKinsey Mind: Understanding and Implementing the Problem-Solving Tools and Management Techniques of the World's Top Strategic Consulting Firm, McGraw-Hill, 2001. [9] Content, ibid., 125 [10] Rem Koolhaas, "Junkspace," in ANY. Nr. 27 (Being and Nothingness). New York: Any Corporation: 7A. [11] Claudia Cornelsen, Lila Kühe leben länger. Ueberreuter, 2003. 123.

do not often occupy the spotlight of media attention.

For instance, architect Helmut Jahn recently did an ad for a Frankfurt newspaper and Frank Lloyd Wright even did one posthumously for GAP's khaki slacks. Not too long ago, fashion designer Jean Paul Gaultier was called upon to upgrade the image of Renault as "créateur d'automobile" and the French carmaker is currently using the slogan "Design instead of Middle-Class" to sell its Megane model. In this connection, it is interesting to note that Ford developed a similar campaign for its Focus, but went with an unknown actor to portray an eccentric fashion guru à la Gaultier. Indeed, mimicking celebrities as a parody of the media circus and PR hype is by no means a recent development in advertising now that the habits of the consumers that make up their target groups have changed in such a way that what they expect from advertising is not necessarily truthful information but entertainment. Strange but true: ads featuring for instance, some sort of scientist in a beard and a white lab coat summarizing test results tend to make viewers suspicious nowadays and come across as unintentionally silly at best.

IN THIS CONTEXT, CREATIVE TYPES, VISIONARIES AND ECCENTRICS ARE MUCH MORE POPULAR WITH AUDIENCES.

One of the reasons is that in this day and age, advertising is generally less a matter of stimulating desires (to say nothing of actually satisfying them); what consumers really desire is to satisfy their need for personal change. And probably the best way to use mass media to depict this desire for change is via creative personalities, whereby the very concept of "creativity" has become a highly elastic one that is now to be found in such spin-doctored neologisms as "behavioral creativity." Precisely this aspect of medial effectiveness and impact can certainly not have escaped the attention of ex-journalist Koolhaas.

A current example of reciprocally beneficial networking among creatives is Coop Himmelb(l)au and Zaha Hadid teaming up with BMW though indeed, in their capacity as architects and not to do TV endorsements for the auto manufacturer. Here, the brand's promise of "Sheer Driving Pleasure" dovetails perfectly with the architects' approach, which entails developing innovative, dynamic and lightweight forms and utilizing state-of-the-art technologies. Whereas corporate architecture often comes across as boring and standardized, this case of a strategic alliance shows that it is capable of providing just the right mise en scène for a brand's specific characteristics. Instead of producing another example of a globally standardized look, the outcome showcases the company's unique identity.

Similar references can be custom tailored to a particular target audience – for instance, shooting an advertising image featuring an Audi posed in front of Oscar Niemeyer's convention center in Brasilia or photographing a woman sleeping on OMA's S,M,L,XL bible for a furniture catalog. Another way to demonstrate taste is to use Mies van der Rohe's Villa Tugendhat as the set for an EA-Generali commercial or applying a large Prada logo to the German Pavilion in Barcelona.

Why the Alliance with B-Celebrities?

The code a particular advertiser uses depends on the target group. There are certain brands like Nike or Pepsi that cast pop stars and top athletes exclusively or deploy the generally understandable codes of popular culture, whereas other brands rely on so-called B-celebrities whose recognition factor is limited to a smaller, more select target group. Aside from stars of bygone days, this list of B-celebrities includes, in particular, outstanding scientists and intellectuals as well as top-name architects and designers. The latter are employed to reach an audience referred to as a community of connoisseurs with a taste for the finer things of life. Sociologist David Brooks calls them Bobos (bourgeois bohemians).[12]
After all, Prada and other luxury brands like Gucci and Armani wish to address their messages solely to an exclusive, affluent public for whom artists like film director Ridley Scott who produced the new five-minute commercial for Prada and Rem Koolhaas are elements of the cultural canon of the lifestyle intended for precisely that target group. An artist like Britney Spears is significantly more

prominent but her style does not appeal to the tastes of the potential buyers. In other words, an alliance with top celebrities would even be detrimental to the image of certain brands, even if the likes of Paris Hilton or Britney Spears would be more than welcome as customers.
Thus, with respect to these luxury brands, "to be" trumps "to have," since sending a message that unmistakably exudes "taste" is what it takes to avoid getting the image of a mass-produced ware that clings to those easily acquired products operating with the codes of youth culture. Indeed, a product's being positioned as a luxury article with a high-end pricing policy absolutely rules out omnipresence on the market and universal availability. That's why there are no commercials on TV for Ferrari or Bentley; the target group already knows what Ferraris and Bentleys are and where they can pick one up if they so desire.
Another factor behind this concept was the crisis of meaning that reared its head during the '90s. Before this, it was still possible to make the Yuppie Generation into dedicated followers of fashion's major brands like Lacoste and Armani but the '90s saw the emergence of Stüssy, Fishbone and other makers of streetwear that is, fashion of the streets, for the streets – while haute couture lost appeal and even Vivien Westwood went about making the punk look presentable in polite society.

SUBSEQUENT YOUTH CULTURE MOVEMENTS LIKE HIP HOP AND GANGSTA RAP EVEN WENT SO FAR AS TO APPROPRIATE BRANDS LIKE GUCCI AND PRADA AND THEREBY TO VIOLATE THE LAW OF "FINE DISTINCTIONS"

that was still being promulgated in the '80s by Pierre Bourdieu in his "Social Critique of the Judgment of Taste." [13]
In his view, an elite today can no longer defend its status with property but rather with taste thus a sales strategy that isn't for sale. Yet even this bastion, as personified by luxury brands, was in serious jeopardy. These brands

12《 David Brooks, Bobos in Paradise. Touchstone, 2000, 11.
13《 Pierre Bourdieu, Die feinen Unterschiede. Suhrkamp, 1987. 405-407.

degenerated to the symbolic props of the entertainment industry as Black ghetto musicians took them to grotesque excess in making vulgar spectacles of themselves. Articles bearing these much sought-after brand logos thus assumed a place in an ensemble with a track suit, a list of prior convictions and a business address in the slums – as if Prada and Gucci had suddenly become streetwear. And as if that weren't enough, the products of Gucci, Lacoste, Vuitton & Co. are being mercilessly knocked off – mostly in East Asia and Africa – and hawked on flea markets around the world. Koolhaas refers to this very thing right on the first page of his book "Content."

IN THE AFTERMATH OF THIS TURN OF EVENTS, WHAT'S LEFT OF A LUXURY BRAND'S VALUE AS A STATUS SYMBOL?

And, incidentally, the same thing had previously happened to Mercedes after the US film industry typecast it as the preferred make of pimps, drug dealers and other criminals. Two strategies to counteract this involuntary downgrading have emerged. One involves irony and exaggeration. The purveyors of such parodies of the popular assume a distanced position in accordance with the motto "See, we can even afford to laugh at ourselves" and, for example, totally plaster the exterior of their handbags and luggage with imprints of their logo. The other involves reduction to the bare essentials, to the iconographic element and the play with our perception that is otherwise conditioned to a deluge of stimuli. Both approaches come into play in the alliance between AMO and Prada that will be discussed below.

Branding along Fashion and Style

For popular brands like Nike and Adidas, it is desirable or even necessary – for reasons having to do with revenue, among other factors – to work with trend scouts and consultants in order to be able to react quickly to fads and to absorb the codes of youth culture into their collections in a timely manner. This also manifests itself in the design of their retail shops; what is called for is to mimic streetwear scenarios and to thus generate atmosphere and emotions with a plethora of staged sensory stimuli. Decisive here is

that decoding them calls for no prerequisites in the way of special insights; thus, they are generally understandable and play to common, familiar patterns of perception. The customers are confronted with causes and situations whose effects and outcomes are pre-established.

WE SEE A STARK DIFFERENCE BETWEEN FASHION AND STYLE.

Whereas style – like fashion – is indeed subject to a certain degree of change, what nevertheless dominates is the criterion of recognizability that constitutes an important element of branding. Accordingly, it doesn't matter if the Prada or Gucci handbag is red, green or whatever; one recognizes a certain "valency" over the years, which is just what the brand stands for. Thus, in the branding process, change and continuity are not mutually exclusive. For instance, the pop greats who have attained the status of icons are the very ones – like Madonna – who undergo constant morphing. In the case of Prada, there's even a formula that, in line with what is called "changeability," calls for 60% continuity and 40% change. [14] Furthermore, an essential aspect of this issue, in our opinion, is that what is fashionable is derived from and meant for the general public, whereas that which is stylish is rooted in the will to display independence and individuality. For brands like Prada that obviously want to position themselves on the market as the epitome of style and not necessarily as trendy, this has two implications. On one hand, what this calls for in their store design is an alliance with B-celebrities in order to appeal to a select target group; on the other hand, these stores should by no means instrumentalized generally familiar codes and patterns of perception since, after all, what they seek to achieve is distinction. The aim is to come across as slightly unsettling and thereby create receptiveness to new experiences that can be tied in to the brand's lifestyle. Customers are confronted unawares with circumstances whose outcomes are not predetermined. Koolhaas' architecture guarantees that.

14◀ Rem Koolhaas, Projects for Prada: Part 1, Fondatione Prada Edizioni, 2001.

Prada in LA and NY

While the other boutiques arrayed along Rodeo Drive present themselves in a conventional retail outlet typology with classic façades featuring display windows, company logos, etc., the look of the new Prada branch dispenses with the logo, the typical storefront and glass enclosure facing the sidewalk. Quite the contrary: the width of the Prada Store's ground floor is open to Rodeo Drive, and moving from street to store requires crossing over subterranean display cases. Carrying on a concept initiated in New York, the shop is conceived as more than just a site for retailing; it enables – or even invites – diversified use as a venue for clubbing, product launches, etc. After all, Koolhaas himself premiered his latest work entitled "Content" on the premises of Mandarina Duck. In contrast to the current tendency in which shopping is increasingly encroaching upon public spaces, AMO brings the public space into the shop and, in doing so, creates the preconditions for unaccustomed forms of perception. This is no doubt why Prada also commissioned Koolhaas to premiere the new Prada commercial produced by Ridley Scott. To do it, he turned Ludwig Hoffmann's turn-of-the-century indoor swimming pool complex in Berlin into an exhibition space, whereby walking about its interior engendered perceptions totally foreign to this type of structure. The entire cross vault, for example, became the projection surface for the film, creating an allusion to the Sistine Chapel. Lifestyle was thus raised to the level of the sacred. Whereas "fashionable" brands (Nike Town, etc.) make customers the passive observers of a set and the spectacle taking place on it, and "arrange" them within the larger configuration, "stylistic" brands like Prada enable customers to star in a show they stage themselves. This means that, in contrast to conventional clientele, the customers have to get active in order to partake of the emotions and experiences associated with the specific lifestyle.

SOME EXPERIENCE THE ARCHITECTURE AS THE STAGE OF A PERFORMANCE THAT ONE ATTENDS LIKE A PLAY; ANOTHER VARIATION IS FOR THE CUSTOMERS THEMSELVES TO BECOME ACTORS AND PRODUCE THEIR OWN SCENE.

With his stage and other features in New York as well as on Rodeo Drive in Los Angeles, Koolhaas has provided a perfect mise en scène for this concept. Moreover, the Peep Show and the Mirror Wall in Prada's New York affiliate underscore the "New Experience" approach. Equally remarkable is the idea of the LA Epicenter – not more of the same old global homogeneity but rather a one-of-a-kind showcase. The only "surprise" that conventional flagship stores usually deliver is the quantity of the wares on sale; the Epicenter impresses with the perception of the offerings.

Thus, conventional shops have to call attention to themselves with garish neon signs, whereas customers of Prada have already been initiated and possess insider status – indeed, as members of a club-like community called Prada Friends, they know where to go (and, in the future, will also be entitled to gather at an online platform conceived by AMO). The outward appearance of the Koolhaas-designed Prada Store on Rodeo Drive – lacking any reference to the brand – also suggests this aspect of a club atmosphere.

THE STRENGTH OF THE CONCEPTS THAT KOOLHAAS/ AMO HAVE COME UP WITH LIES IN THEIR OPERATIVE POTENTIAL TO ENABLE CUSTOMERS TO IMMEDIATELY EXPERIENCE THE BRAND, TO LIVE IT OUT.

They offer a stark contrast to conventional strategies that merely attempt to communicate a brand's message using aesthetic means. The former approach heightens the affinity with the brand and also illustrates the enormous potential of an interdisciplinary think tank as exemplified by the successful AMO-Prada alliance.

Conventional store	AMO/Prada store
fashion	style
CI due to global uniformity	CI due to local variations (Epicenter)
shopping	attention
shopping within public space	public space inside the shop
marketing tools in space	space as marketing tool
„productive" space	„wasted" space (as luxury)
decision	clarity
observer	protagonist
cause with pre-given effect	effect due to open cause

Prada Store LA

DESIGNING
COMMUNICATIONS ❮

THOMAS DUSCHLBAUER ‹

Media philosopher Norbert Bolz was the first – followed, most recently, by architect Rem Koolhaas – to cite the example of the post-Biblical Babel that is modern-day united Europe to demonstrate the considerable importance currently being attached to all those whose business it is to deal with design or architecture. After all, the enormous complexity of an apparatus erected amidst the field of tension and interplay at the nexus of vastly divergent interests and one whose identity actually manifests itself solely in a vague acknowledgment of pluralism can only be grasped and made tangible when it assumes a clear, definite form.

THE FALL OF BABEL IS ALSO A CASE STUDY ILLUSTRATING THE GREAT URGENCY OF THIS UNDERTAKING.

Moreover, the fact that more and more design these days is communications design gives rise to the presumption that we have learned the lesson from this tale.
One of the first to initiate this process on a theoretical level was Marshall McLuhan, who had already recognized content in the medial form of communication itself and saw this as the actual message. Indeed, it is precisely the analysis of communication that clearly shows us that it is so-called content in particular that, due to its complexity, its contradictoriness and other factors, is slowly but surely receding from our capacity to comprehend it. Even the act of redundancy is no longer capable of doing anything to change this, since even the most contradictory messages are communicated in redundant form and across the entire spectrum of channels.
What is called for is to link communication much more closely with people's own experiences and with their subsequent actions – that is to say, to make communication "livable." After all, language is not just something within us; rather, our identity lies in our linguistic capabilities as

a possibility of articulation. This "means" of verbalization is to be regarded as the "capital" of the future and it is incumbent upon the designers of it to not merely manage it but rather to make it increase abundant in such a way that mutually agreed-upon meaning can be derived from even the most complex processes.
In this regard, Ole Bouman, publisher of a prominent magazine for architecture and communication, has rediscovered something that perhaps has even more to do with a happening than commonly with an event. The happening is characterized by the fact that it is not necessarily designed to achieve a particular objective or is not what we would today call "a project". Instead, it derives its meaning solely from a shared experience. Here, progress exists first and foremost in the process of transpiring, in the experimental occurrence, which serves as a basis for an ongoing process of discussion. Instead of talking at length so that nothing can happen, this is a case of the occurrence of something that is then talked about, that is taken up in a productive discourse.
This is not a matter of a bitter struggle to wrest power over a discourse and henceforth to direct its course, but rather to impart a structure to it and to offer a variety of possibilities of dialog. This is why, in the case of Archis, communication is also endowed with a certain form in order to allow for joint communication about complex design issues, whereby design achieves separation and independence from concrete, objective representation in order to enable new approaches to the material world via structured forms of communication.

Designed communication or rather the well thought-out strategic interweaving between material and immaterial that has long been utilized in advertising and marketing communications on the consumer level as a means of arousing identification with a product on the part of a target group – also serves in this respect on complex levels of production as a possibility to make processes easier to grasp and to organize them better.

One has good reason to doubt the meaning of the term "global society" but it makes no sense to doubt the globalization of the economy, the supra-nationalization of politics and the everyday phenomena of global communications. Accordingly, my hypothesis is:

MODERNISM, WHICH HAS BEEN REFLECTED IN AND CONFIRMED BY POST-MODERNISM ITSELF, IS THE TIME OF GLOBAL COMMUNICATION.

It is ruled not by the sign of Prometheus (production) but by that of Hermes (communication).

The Age of Global Communication is characterized first and foremost by the fact that the perception of communication has taken the place of the perception of the world. We are meant to infer from global communication that the world is everything that is communicated. This is not the same as the term "(lived-in) world" as employed in phenomenology, nor is it identical to the term "world" in the field of systems theory – i.e. a formula designating the state of being unmarked and unobserved. Instead, we understand "world" to refer to the framework of communicative accessibility.

Especially in the wake of the PR campaign successfully promoting "interactivity" within Internet culture, one has to make it clear that the formation of social systems has less and less to do with interaction. And this is why interaction no longer opens up any access – at least no privileged access – to society.

Global communication means sacrificing space in order to gain time. The diminishing significance of space manifests itself above all in the fact that communications networks are emancipating themselves to an increasing extent from transportation networks. The exact geographical position of global society can no longer be specified. All that still matters is time, which is always scarce. All problems are solved by temporalization. Hurry, urgency, acceleration and set time limits are the great themes of our time.

Of course, global communication is also that which the news agencies make possible via mass media: the simultaneity of elsewhere. The critique of mass media having fossilized into the feuilletonists' standard operating procedure has shifted their function into a more advantageous angle of observation.

PROBABLY THE MOST IMPORTANT SOCIAL FUNCTION OF THE MASS MEDIA IS TO PRODUCE A SORT OF FUNDAMENTAL TRUST IN SOCIETY.

TV, radio and the print media make it possible to partake of events taking place around the world in a distanced, impersonal manner, and that means accessibility as a matter of principle and, above all, the technically assured passivity of the viewer. The usual fare is meant to satisfy curiosity and the desire for sensation and exposé.

But, as we all know, the mass media are not the new media. The global communication network condenses and intensifies most spectacularly there where its name calls a spade a spade right up front: in the Internet.

THIS COMMUNICATIONS CULTURE DOESN'T APPEAR AS AN OPTION BUT RATHER AS A MUST.

It is communications technology in particular that exerts such tremendous pressure to get connected that, ultimately, no one can resist. Anyone without an Internet address these days is dismissed as a maladapted mutant of media evolution.

Media fascinates the consciousness, which is why many people display an interest in their technology that approaches fetishism. As hackers, they are the nightmare of the media industry and as "prosumers" their darlings. When technology is the structure demarcating the boundary between society and nature, we are in the world of artifacts. To the extent that technology is characterized by engineers and not by designers, it is the case that the more technical the facts of a matter are, the more irrelevant is its context. Technology is not complex; at most it is complicated – a paradise for people who like finicky jobs and niggling problems. In the technical world of programs, total agreement prevails about the problem and perfect knowledge exists. What is characteristic of the social world of risk, on the other hand, is that one never knows enough and there is disagreement about the consequences.

The term global communication asserts the primacy of the perception of communication. This is why sociologists have to be interested in design, since design is what makes communications perceptible. Design mediates between (social) communication and (psychic) perception. Its artifacts are interfaces and to be precise, two-sided user interfaces that simultaneously conceal two black boxes: the psychic system and the complicated technology. In other words, one need not understand either the souls or the technologies in order to describe the communications design of our world.

The new media makes up the domain in which we feel most clearly today the painful consequences of modernization in that the evolution of the media and computer technologies is consummated without any consideration for human beings' capacity to process and deal with it. This is why mankind needs techniques that provide relief and endow meaning. We can live only when we selectively – according to anthropomorphous schema – partake of the data of a world that violates the human scale. The media-technologically staged One World provokes the specific post-modern parallel world of lifestyle pluralism. In other words, identity discourses circulate as compensation for the universalism of global communication.

- *It is precisely because all signs point to globalization and global communication that people need cultural preserves of diversity. New tribalisms compensate for the impositions of global society.*
- *It is precisely because virtual reality has become a part of the media-technological infrastructure of our postindustrial everyday life that there have emerged what are tantamount to antidotes to immaterialization – a cult of the body, wellness as philosophy of life, a new aesthetic of existence.*
- *It is precisely because everyone senses that the media and their power to stage events are penetrating deeper and deeper into reality that people increasingly long for the "real reality." In the world of simulation, the real becomes an obsession.*

Modernism features an indissoluble inter-relationship among complexity, contingency and artificiality. No effect without side-effects, no function without dysfunction, no theme without anathema, no artifact without the experience of the guile of the object. All that is certain here is uncertainty and you can rest assured only that the others have no assurance either. Modern men and women suffer from options overload; for them reality means always being forced to choose. Thus, reality is no longer the most natural thing in the world. And this loss of something taken completely as a matter of course is itself already being taken for granted. This is why there are designers who are opening up a world by design. Design comes about when there are no more valid, generally prevailing forms. It creates an artificial environment for people, one in which they can exist in a way that makes sense.

Global communication opens up a wide variety of options that are absolutely disproportionate to our available time resources. The fact that everyone can communicate with everyone else overloads our capacity to pay attention. In a world of manifold possibilities, the everyday shortage of time turns life into a competition for attention. This can be formulated with greater precision by using mathematics. The arithmetical increase in the number of elements in the network of global communication yields a geometric increase in the number of possible relationships among those elements. And this is why it is precisely the culture of the Internet that needs organization – namely, as a limitation placed on the possibility of everyone talking to everyone about everything.
With this,

WE ARRIVE AT AN INTERESTING PARADOX. IN MULTI-MEDIATIZED SOCIETY'S DELUGE OF DATA, "SURPLUS VALUE" CAN ONLY MEAN LESS INFORMATION.

"Information at your fingertips" doesn't quite do the job. Under the pressure exerted by the new information technologies, though, one tends to interpret all problems as being attributable to a lack of knowledge. But the proper response to questions of meaning and problems of orientation cannot be with information. The problem is not a lack of knowledge but rather confusion. And in a complex situation in which it is difficult to achieve an overview, the more information that is available, the greater the insecurity and the less the acceptance. Thus, the modern world forces us to compensate for growing ignorance through trust.

A knowledge-based society is ipso facto an ignorance-based society. And the less that status and authority vouch for the credibility of knowledge, the more a society has to rely on trust. The Internet in particular presents a sharply focused illustration of the problem of the credibility of knowledge. From this perspective, our culture seems to have been dispensing with the truth for some time now. Its place has been taken by trust in the competition among information sources.

Internet culture's sphere of information is, in the mathematician's vocabulary, infinitely dimensional. It has no natural topography. Accordingly, cyberspace is not a territory that can be mapped. In coping with this circumstance, the respective social systems of modern society are displaying varying degrees of success. Law and politics are most strongly oriented on the principle of territoriality and this leaves them helpless in a time of total mobility and global communication. Nowadays, we must acknowledge the fact that national borders are no longer society's borders. The operative principle here: The more complex a system is, the more abstract its boundaries are. It used to be that territorial borders made the limitlessness of the universe bearable. But what now?

Thus, society has only abstract borders – that's one part of it. The other is that its evolution is blind, meaning that, in communicating, it operates in the absence of contact with its environment. So how are you supposed to design that? Neue Unübersichtlichkeit (new incomprehensibility) is the now rather long-in-the-tooth term coined to describe the facts of this matter. Here, a policy of muddling through is much more successful than a strategy of sustainability and anticipation.

NEEDLESS TO SAY, THAT INSULTS BOTH MORALITY AND INTELLIGENCE.

Ethics must live with the fact that there are no more hierarchies of values. Instead all values revolve in the circularity of value preferences. And reason must live with the fact that human beings cannot get an overall picture of complex situations.

In human beings, life, consciousness and communication are interlocking. Human beings are interwoven in systems but are not themselves elements of social systems.

The human being is not the standard of measurement of either technological evolution or the autopoietic systems in which he is enmeshed. He can assert himself only as the frozen contingency referred to as an individual. And this is how the human being assumes the position of a god; he becomes transcendent.

OR TO PUT IT IN OTHER TERMS, HE BECOMES SOCIETY'S ENVIRONMENTAL PROBLEM.

The borders of human existence are thus not the borders of society. That social systems are unable to deal with human beings is, however, the precondition for freedom. After all, for each and every individual, other people's freedom manifests itself in and as its unpredictability. Ones expectation of the Other is always as one who could also be otherwise. Thus, freedom here is not an essential determinant of the human being but rather conceived in strictly operational terms. The human being surprises society with freedom – i.e. uncomputability.

Money, power and the law are the most important symbolically generalized communications media; print, TV and the Internet are the most important technological propagation media. The task of designing global communication is made significantly easier by a set of facts that can be observed in both hierarchical structures and emergent phenomena namely, by decomposability. This means that one can ignore the respective underlying levels or give them compact treatment (e.g. statistically). One can, for example, describe a computer functionally without giving any consideration to the hardware. One can characterize networks according to their behavior without going into computers. Communications react to communications, not to switches.

Symbolically generalized communications media or to use Habermas' "critical" formulation, media of control such as money but also power as well as love already provide in the present the sense of security that unforeseen future problems will be able to be solved. They are equivalents of certainty and allow us to dispense with information and/or foresight. They unburden the consciousness and thereby heighten its capacity to encounter random phenomena and surprises. This capability becomes increasingly important in the age of mass media and multimedia, of course. The actual problem one that the term "deluge of information" coined by the feuilletonists does a better job of concealing than of naming – is that the difference between that which one registers as information and that which one operatively controls is constantly increasing.

Politics is not dominant in global communication. Global society esteems the readiness to learn, that is, cognitive anticipatory styles.

THE ECONOMY (WITH ITS MARKET ORIENTATION) AND THE WORLD OF SCIENCE (WITH ITS FALSIFICATION PRINCIPLE) ARE EAGER TO LEARN. POLITICS AND THE LAW, ON THE OTHER HAND, TEND TOWARDS NORMATIVITY.

Needless to say, global communication has a prior history. This began in Europe, from whence it proliferated across the face of the earth with the dual dynamism of Occidental rationalism and colonialism. Incidentally, it was the emergence of a global society that also launched the successful career of the concept of culture. After all, the comparison of cultures and regions only makes sense before the backdrop of this shared global horizon. And today, doesn't humanity have the same global horizon of expectations and live in the same society?

And, indeed, why do appearances speak against the hypothesis of a global society? Basically, there are two reasons for this.

• *First, globalization does not establish itself on "the whole," but rather on individual functional systems such as the economy, the scientific community and the mass media. Positive feedback in these subsystems then gives rise to enormous regional differences. He who has, keeps getting more. This is also referred to as the intensification of deviation. The greater the degree of global interdependence, the greater the regional*

differences become.
• *Second, the media-technologically staged One World provokes the specific post-modern compensation of lifestyle pluralism. In other words, identity discourses circulate as compensation for the universalism of global communication. In the politics of everyday life as well, globalization and local self-organization are complementary. The more complex and spatially wide-ranging living conditions and circumstances become, the more people need the local self-organization of communities of choice.*

The network of global communication condenses and intensifies in the Internet, and here, above all, with the killer application e-mail. Of course, global communication is also that which the news agencies make possible via mass media: the simultaneity of elsewhere. And what is especially important here: where one watches or what one views on TV makes absolutely no difference. Naturally, the diffusion of the topics of public opinion also belongs in this context. Furthermore, instead of referring to a public sphere, it would be logically consistent with the considerations I have elaborated here to speak of global communication. And finally we come to globally accessible scientific knowledge: Computer-supported knowledge provides a spatially unbounded network of data. The way information functions in the system of global communication is an extremely demanding question that leads to a whole cascade of differentiations.

HERE, I'LL JUST BRIEFLY TOUCH ON A FEW IMPORTANT POINTS:

• *Mechanical data processing has a totally different logic than sensory processing of experiences.*
• *There is no continuum leading from information to intentionality.*
• *Technical media function differently than social media.*
• *Information is not knowledge. In light of the Internet, one could speak of the anarchy of information. There is no longer any possibility of control.*
• *That which is certain is not informative; that which is informative is uncertain. Therefore, it holds that: The more information, the less acceptance.*

Kierkegaard formulated this beautifully: "Freedom is eternally 'communicative.'" Today, one might well reformulate this as: In the Age of Global Communication, freedom is epitomized by the chance to communicate. And everybody is joining in. Nevertheless, logic and history teach us that there is no inclusion without exclusion, no theme without anathema. And this raises the question: What possibilities are excluded by the Global Society? According to our theoretical suppositions, the answer can only be: Global Society excludes everything that isn't communication. Beyond the realm of society is speechlessness. But even on this side of the boundary, one has to differentiate.

3

INCLUSION IN GLOBAL COMMUNICATION MEANS: NOT EVERYONE CAN BE A DESIGNER, BUT EVERYONE HAS TO BE ABLE TO BE A USER.

When business executives are asked to cite the watchwords they live by, it's a fair bet they're going to say that change is the only constant in life.

IN THE MEDIA AND NEEDLESS TO SAY IN SPEECHES BY POLITICIANS AND ECONOMISTS, CHANGE AND ITS OSTENSIBLE NECESSITY ARE PRACTICALLY UBIQUITOUS AND THIS HAS HELD TRUE FOR AS FAR BACK AS I CAN REMEMBER.

Change is tracked by trend watchers, adapted to standard corporate operating procedures by innovation consultants, and now there are even experts in change management engaged to tame it so that change loses its wild countenance and becomes an obedient servant. After all, we need not fear change (at least as far as management is concerned). For those capable of domesticating or even making a profit from it, change poses not a problem but a welcome challenge.

Nowadays, change is treated and traded in like a resource, although, in contrast to other resources, its subsequent use is open. And this is precisely what makes change so valuable, since it can only prove its great worth once it has occurred. If, on the other hand, it turns out to have been unnecessary or even detrimental, then this really does produce a need to take incisive action, or else this particular change can be dismissed as something that was unfortunately too far ahead of its time.

The Logic of the Itinerant Preacher of Change

Change is thus an immaterial resource that, as the narrative plot of the future or what one might refer to today as a select form of storytelling, is constantly capable of getting our attention. Change is something no one can escape after all the whole of mankind is said to be living during an age of drastic change.

THUS, CHANGE AUTOMATICALLY INCLUDES US AMONG THE RANKS OF THE AFFECTED BECAUSE IT AFFECTS US ALL.

It has by now come to have such a dramatic impact on us that we can't escape the feeling of having to endure an ongoing personal makeover in order to keep pace with change. That's why we develop the storytelling of our self-transformations, the very stuff that trend researchers then interpret as individual processes of unfolding growth and branded as "Selfness" for instance are successfully selling back to us. What this actually amounts to, though, is a helpless attempt to adapt to change. As a rule, this effort goes hand in hand with various manifestations of retail consumption which in turn imparts sufficient impetus to the economy to keep the dynamics of change up and running. In this connection, Douglas Rushkoff calls for scholars of culture to critique the new "long boom" theories and the "galloping lunacy" that is being pawned off on us as the expansion of democracy. He also poses a very interesting question, which he proceeds to answer himself: "But how can playing the game and the success with which this society rewards us provide lasting satisfaction? It can't, because these systems that we're caught up in are there

for the sole purpose of reproducing the same thing over and over again." 1<

Accordingly, the concept of the itinerant preacher of change too succeeds as a self-fulfilling prophesy in that it is coupled with a promise of salvation.

AS LONG AS WE ARE IN A POSITION TO CONTRIBUTE TO THE MAKING OF OR CONSUME THE FRUITS OF THIS PROCESS OF CHANGE, WE WILL ALSO REMAIN UNSCATHED BY THE NEGATIVE ASPECTS OF CHANGE.

Since what was available 50 years ago did not even come close to the great diversity of what's out there today, one had to accumulate a reserve with iron discipline back then in order to be able to afford the changes that reared their head in ones own private sphere.

The way it's done today is to consume and to willingly undergo a constant process of personal change in order to create diversity. Accordingly, new needs emerge one after the other as if they had been developed on a drawing board as a source of viable business models. Change is to be regarded for the most part as an end in itself, as a post-capitalist fetish, which is why, even on a meta-level, everything having to do with trends or longer-term socio-cultural developments is itself downgraded to a fad.

The Paradoxes of Change

In this day and age, the only ones able to really undergo a process of personal growth are those who, despite consumption, are in the privileged position to safeguard themselves financially from the vagaries of change. Thus it is also no contradiction that, on one hand, there's continual talk of transformation and change but on the other hand, the need for security has never been as great as it is right now. Nor is it a coincidence that, for example, a TV commercial for Zürich Insurance featuring the slogan "Because change happens" poses the question of what you would do if your own retail shop's business model changed every four hours.

Although we purportedly live in a thrill-seeking society, we can take out insurance policies against any conceivable risk and even the most child-proof devices come plastered with an array of dire warning labels. Evidently, the emergence of a thrill-seeking society has proceeded in lockstep with risk management's march to victory.

Obviously, change – even when it's sold to us as something necessary and even positive leads to a feeling of uneasiness. Indeed, this is not a sense of real existential apprehension as in the past, rather this is primarily angst about possibly no longer being able to get in on the process of transformation, its dynamism and its promise. Douglas Rushkoff's analysis of this conflict is once again right on the mark: "Wherever we look, from the media to politics to the financial world, we encounter systems that have been ingeniously designed to put our common sense out of commission and to confirm our greatest fear: that we have to do more to simply be able to be the way we are." [2]

This uneasiness also manifests itself in a sort of regressive behavior that is anticipated by advertising. What is meant by this is seeking refuge in ones own childhood, which is often labeled as the Retro trend. This wish for or rediscovery of the products of our youth points up a longing for the sense of warmth and security that was still intact in the '70s and '80s. Thus, the Barbapapas and their family idyll are now featured in ads for flexible mortgages, and the pablum that used to be fed strictly to infants is now chalking up big sales among adult market segments too.

Of course, the preachers of change have not failed to take note of this uneasiness even as they continue to evoke concepts like "long-term sustainability." Simultaneously, what is said to be original and authentic is now being sold at a premium as well.
This is another indication that change per se is not

---

[1] Douglas Rushkoff, Der Anschlag auf die Psyche. Stuttgart/Munich: DVA, 2000, p. 324. [2] ibid., p. 324

necessarily associated with something radically new; instead, it certainly may be regarded as something of a system-stabilizing nature or merely as the heightened diversification of the same old thing.

Architecture as Expression of Uneasiness

Another manifestation of uneasiness is the inflationary use of the word "architecture" in tandem with other terms – e.g. computer architecture, security architecture and educational architecture. In such pairings, architecture functions as a metaphor for something stable, something binding or even for the consensus that does not as for example Jean-François Lyotard calls for [3] – have to be called into question over and over again or cannot be subordinated by the process of change. Architecture in this form exists not merely as an expression of a longing for steadfastness; what it is also supposed to assure thereby is that change does not fall victim to itself or that its basic principles remain intact and are not themselves subjected to a process of transformation.

We thus cannot immediately proceed at least not on the basis of this terminological usage to the conclusion that this constitutes the enhancement of the status ascribed to a profession whose know-how is suddenly required in other disciplines in order to push ahead with change.

RATHER, THIS HAS TO DO WITH THE STATIC ELEMENT ASSOCIATED WITH ARCHITECTURE AND WHICH NOW HAS TAKEN ON CENTRAL SIGNIFICANCE FOR THE DOMESTICATION AND EXPLOITATION OF CHANGE.

Instead, architecture and especially design are impacted by the fact that they on one hand, are considered artistic or at least creative disciplines but on the other hand, are subordinate to certain market mechanisms. Architecture and design have to pursue a functional aspect determined by the client commissioning the project. In contrast to other artistic fields, the creative work of an architect or a designer is generally perceived as not authentic but rather as significantly determined by commercial considerations.

Boris Groys described this in the following terms: "A fundamental inability to bring forth something really new is ascribed to the faculty of reason working according to a strategic plan since it is said to be ruled solely by thoughts of success and of gaining an advantage." [4] Thus, Postmodernism tends to regard that which is novel and innovative in architecture and design as a specific solution to the demands of the marketplace, whereas in Modernism, this was still being celebrated as a social utopia or was letting itself be celebrated as such.

AND AS GROYS HIMSELF POINTS OUT, IN ACTUAL PRACTICE IT IS IMPOSSIBLE TO DIFFERENTIATE BETWEEN THE "AUTHENTICALLY NEW AND THE NON-AUTHENTIC."

In his view, the intimation of authenticity ultimately constitutes merely a sort of advertisement, a marketing strategy designed to endow the artist with a certain image, and is by no means a criterion for originality. [5]

With respect to change and the associated fickleness of our behavior as consumers, it is definitely the case however, that the disciplines of architecture and design also delegated responsibility for simplifying that which is increasingly complex. After all, a continually changing context and the increasing diversity of similar or equivalent goods and services means we incessantly face new decisions. Amidst an ever more immense deluge of information, it becomes more than ever incumbent on architecture and design to provide emotional stimuli and to impart feelings to bring about decisions on the part of consumers and to facilitate orientation.

[3] Jean-François Lyotard, Das postmoderne Wissen. Vienna: Passagen Verlag, 1999, pp. 190-191.
[4] Boris Groys, Über das Neue. Frankfurt: Fischer Taschenbuch Verlag, 2004, p. 35. [5] ibid., p. 36

MICHAEL SHAMIYEH 〈
and DOM Research Laboratory (Ed.)

ORGANIZING
FOR Ǝ⅁ИAHƆ\
SPACE Integrating architectural
thinking in other fields

Birkhäuser – Publishers for Architecture
Basel | Boston | Berlin

TABLE OF CONTENTS ❮

3

SPEAKERS ❮

Kari Jormakka ❮ is O. Univ. Professor for architecture theory at the TU Vienna; previously, he has taught at the Bauhaus University in Weimar, the University of Illinois at Chicago, the Ohio State University and the TU Tampere . He he studied architecture and philosophy in Finland and holds a Ph. D. and a Habilitation in architectural theory and history. Author of ten books and about 80 papers, his books include a Geschichte der Architekturtheorie, Flying Dutchmen and Heimlich Manoeuvres; the next to appear is Genius locomotionis, a study on motion in architecture.

Christian Kühn❮ Christian Kühn was born in Vienna in 1962. He studied architecture at TU Vienna (Dipl.Ing) and at ETH Zurich (Dr.sc.tech.). He is assistant professor at the department for Building Theory and Design at TU Vienna. He has been board member of the Austrian Society for Architecture since 1995 and is chairman of the Austrian Architectural Foundation since 2000. He has published about a wide range of topics including architectural theory and CAAD, among them: Das Schöne, das Wahre und das Richtige Adolf Loos und das Haus Müller in Prag, Vieweg 1989; Stilverzicht Typologie und CAAD als Werkzeuge einer autonomen Architektur, Vieweg 1998; Anton Schweighofer Der stille Radikale, Springer 2000 (forthcoming). His essays have appeared in Architektur- und Bauforum, Arch+, Archithese, Daidalus and Architecture d'aujourd`hui and on a regular basis in the Viennese newspaper Die Presse.

Andreas Ruby ❮ Andreas Ruby studied History of Art at University of Cologne/ Germany before undertaking post-graduate studies in Theory and History of Architecture at the Ecole Spéciale d'Architecture Paris with Paul Virilio and at Columbia University New York with Bernard Tschumi. He is currently Visiting Professor for Architectural Theory at University of Kassel, Germany. In 2001 he founded together with Ilka Ruby textbild, an agency for architectural communication. Recent publications include: Images. A Picturebook of Architecture. Prestel, 2004; and „The Challenge of Suburbia", Wiley-Academy 2004; and „R&Sie/François Roche: Spoiled Climate", Birkhäuser 2004.

Michael Shamiyeh ❮ Is a licensed architect. He Graduated with distinction as an architect from the Technical University Vienna and as a Master in Architecture from Harvard University. He has done extensive research work in Jerusalem and Berlin. Together with the cultural theorist Thomas Duschlbauer he founded the interdisciplinary Bureau for Architecture, Urbanism and Culture (BAU|KULTUR) that seeks to define new relationships – as much theoretical as practical – between a contemporary architectural production and a contemporary cultural situation. Thus, the firm concerns itself with realizing projects, teaching and investigating matters of cultural phenomena. Michael Shamiyeh is also founder and director of the Design-Organisation-Media Research Laboratory (DOM).

Michael Speaks ❮ Michael Speaks completed a Ph.D. in Literature at Duke University in 1993. He is the founding editor of Polygraph, and has been the Senior Editor at ANY magazine in New York, where he was also the Series Editor for "Writing Architecture," published by the MIT Press. He has published and lectured internationally on art, architecture, urban design and scenario planning. Speaks is a contributing editor for Architectural Record, and serves on the editorial advisory board of A+U (Japan) and on the advisory board for the Storefront for Art and Architecture in New York. Currently Head of the Metropolitan Research and Design Post Graduate Degree at the Southern California Institute of Architecture in Los Angeles, Speaks has also taught in the graphic design department at the Yale School of Art, and in the architecture departments at Harvard University, Columbia University, Parsons School of Design and The Berlage Institute in Rotterdam. He has also been a research fellow on the architecture faculty at the TU-Delft in the Netherlands, and currently heads the Los Angeles-based urban research group, BIG SOFT ORANGE.

Roemer van Toorn ❮ Roemer van Toorn (1960) is an architect, critic, photographer, and exhibition curator in the fields of architecture, urbanism, and art. After graduating from the Uiversity of Technology Delft, he published The Invisible in Architecture in 1994, in collaboration with Ole Bouman; in this acclaimed encyclopedic manifest he dissects the varied range of cultural, economic,political and philosophic outlook within the contemporary architectural discourse with the aim of outlining different positions and issues of today's architecture. As a teacher, he runs and coordinates the Projective Theory program as well as the Advanced PhD research at the Berlage Institute together with Wiel Arets and Alejandro Zaera-Polo, at the same time pursuing a career as an international lecturer. He has several times been co-editor of the annual publication The yearbook of Architecture in the Netherlands, as well as being an advisor of the magazine Archis and Domus, and, as an author and photographer, he also contributes to many other publications. As a photographer, his work The Rise of the Megacity was exhibited in the Plug In ICA Gallery, Winnipeg and part of the traveling exhibition Cities on the Move curated by Hou Hanru and Hans-Ulrich Obrist. In 2004 his photos on the Society of The And were exhibited at the Archilab exhibition "The Naked City" curated by Bart Lootsma, Orleans, France. Forthcoming is his photobook Society of the And (Spring 2005) and In Search of Freedom in Contemporary Architecture: From Fresh Conservatism to Radical Democracy" (Spring 2006).

6

7

POSITIONS OF
NEOREALISM 〈

ANDREAS RUBY ‹

The architecture of the avant-garde was based on its practitioners' certitude of having come up with an alternative to what was already there: a plan for a better world. With what Lyotard called the end of the great narratives, architecture lost this certainty and the utopia left behind was scorched earth. But in a development that went generally unnoticed at first, a new generation of visionaries began to tend this wasteland. Today, their field is abloom with the "retropia" of New Urbanism, which purports to redeem Modernism's unfulfilled pledge of a better life in the post-historical present of an eternal yesterday. To this extent, New Urbanism is the de facto heir of the avant-garde, and not the least of the reasons why is that it can lay absolutely uncontested claim today to the public popularity that the avant-garde had postulated in rather prophylactic fashion back in its day. Thus, the topos of utopia is already occupied and no longer available to contemporary architecture, which has no alternative than to deal with the status quo. Architects – assuming that intervening in reality is even on their agenda – must face it and come to terms with it. Accordingly, it's not "Fuck …" but rather "Face the Context" that becomes their motto. To do so, they have to renounce the avant-garde's bipolar worldview in which architecture rides in like the good guy in the white hat to deliver society from the evils besetting it. That all-too-familiar sermon preaching replacement of the conventional Old by the progressive New now gives way to a practice of mutation whereby it is precisely that which already exists that constitutes the material for its own renewal.

This absence of an alternative to the status quo explains the interest that certain contemporary architects show in all that they had been previously forced to ignore in order to credibly maintain their claim to cultural superiority. Instead of doing everything in their power to place themselves high above that which is already in place, they work with its codes and investigate the mythologies of our everyday life. They are just as interested in the values of popular culture as they are in the concrete stuff that makes up the straitjackets of administratively regimented life, and no longer look down on it from the high horse of a Dutch variety of Dirty Realism. They are not out to impart an ironic spin to the world in order to keep it at arms length; rather, they assume a position of Neo-Realism so that their confrontation with what is real can be one in which they look it straight in the eye. Once they've ventured outside the sheltered studio world of architecture's interlocking network of ivory towers, they are suddenly struck by the completely obsolete arbitrariness of Modernism's canon of dos & don'ts including its passé proscription of the gabled roof, the transgression of which is, even today, capable of plunging architecture's good ideological conscience into a state of seething turmoil. For Le Corbusier, the flat roof had a performative function: the ground floor, which modern architecture had ceded to the urban sphere through its withdrawal from that earthbound level, would be restituted to it on the roof. Nevertheless, most flat roofs are not even designed to accommodate pedestrian traffic – thus, they are purely formal, or even ideological, relics.

Some contemporary architects are interested precisely in this ambiguous multiplicity of meanings of the symbolism built into our constructed environment. They seek the element that makes it difficult to decide what's new and what's old, good or bad, commercially generated or consecrated with the architectural seal of approval. They prefer to be seen in some eyes as having descended into the teeming mass of the common and everyday than to persist in the ghetto of good taste that does not reflect its historical relativity. They would rather submit to the demanding cognitive discipline of perceiving their environment as impartially as possible. They make a concerted effort to comprehend the cliché's power to fascinate (as attested to by the reality that surrounds us), the seductiveness of tradition and the omnipotence of recognition as topographic facts dotting a democracy's landscape of opinions. They do not attempt to juxtapose some countervailing model opposite – and far removed from – these social estimations; instead, they put them on trial, take them literally, test their viability, sometimes to the point of collapse. Thus, they no longer derive the premises of their actions a priori from assumptions but rather a posteriori from experience. There are, no doubt, hidden risks in this practice, since the results of the experiment are not already known in advance and failure is one of the possible outcomes. On the other hand, this is precisely what makes the experiment necessary. Anything else would be business as usual, and ultimately something that would make architecture itself superfluous.

1

Management thinker Peter Drucker has drawn an important distinction between problem solving and innovation that many of these post-vanguard practices have taken to heart and that architects in general would do well to better understand.

PROBLEM SOLVING, DRUCKER ARGUES, SIMPLY ACCEPTS THE PARAMETERS OF A PROBLEM GIVEN, IN THE CASE OF ARCHITECTURE, BY THE CLIENT.

The designer is then to work within those parameters until a solution to the problem is reached, a final design. Innovation, Drucker tells us, works by a different, more entrepreneurial logic where, by rigorous analysis, opportunities are discovered that can be exploited and transformed into innovations. While problem-solving works within a given paradigm to create new solutions to known problems, innovation risks working with the existent but unknown in order to discover opportunities for design solutions that could not have been predicted in advance.

Schools

Over the last several years, some of our most prestigious schools and institutes of architecture have drawn up balance sheets in an effort to document where the discipline has been and to propose where it might be going. Some of these accountings have taken the form of public lectures held to inform the search for a new dean, as occurred at the Architectural Association in London this past year. Others have been recorded in school publications like "Stocktaking 2004," an issue of the Harvard Design Magazine, in which educators and practitioners were asked their opinions on the future of design and design education. Others still have marked the end rather than beginning of an academic career, as did the symposium and publication, The State of Architecture at the Beginning of the 21st Century, a celebration of Bernard Tschumi's tenure as Dean of Columbia University's Graduate School of Architecture, Planning and Preservation in New York City. However different and whether marked by the palpable sense of urgency and mission spelled out in this latter title or by the cheeky bravado of "How to Become a Star," a public debate hosted by Wolf Prix and his studio at the Academy of Applied Arts in Vienna this past spring, these various attempts to "take stock" all seem to suggest that architecture faces unprecedented challenges in a world increasingly dominated by technological change and marketization.

Despite the obvious concern exhibited in these and other symposia and publications, schools and institutes of architecture have nonetheless been slow to recognize the fundamental nature of these changes.

As a result, they have approached with timidity the curricular and institutional transformation necessary to provide students with the skills needed to compete in a world that places such a high value on innovation. There are exceptions, of course and with so many new architecture deans and department heads hired in the last few years, one can only be encouraged that the situation might change.

IT IS NOT ENTIRELY THE FAULT OF SCHOOL LEADERSHIP, HOWEVER, THAT SCHOOLS HAVE NOT FULLY EMBRACED A CULTURE OF INNOVATION.

Schools are by nature slow to change and though it may seem paradoxical, this is especially true of our most advanced schools of architecture. One reason may be that since the 1970s, many of the so called elite schools have embraced a form of academic vanguardism shrouded in Deconstruction and Marxism and an almost constitutional aversion to commerce and the marketplace, the very milieu

of innovation and shaper of any future architecture whether in Boston, Beijing or Buenos Aires.

In such an atmosphere, raising the issue of how design adds value to the commercial equation is met with scorn and derision, as occurred last year in my exchange in the journal Praxis with Hal Foster, an art historian who teaches in the School of Architecture at Princeton. More recently, Reinhold Martin, an assistant professor of architecture at Columbia University, in a paranoid and misguided attempt to condemn my use of the term "intelligence" to describe an emerging form of architectural knowledge, suggests that I am somehow associated with right wing think tanks and the CIA. This, presumably, because in a lecture he attended, I favorably cited the Iowa Electronic Markets, developed by the Business School at the University of Iowa and other decision markets like those being developed for the real estate market by the MAZE Corporation in Rotterdam, as particularly efficacious aggregators of market based information. Both Foster and Martin assume that the mere suggestion of a connection to commerce—a brochure or market based analysis—is sufficient to cast doubts on the legitimacy of any argument. And that is too bad; not for me, but for students of architecture who now more than ever need to understand the relationship between their discipline and the market.

Theory

WHAT DO I MEAN BY THEORY?

By theory I mean that set of mostly French, German and Italian philosophical tracts that arrived in the US in the late 1970s through departments of comparative literature and were disseminated to the American university system as a wonderful new mode of contemporary thought. Theory was detached from its continental origins and replanted in the US where it took on a lighter, more occasional existence. Theory was portable—it could be attached to almost any field of study, film, literature, anthropology, even architecture. Theory carried all the punch of philosophy without the windy German preambles and recondite French qualifications, without, that is, years of study, political affiliation or deep knowledge. Theory was a weapon of the young, the post-68 generation, wearied by the morality and slowness of their elders who seemed so untheoretical whether they embraced or rejected theory. Theory was fast philosophy and it made its way through various sectors of the US academy in the 1970s and 1980s and arrived to architecture, late, as Mark Wigley has so famously and so frequently pointed out. The emergence of theory was especially important for the vanguard architects whose work and writing came to dominate scholarly journals, school curricula and indeed much of what passed for

intellectual discourse and debate in architecture from the 1970s until the late 1990s. Whether articulated in the form of Tafurian or Frankfurt school analysis or Derridean deconstruction, these theory-inspired vanguards asserted the impossibility of affirmatively intervening in a world dominated by capitalistic and/or metaphysical oppressors.

CONTINUOUS CRITIQUE AND RESISTANCE INSTEAD GUIDED THEIR RESOLUTELY NEGATIVE PRACTICES.

But as the 1990s drew to a close, theory-vanguardism began to wither as new architecture practices better suited to meet the challenges issued by globalization arose to claim the mantle of experimentation that the vanguard, whether in philosophical or theoretical guise, had so long held. Identified as post-critical, fresh and ideologically smooth, these practices embraced much of the market-driven world their theory-hamstrung predecessors held in contempt.

Chatter to Intelligence

According to comscore.com, a consultancy that tracks Internet consumer traffic, Americans conduct around 3.5 billion Internet searches per month. These numbers will soon explode beyond comprehension as China, India and the rest of the world come online in increasing numbers. Open source information, available to Google and other search engines users, however, is only a small part of a much larger story. Clandestine information—what we know of it—is generated and stored in equally staggering quantities. According to those in the know, satellites operated by the National Security Administration, the US agency responsible for electronic eavesdropping, collect enough information every three hours to fill all 530 miles of shelves in the Library of Congress. Commercial stores of proprietary information, like those generated for inventory control purposes by retail giants such as Walmart, are similarly outsized and will grow exponentially as RFID (small radio chips that emit information via radio frequencies) are embedded in almost every product, and indeed, potentially in every conceivable thing on earth, including our own bodies.

We are today awash with more information about more things than at any time in human history. And yet, we seem to know with certainty less rather than more. One reason is the speed at which information becomes appears and becomes redundant. Take, for example, stock tips, or the location of a terrorist operative, almost as soon as these bits of information are drawn from depths of chaos to inform our actions, they are sucked by time back into the black hole of irrelevance. We must act sooner, quicker, and with greater deliberation because the world around us is

subject to almost constant change. Propelled by technology and global marketization, the twin engines of contemporary modernization, information has proliferated into an incomprehensible, living swarm of chatter, a term that before 11 September 2001 referred to trivial, rapidly articulated communication such as bird chirping and children's babble, but has since come to refer to a vast global data stream – both open and closed source – sifted by security organizations in search of leads about potential threats. We now live in a "global risk society," as sociologist Ulrich Beck informs us, where sifting and resifting chatter is not just a security concern but is increasingly important to nation states, corporations, and even small architecture firms looking for competitive advantage in a global marketplace where winning is often a matter of life and death.

RISK THREATENS, AND SO WE NEED TO SECURE OUR INTERESTS; BUT RISK ALSO CREATES OPPORTUNITIES: FOR INVENTION AND INNOVATION.

Advantage, however, offers itself only to those willing and able to transform this global swarm of chatter into knowledge that can be used to achieve competitive advantage.

As management pioneer Peter Drucker has argued, the accession of modern capitalism to world system status was enabled by a fundamental change whereby knowledge was no longer concerned with philosophical or religious truth, but with doing, with action. After the Second World War this transformation ushered in the management revolution and signaled the emergence of what Drucker calls "the knowledge society," a post-capitalist paradigm enabled by globalization.

TAKING A MORE PESSIMISTIC VIEW OF WHAT THEY PREFER TO CALL THE "SOCIETY OF CONTROL,"

Michael Hardt and Antonio Negri, authors of Empire (2000), the highly acclaimed neo-Marxist study of globalization and politics, nonetheless agree with Drucker's assertion that the new economic order ushered in by globalization is knowledge-based. Though states still exist as filters of power and control, Hardt and Negri argue that real command and control is now in the hands of mobile and constantly evolving global organizations free from national obligation to roam the planet in search of affiliations that provide competitive advantage. No longer stored in banks of metaphysical truths, today knowledge is manifest as intelligence used to manage these organizations in a world where remaining competitive is often a matter of life and death. As Hardt, Negri and Drucker suggest, the great ideas

of philosophy and theory have given way to the "chatter" of intelligence. Philosophical, political, and scientific truth have fragmented into proliferating swarms of "little" truths appearing and disappearing so fast that ascertaining whether they are really true is impractical if not altogether impossible. No longer dictated by ideas or ideologies nor dependent on whether something is really true, everything now depends on credible intelligence, on whether something might be true.

Design Intelligencers

If philosophy was the intellectual dominant of early 20th century vanguards and theory the intellectual dominant of late 20th century vanguards, then intelligence has become the intellectual dominant of early 21st century post-vanguards. While vanguard practices are reliant on ideas, theories and concepts given in advance, intelligence-based practices are more entrepreneurial in seeking opportunities for innovation that cannot be predicted by any idea, theory or concept. Indeed, it is their unique, produced design intelligence that enables them to innovate by learning from and adapting to instability. The most innovative of these new practices are thus more concerned with the "plausible truths" generated through prototyping than with the received "truths" of theory or philosophy. Plausible truths offer a way to quickly test thinking or ideas by doing, by making them and are thus the engines for innovation rather than its final product.

George Yu put it this way in response to a question about how his office, George Yu Architects, in Los Angeles, conducts research.

The traditional distinction between research and doing or making is something that's becoming blurred for us. Doing has become research and research has become doing at this point. For us, research is not something that comes before doing—it's maybe even the other way around. Doing is in fact a kind of research. But the bigger question is: Why do research in the first place? I think that the starting point for all our projects is shaped by an attempt to understand and accept the givens of the project in a really optimistic way. To understand the real parameters of the problem at hand and add something unexpected, something that the client may not have been expecting. This kind of research is an absolute necessity given that many of our recent clients were looking for someone to help them develop an organizational vision for the company.

Other forms of interactive prototyping, especially those associated with 3D modeling, have transformed the way buildings are designed and built. Commenting on the use of such modeling in the design and fabrication of the Greenwich Street Project in Lower Manhattan, completed

this year, Winka Dubbeldam, principal of Archi-Tectonics in New York, noted the following about the building's folded façade.

The folds in the façade are diagonal which means the whole space folds inside out and is pulled unlike if it were a simple fold. But this can only be controlled with the kind of precision 3D computer modeling makes possible. During the design phase the slightest change in the fold—whether for code or aesthetic reasons—affected the entire building because it was all one performative system. This also meant that with fabrication everything was controlled by mathematics, by an abstract system rather than by traditional site measurements. This leads to a completely different way of building. When the pieces arrived, they all fit together like a glove. When you see this you realize there is something very beautiful about working from abstract rules. If everyone works by them, and if all the material tolerances are observed, then making the building is all about agreements, codes, notations, not about construction in the conventional sense.

Prototypes create "design intelligence" by generating plausible solutions that become part of an office's overall design intelligence. Rapid prototyping and the use of scenarios, for example, enables mass production of uniqueness in which the "final" product is both the design and the array of specialized techniques invented and deployed. Commenting on the kind of design intelligence generated through the use of scenarios and rapid prototyping, Oliver Lang, of LWPAC in Vancouver, observed the following about an extremely fast-pace project then underway in China.

The scenario exercises utilized in earlier projects have become extremely important in helping us test the building and its ability to adapt. We got the job, in fact, because of our approach to phasing and time based design with scenarios... Platform design and rapid prototyping have been invaluable in developing this aspect of the project. All the research and intelligence generation that we have been developing over the last several years is now paying off and indeed has made it possible for a small, Vancouver based office like ours to take on such immense and complex projects as these in China.

Similarly, offices like Rotterdam based Max.1 and Crimson focus on the development of what they call "orgware," the organizational design intelligence that negotiates between the software of policy directives, zoning and legal codes and building or infrastructural hardware. In the mid-1990s Max.1 was offered a commission to develop a master plan for Leidsche Rijn, a new town extension for the city of Utrecht. One of the first large-scale urban planning projects in the Netherlands that reflected a turn away from subsidized to market rate housing, Leidsche Rijn required

an innovative urban planning approach flexible enough to accommodate the dramatic social and economic changes then occurring in the Netherlands but strong enough to create a new town with its own unique urban character. Working with Crimson, a research and planning office also from Rotterdam, Max.1 developed a mater plan guided by what Crimson called "orgware," the organizational intelligence used to transform the "software" of public and private policy directives into the "hardware" of buildings and infrastructure. Rather than focusing their efforts on an over-designed, inflexible master plan, Max.1 instead designed a plan of negotiation that required certain things to be built while allowing, through built in redundancies, for other elements in the plan to be sacrificed. This same approach of engendering flexibility through enforced inflexibility, guided Max.1's innovative "Logica" plan for Hoogvliet, a suburb of Rotterdam, also developed in conjunction with Crimson. Logica, an exemplary form of design intelligence, requires stakeholders to make definitive choices about how the city will develop. The choices were designed by Max.1 after a period of rigorous analysis and were issued as a challenge to politicians and stakeholders to take immediate action. Once made, these choices become the planning infrastructure that allows other, more flexible choices at different scales to be made over time as the city is rebuilt. As Rients Dijkstra, principal of Max.1 remarked at the conclusion of the process.

Logica has now been accepted by the city as the official planning document. All of the choices were made by the council and now cannot be changed. They are the equivalent to the large-scale projects at Leidsche Rijn. That is, they are inflexible, not negotiable. The negotiable part comes in how the choices are implemented by the city of Hoogvliet. The choices are yes-no and once made, they are inflexible. They are what allow things to actually get done. They are the first, necessary step that must be taken. Now the work of filling in those choices begins.

Part of a one-year, "design intelligence" interview series I published in a+u (2003), these four examples of intelligence-based practices cannot be categorized under any existing classification system. Some design boxes, some blobs while others script complex ballets of urban movement.

Holding to no philosophical or professional truth, making use of no specialized theory, these practices are open to the influence of "chatter" and are by disposition willing to learn. Accustomed in ways that their vanguard predecessors can never be to open source intelligence gathered from the little truths published on the web, found in popular culture and gleaned from other professions and design disciplines, these practices are adaptable to almost any circumstance almost anywhere.

Though we live in uncertain times, one thing is certain: experimental architecture practices are no longer driven by grand ideas or theories realized in visionary form. Instead, the most influential architecture practices are today compelled by the need to innovate, to create solutions to problems the larger implications of which have not yet been formulated. This, I argue, can only be accomplished with intelligence. Otherwise, design is simply a matter of completing a problem given without adding anything new. Architecture should be more ambitious than to settle for that. Each of the offices mentioned above (and there are many more) have not settled on practices focused on what Drucker calls problem solving; they have instead developed unique design intelligences that enable them to innovate by adding something not given in the formulation of whatever problem they have been asked to solve.

THEY ARE BUT THE FIRST WAVE OF A REMARKABLE CHANGE IN ARCHITECTURE PRACTICE, AND I FOR ONE INTEND TO KEEP TRACK OF THEM EVEN IF OTHERS ARE CONTENT TO CONTINUE DEBATING STYLE, FORM, SHAPE, POLITICS AND FASHION.

ROEMER VAN TOORN ❮

After Criticality – The Passion for Extreme Reality in Recent Architecture . . . and Its Limitations

9

IN CONTRAST TO BOTH THE CRITICALITY
OF DECONSTRUCTION AND CRITICAL
REGIONALISM, "PROJECTIVE PRACTICES"
AIM TO ENGAGE REALITIES FOUND IN
SPECIFIC LOCAL CONTEXTS. INSTEAD OF
HANGING IDEOLOGICAL PREJUDICES ON
BUILT FORM, (DERIVED FROM KNOWING
THE FUTURE TO COME OR FROM NEGATIVE
CRITIQUE AGAINST REITIFICATION
(VERDINGLICHUNG)) THE ARCHITECTURAL
PROJECT MUST BE RENDERED CAPABLE
OF FUNCTIONING WITHIN EXTREME
REALITY. WITH A PROJECTIVE PRACTICE
THE DISTANCING OF CRITICAL THEORY IS
REPLACED BY A CURATORIAL ATTITUDE.

1) The failure of Criticality

A lot of Western (great) criticsm draws the research (and its readers) away from experience and pushes them toward the side of deconstruction or criticality". This critical attitude finds its origin in for instance the work of Michel Foucault and the Frankfurter School theorists who accord a paramount place to ideology and culture critique but minimize the possibility of emergent or alternative consciousness allied to emergent and alternative phenomena and groups within the dominant society. The problem with the correct ideas of criticality is that they conform to dominant meanings or established passwords; that it is always ideas that verify something, even if this something is yet to come. Criticality, is trapped in "winner loses". The more Foucault wins by portraying society as corrupt the more he loses as his critical voice of refusal allows him to do anything about it.

HIS CRITIQUE MAKES HIM INCREASINGLY PARALYZED THE BETTER HE EXPLAINS HOW CURRUPT THE WORLD IS.

That kind of criticality is proof of a kind of sado-machoism... Raymond Williams says that "however dominant a social system may be, the very meaning of its domination involves a limitation or selection of the activities it covers, so that by definition it cannot exhaust all social experience, which therefore always potentially contains space for alternative intentions which are not yet articulated as a social institution or even project." What seems guarded against in this approach from Williams is immediacy, the unknown, that untreated bolus of direct experience, experiences that cannot be reflected as a whole.

The criticality of Foucault and others looks backward, is armed with prior theory. But what you could call the projective attitude of Williams is not one which comes armed with prior theory, but rather one who helps formulate new problems or suggests new concepts to be operational within actuality.
The very act of doing, entails a commitment to the future, more particulary a commitment to appearing in, making a contribution to, or in various other ways forming and affecting the future.

In light of this Sarah Whiting, Bob Somol and myself, instead of critical architecture, proposed the term Projective. Why the word *projective*? Because it includes the term project – that is, it is more about an approach, a strategy, than a product. The projective looks forward [projects], unlike criticality, which always looks backwards.
Criticality in architecture rests like critical theory on a self-affirming system of theoretical and ideological convictions.

CRITICALITY IN ARCHITECTURE PROCEEDS FROM A PRECONCEIVED LEGIBILITY. IT IS AN ARCHITECTURE THAT BROOKS NO ALTERNATIVE INTERPRETATIONS.

Unless the critical theory and vision are legible in the object, the object fails. One form of critical architecture exemplified by the work of Peter Eisenman, Daniel Libeskind, and Diller + Scofidio offers comments within architectural/social discourse and avoids looking for any alternatives in reality. The Frank House by Eisenman, for example, forces the couple living in it to think about the psychology of their cohabitation by placing a slot in the floor between their beds (as here in the image). Critical Regionalism in Europe, Asia, and Australia – exemplified by the works of Ando, Hertzberger, Siza, and Murcutt – tries, out of disgust with contemporary society, to overcome estrangement, commodification, and the destruction of nature. Critical Regionalism does not strive to make difficult or playful comments on society – as Eisenman or Tschumi do, but invests in alternative spaces far from the wild city of late capitalism (as we see here in the image).

Critical regionalism hopes to locate moments of authenticity – to calm the mind and the body – in order to survive in our runaway world. While critical architecture deconstructs the discourse of architecture, de-mystifies the status quo, or locates alternative worlds in the margin, it believes that constructing liberating realities in the center of society is impossible.

IN CONTRAST TO BOTH THE CRITICALITY OF DE-CONSTRUCTION AND CRITICAL REGIONALISM, "PROJECTIVE PRACTICES" AIM TO ENGAGE REALITIES FOUND IN SPECIFIC LOCAL CONTEXTS.

Instead of hanging ideological prejudices on built form, (derived from knowing the future to come or from negative critique against reification (verdinglichung)) the architectural project must be rendered capable of functioning within extreme reality.

With a projective practice the distancing of critical theory is replaced by a curatorial attitude. By systematically researching reality as found with the help of diagrams and other analytical measures, all kinds of latent beauties, forces, and unknown possibilities can be brought to the surface. Preferable, it seems to me, is a projective practice that operates with and within society at large and that set

a collective and public agenda in direct communication with modernization.The victimology (pityscience) of critical theory leaves no running room for plausible readings capable of completing a project in the mundane context of the everyday including that of alienation and commodification. Estrangement and schizophrenia must not be thought of as something to overcome, but as a position from within which new horizons can open. Although the urban, capitalist, and modern everyday is pushing towards increased homogeneity in daily life, the irreconcilable disjunctions born in a postindustrial city full of anachronistic interstices make it impossible to think of modernization as only negative.

Although the urban, capitalist, and modern everyday is pushing towards increased homogeneity in daily life, the irreconcilable disjunctions born in a postindustrial city full of anachronistic interstices make it impossible to think of modernization as only negative. Critical practices reject and react unsubtly to the positive things that have been achieved in contemporary society, such as the vitality of much popular culture, including its hedonism, luxury, laughter, even folklore and innovative technologies. *So what instead of criticality does the projective produce?*

Addiction to extreme realism

In many practices of experiment – what I called earlier projective practices -- the architect waits and sees in the process of creation where information leads him or her. Much of the strange shapes of for instance recent Dutch architecture can be attributed to the devotion to the diagram, and the authorial absolution it grants. By taking traditional Dutch pragmatism to absurd, deadpan extremes, the designer generates new, wholly unexpected forms. Some of "Droog Design" embodies this absurdist-hyper-rationalism.

THE DESIGNER SIMPLY CONTINUES TO APPLY THE SYSTEM UNTIL THE FORM APPEARS IN ALL ITS STRANGENESS.

(explain zapper and beer). The touchstone here is not subjective vision but an addiction to extreme realism, a realism that is intended to show no theoretical or political

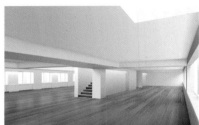

mediation, a kind of degree zero of the political, without thought about the consequences of the social construction it would lead to in reality. The extreme realities the projective is obliged to deal with are the cyborg; the information society; the global migration of money, people, and imagination; shopping; fashion; media; leisure; and the coincidence of the enormous effectiveness and absolute abstraction of digitization. In other words, this practice brings to its extreme the consequences of the processes of commodification, alienation, and estrangement that constitute the contemporary motor of modernity. According to projective practices, involvement, even complicity with given conditions, rather than aloofness, is more productive than dreaming of a new world. The paternalistic "we know best" attitude that has long hindered critical architecture is a thing of the past. From my perspective, we can see three basic types in many recent realized projects in the Netherlands and abroad, types that display

1) *"projective autonomy,"*
2) *"projective mise-en-scène," and*
3) *"projective naturalization."*

Projective autonomy

The architecture of John Pawson and other minimalists) reveals what I am calling "projective autonomy." It is what you could call a simple projective practice. Not movement, not becomings, but in opposition to organization they promote form. The meticulously crafted intesity of forms characteristic of their projective strategy offer stability and often comfort. Projective autonomy revolves around the self-sufficiency of tasteful form, which, notwithstanding the wildness of life, is in theory capable of enduring for centuries. For Claus & Kaan, a dutch office, the organizing principal is not typology but the typographic autonomy of a building. Just as the typographer selects his typeface and searches for the most appropriate spacing, so Claus & Kaan deal in a craftsmanly and repetitive manner with windows, columns, doors, facade panels, and volumes. They pursue a conventional architecture that inspires confidence and eschews controversy, that is about mass, monumentality, boxy volumes, light, beauty, and style. This minimal chic glosses over vulgarities with its abstract perfection. It is a kind of contemporary baroque. A minimum chique within maximum drag. It's boxy attitude is drasticaly on the rise.

Projective mise-en-scène

In the projective mise-en-scène favored by for instance NL and MVRDV, the user becomes an actor invited to take an active part in the theater choreographed by the architects. In these projective practices, projects are not to be contemplated; rather they throw reality forward through the help of scenarios inspired by the theatrical programs theze architects write based upon the data they find within "extreme reality."

THEY TURN LIFE INTO AN OPTIMISTIC AND CHEERFUL PLAY THAT GENERATES NEW SOLUTIONS WHILE MAKING JOKES ABOUT OUR CONSTANTLY MUTATING REALITY.

MVRDV translates the program into a carefully choreographed spatial experience that incorporates the user into latent science fictions in the everyday. While NL makes jokes and develops a trendy lifestyle, MVRDV looks for new spatial concepts capable of giving our de-regulated society the best imaginable and spectacular shape. In projective mise-en-scène, it is not the autonomous force of the type of maximum minimalism that is given free reign – as in projective autonomy – but the daydreams alive in society. Objects are not important as things in a projective mise-en-scène they are there to be used as a screen onto which fragments of our extreme reality can be projected.

As in the social sciences, objects are seen as the carriers of everyday culture and lifestyle. The architecture is a co-producer in the embodiment of cultural and social meaning. The shock effect of the surreal and pragmatic mise-en-scène – like the Benetton billboards by Olivier Toscani with an AIDS patient dying in a living room – will immediately grab attention. But if this bewildering realistic mode of representation is interested in either a better world or in exposing our "Brave New World" remains uncertain.

The fables that lie hidden in the everyday are made visible by MVRDV's opportunistic imagination and make users

❮ When you stack all the village libraries from the province of Brabant in one huge skyscraper with the looks of an updated tower of Pisa and make individual study rooms into elevators zipping up and down the facade of books, the user suddenly takes part in a futuristic mise-en-scène.

❮ Instead of continuing to hide the more than sixteen million pigs in thousands of pitch-roofed bioindustry barns spread over the picturesque countryside of the Netherlands, MVRDV proposes that it is more efficient and animal-friendly to house pigs in high-rise flats in the harbor of Rotterdam. Suddenly—without any value judgment—the facts that there are more pigs than people in the Netherlands and that pigs can be happy in high-rises with a view—looks plausible.

❮ Giving the flat roof of the bar in Utrecht an added function is not just a clever use of space; by putting a basketball court on the roof of this student bar, NL Architects also achieve a delightfully absurd juxtaposition of two quite different milieus.

into leading actors, as in the "Medical Center Pajama Garden" in Veldhoven. Like Steven Spielberg, architects must provide new representations that everyone can enjoy. Entertainment first confronts you even with the dystopias (e.g., sixteen million stacked pigs), then guarantees a happy ending by glossing them over with "pragmatic solutions" ensuring conformity. The attitude is the putatively cool "Whatever." As long as it generates difference.

Projective naturalization

WHILE THE PORJECTIVE MISE-EN-SCENE IS BUSILY PROJECTING MEANING ONTO THINGS,

it forgets that materials and structures can themselves convey meaning, can be sensitive and active, and can activate processes in both the eye and the body. That performative capacity is at the heart of practices that follow the route of what could be called "projective naturalization."

In the Netherlands, projective naturalizations have been developed by, among others, Oosterhuis.nl, UN Studio, Maurice Nio, and NOX Architekten.

PROJECTIVE NATURALIZATION IS NOT ABOUT SIGNS, MESSAGES, CODES, PROGRAMS, OR COLLAGES OF IDEAS PROJECTED ONTO AN OBJECT, BUT ABOUT TECHNOLOGIES THAT ALLOW MATTER TO BE PERFORMATIVE.

Architect Lars Spuybroek of NOX is not interested in technology as a way of regulating functions and comfort. He sees it as a destabilizing force whose function is to fulfill our craving for the accidental by providing a variety of potentialities and events. What geology, biology, and even history have taught the architects of projective naturalization is that mutable processes generate far more intelligent, refined, and complex systems than ready-made ideas ever can. This non-conventional architecture

❮ A blobbish interactive "D-tower" designed by NOX is connected to a website at which the city's inhabitants can record responses to a questionnaire, designed and written by artist Q.S. Serafijn, about their everyday emotions: hate, love, happiness, and fear. The answers are graphed in different "landscapes" on the website that show the valleys and peaks of emotions for each of the city's postal codes. The four emotions are represented by green, red, blue, and yellow, and determine the colors of the lamps illuminating the tower. Each night, driving through the city of Doetinchem, one can see which emotion is most deeply felt that day.

comprehends many shapes and schools.

WHAT THESE MANIFESTATIONS HAVE IN COMMON WITH NATURE IS THAT THE SHAPES THEY PRODUCE EXHIBIT SIMILARITIES WITH THE STRUCTURES, PROCESSES, AND SHAPES OF BIOLOGY.

A facade is not simply a shell, but a skin with depth that changes in response to activity, light, temperature, and sometimes even emotions of its inhabitants. Another example, perhaps the best realized until now is the Yokohama terminal by Foreign Office Archtects in Japan. A host of measurable data and technologies gives rise to a sophisticated metabolism that, as in Foreign Office Architects' Yokohama Terminal, channels the flows of people, cars, ships, and information like blood cells through and near the organism of the building.

THE PROJECT TRIES TO FUNCTION WITHOUT OBSTACLES OR OTHER COMPLICATIONS AND AVOIDS COMMUNICATING CULTURAL MEANING THROUGH SHOCK, AS DOES THE WORK OF MVRDV.

It is not ideology but the (wished for) instinct of artificial organisms that ensures that complex processes are operating appropriately. Buildings are intended to function like bodies without heads (as the schizo) following complex biomechanical logic.

When Foreign Office Architects exhibited their Yokohama terminal at the Venice Biennale, they showed sections of a body scan parallel to the one of the terminals, suggesting that the logic of a building should resemble the body's. In contrast to projective mises-en-scène, projective naturalizations are not interested in projecting scenarios onto objects related to society, religion, power, politics, globalization, or individuals.
Projective naturalizations possess a super-functionality that revolves around movement, self-organization, and interactivity. Projective naturalizations are about modulating precise and local decisions from a mechanistic perspective interested in self-organizing systems that allow flows of consensus to follow their different trajectories.
While concentrating on organic abstractions, projective naturalizations totally neglect the fact that every appropriation of a project depends on narratives of use – it is about the interaction between social behavior and a given objective condition. What projective naturalizations

tend to forget is that our social actions and behavior, not our biological bodies constitute our identities.

I am always surprized when Ben van Berkel of UN-studio shows his manimal metapor for a new architectural practice – an image hybridizing a lion, a snake, and a human, and only talks about the process of generating the manimal but never about its cultural, ideological, and symbolic implications. For them it's all about process and not how social practices of use unlock such a metaphor.

Projective naturalizations have fresh and new ambitions but they are purely operational. They have gone beyond form to sheer performance and they claim that they had gone beyond the semantic into the purely instrumental and the strictly operational.

What I find still baffling is their hostility to the semantic. Semiotics is more triumphant than ever as evidenced for example, in the corporate world or in branding, a semantic critique may be more usefull than ever. You cannot escape representation and escape in purely instrumental presence or performance my conviction.

Larger ambitions

Breaking with criticality, a passion for extreme reality and a return to what architecture as a discipline is capable of projecting are essential to make the most of the many possibilities inherent in our "second modernity." Instead of predicting the future, we have to be attentive to the unknown knocking at the door.

PROJECTIVE PRACTICES ALSO DEMONSTRATE THAT THE QUESTION IS NOT WHETHER ARCHITECTURE SHOULD PARTICIPATE IN LATE CAPITALISM. THAT IS A GIVEN.

But what form this relationship with the market realism should take is an ethical and political question that cannot be curated only in pragmatic, technical or aesthetic terms. The projective practices described here create spaces cut from the same cloth as the garments of the ruling systems. As such they confine themselves to forms of comfort enjoyed in particular by the global middle class. Apart from fear of confrontation with the unknown, the imigrant should become just like them, otherwise the chief concerns of this middle class are the smooth processes that guarantee its rights to power, their kind of individualism, career, identity, luxury, amusement, consuming and the infrastructure that makes all this possible.

The projective practice I spoke of so far is a strategy

without political ideals, without political or socio-historical awareness that is in danger of becoming the victim of a dictatorship of aesthetics, technology and the pragmatism of the blindly onrushing global economy. Instead of taking responsibility for the design, instead of having the courage to steer flows in a certain direction, the ethical and political consequences arising from the design decisions are left to the market and the architect retreats into the givens of his discipline. In that way, all three projective practices described so far are formalistic and politicilily blind. It's the politics of what I call Fresh Conservatism or what you can call Revolutionary Concervatism that embraces the many transformations of our reflexive modernization without willing to see what the consequences are of the many subversive, cool and transgressive (thus fresh) lifestyles they design within the contemporarity.

WHILE THE FRESHNESS OF THEIR DESIGN GENERATES ENDLESS DIFFERENCES ON THE CULTURAL LEVEL, THEY GENERATE A NEW HOMOGENIZATION ON THE LEVEL OF THE POLITICAL.

(It neutralizes, immobilizes political and economical differences). (explain image). According to me, we face a huge dilemma that both the Right – which Acts big now – while the Left is still disenchanted after the failure of any grand-narrative, are both convinced that we can only progress through the multitude. Present-day capitalism has bid farewell to totalising regulation. Digital capitalism has even turned Deleuzian.

Just as the innovative architecture I have discussed– is based on swarm, spontaneity and self-organizational systems. The carnivalesque character of everyday life now guarantees high profits through the permanent revolution of its own order. And the projective practices I discussed give this Revolutionary concervatism its dynamic material organization.

Beyond Fresh Conservatism.

The positive thing about projective practices is that in the making of a project, under the influence of the material, the economy, the construction, the form, the program, a specific context, and with the help of architectural knowledge, projections can be tested and developed. In the very act of walking, projective practices create their paths. Not apriori ideas, but the intelligence of a certain condition is used to the full. In the making of work, reality projects itself. As the Chinese say: in troubled water you can not catch any fish.

So the urgent question is how we can develop a more progressive projective practice operating within late

capitalism but overcoming fresh conservatism?

The projective practice I am after should take the following into account:

1) ONE, **Architecture should be understood as a quasi-object.**

In human sciences, the object has no meaning as a thing; it only exists to be used as a white screen onto which society projects its ideals. Projective mise-en-scenes look that way to objects, how matter is performative as an experience is not understood. For the natural sciences, the objective powers of the thing are so strong that they alone are of overriding importance. This is the mistake the projective naturalizations make. They have no clue about the semantics or complex forms of representation. It is this duality of objects between the "soft" and "hard" that must be urgently reconsidered. It is precisely as if, in most reflections on architecture narratives of use are totally divorced from the diverse architectural qualities of an object. Time and again, it goes unnoticed that objects only acquire meaning once their cultural capital is activated by different formations of use in context and time. Things are imparted by meaning, by use and perception, by touch, by looking at and being looked at, by habit and tactile appropriation, by a coincidental discovery during a walk or conversation.

The research into either the "hard" or "soft" qualities of an object are naturally applied in practice, but how these two cultures function together, forming a complex whole, goes unnoticed. This is remarkable to say the least because in reality we do not make a distinction into two cultures; quite the opposite, we assume hybrid relations. For this reason it is better to talk of the quasi-object. The quasi-object equips us to develop a new model of knowledge that goes beyond dividing an object into two cultures. Rather than considering an object as a fact or a value, to see it simply as a (stylistic) form or social function, we must begin to grasp the facts/values as intrinsically inter-related wholes. The point of a quasi-object is that relationships are forged between values and facts by different frameworks. Neither the projection on … nor the objective fact are central in a quasi-object but the relations and interferences which are activated by the framing at different scale levels. The whole is held together by that which agitates or constantly attempts to pull it apart and bring it back together. The quasi-object is an astonishing constructor of intersubjectivity. A quasi-object is about inserting itself between, to underline that we live only by relations.

2) TWO **we face a crisis or representation.**

Until recently we could still confine our ecology, economics, our infrastructure, our computers, our economies and our politics to scientist managers and engineers who know better and see forward. But the sciences that were part of the solution have become, one after the other, part of the problem. The objects of science, architecture and technology have become so controversial and

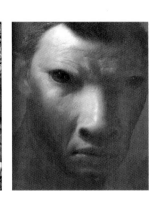

so entangled that the delegation of power to experts appears no easier than the older delegation of power to members of parliament. This could be diagnosed as the crisis of representation. With the rise of globalization and individualization in our information age, democratic institutions taking care of the many, the common good, had to give in to privatization. The nation-state taking care for the collective, came under pressure through the paradigm of difference as self fulfilling prophecy. We arrived in a culture of sprawl and mobility, where everybody works on his or her own do it yourself biography. All forms of life are experienced as a matter of the free choice of a lifestyle. The "Promised Land" we no longer imagine being in heaven but is brought by us by the desire of design (closely related and motivated by Leisure). The desire for Design replaces God as a new form of religion (Design as religion).

Through the fulfilment of desires (by intelligent design: a form follows experience) we moved from a functional landscape (of the nation-state) to landscapes of (individuated) desires, often operating with the very similar logic of control as analysed by Deleuze.

SOMEHOW WE FACE A CRISIS OF REPRESENTATION.

Now the blind are leading the blind. Of course we are freed from the nightmare scenarios concocted for us by the know-it-alls. And yet we have to be led; we have to come to some sort of agreement about controversial states of affairs. Although the crisis of representation is everywhere in science, in law, in ethics, in architecture, in art and in politics, it has to be overcome.
We have to reinvented democracy in space. Or ask – as Bruno Latour does in his upcoming exhition opening this month with Peter Weibel in Karlsruhe: How can we make things public?

What it comes down to is that we have to develop a so-called democracy of the multitude now that the nation-state is bankrupt under the siege of globalization. We need a new science, that is, a new theoretical paradigm to confront the new situation.
With the idea of the multitude we start to understand that we can no longer speak of the PEOPLE, or the MASSES (the

crowd behaves primitive, has only an instinct, etc). We have to start to understand the public as a multitude consisting of many different singularities (reflexive subjects). It is a new notion of the public, the question is how institutions of political representation can allow citizens to express their plural desires and demands while at the same time allowing the state to synthesize them as one coherent unity.
I am not going to analyse the crisis of representation.
We don't have time for that.

IMPORTANT IS THAT WE HAVE TO RADICALLY RETHINK DEMOCRACY THROUGH CONCRETE PRACTICES AND EXPERIMENTS AS ARCHITECTS.

The collective decisions motivated by bottom-up strategies – even with the support of institutions as in the projective mise-en-scene and the projective naturalizaion will remain limited to the technical data flow, cultural issues of religious, sexual, ethnic and other way-of-life differences and techniques, without actually encroaching upon the level at which long term decisions that affect us all are made.

What we need is not an administration of social affairs or a new hyperfunctional technology but we need a proper political constitution which undermines the depolitization of economics to the common acceptance of capital and market mechanism as neutral tools/procedures to be

exploited. So instead of celebrating the new freedoms and responsibilities brought about by extreme reality full of endless differences, it is much more crucial to focus on what should stay the same in the global fluidity and reflexivity. Bottom-up strategies are simply not enough to counter the invisible (sameness disguised as difference) tendencies of geopolitical capital, even when they are foreign or subversive it does not help to develop a route towards a progressive future.

WHICH DIMENSIONS COULD HELP THESE NEW FORMS OF PARLIAMENT TO OVERCOME THE CRISIS OF REPRESENTATION IN URBANISM AND ARCHITECTURE, IN ORGANIZATION AND FORM (WHAT DOES PUBLICITY MEAN).

What the projective practices of autonomy, mise-en-scene and naturalization fail to see, is that utopias – as a principle of hope - are necessary in order to develop in a project a perspective that reaches beyond the status quo. I am not suggesting that utopias should be realized, but that such utopian dreams provide frames of reference for political action. Utopian dreams also enable us to make a detached diagnoses of the present. This moment of exile from the addiction to extreme reality could make us aware of our own inevitable and implicit value judgments, of the fact that

excluding political and social direction itself sets a political and social direction.

It is the interaction between the moment of utopia with reality that could help a projective practice develop a new social perspective. What should fascinate a projective practice is how it might inflect capitalism towards democracy.

The only problem is that so far almost nobody has been prepared to rethink the now eroded concept of democracy or to carry out research into what democracy could mean today in spatial terms.

At times, the practice of Rem Koolhaas (although he refuses to talk about it) seems to experiment with new notions of democracy in space. Alongside the three projective practices mentioned there are also "projective juxtapositions," in which the permanent crisis of late capitalism is a source of inspiration. Projective juxtapositions are characterized by an indefinable critical detachment that continually places the program and with it the organization of society in a state of crisis. In projective juxtapositions – such as the ones of OMA – a project never reaches a conclusion but instead provokes a never-ending subjective interpretation and inhabitation.

The early projective juxtapositions of OMA were a vessel to experiment with new freedoms, as for example the Kunsthal resisting the current idea that a museum needs to be a temple with quasi-neutral white exhibition spaces.

There a projective juxtaposition is combined with what Immanuel Wallerstein calls Utopistics. With Utopistics Wallerstein is not referring to a progressivism that already knows what is to come, but is pleading for a science that seriously assesses liberating historical alternatives – what best possible path for a far (and uncertain) future can be followed. Reassessing Utopistic examples – which proved successful in creating freedom in the past – can help in the creation of new situations of freedom.

Such an approach can be found in the OMA's Seattle library, which to a large extent reworks the public library of Hans Sharoun in Berlin. When Utopistics are combined with a projective juxtaposition, we come close to what I am after. Talking about democracy is simultaneously a taboo and a fetish. We treat the word democracy as a palliative that relieves us from having to think hard about its realization. If we were to dream about new formations of democracy in space and time, we would develop visions that shake off the current political ennui, the blind pursuit of the market (as seen in this image along the highway in Graz), and our incessant navel-gazing.

Although time is very limited I will sum up as a kind of conclusion of this talk what a new democracy in architecture could be concerned with (and we should understand that democracy in architecture has nothing

to do with giving a voting advise). So a projective radical democratic practice – my working title for the approach I am after, is concerned with:

(1) Determine who is the enemy.

One of our greatest enemies is the modern world of stupifying banality, routine, generalizations, mechanical reproduction or automatism. Not the image in our culture of sprawl full of semantics is the problem but rather the cliché. We don't live a civilization of the image but of the cliché (the visual). We have to release ourselves from the suffocation of the cliché both visual as organizational.

(2) A work of **architecture should not lead to contemplate the world, or build found data, but should change it,** it should distribute and produce meaning in order to transform conventions.

We have to develop other programs, (first) we analyse a specific situation, look for the latent liberating energies. (second) we (almost as if from exile) plug-in a new developed program. And Utopistics (the rich history of realized utopias) can help us.

(3) With democracy in architecture I **look for what you could call dialogical spaces or with another word for reflexive spaces.** I am against spaces that judge for you (through the salvation of the design or organizations like Disney as here in Celebration City or Singapore). They are about judgement and not experimentation. I am against the idea that the object or design dictates the use how to behave, how to look, how to be. With Reflexivity or the dialogical I look for works that call attention to the factitiousness of their own constructs. The architect must make his own manipulation and that of the client and context visible in the work by incorporating references to the accepted codings, to the ones of the everyday, should invite the use, the program of life to establish meaning. The work is recognizably artificial, a construct, an ideological instrument in the permanent discussion about contrasts in social reality. A cultural product of the kind has the metaphorical quality of self re-evaluation. It is a strategy of reflexivity which aims to establish a continuous openness.

To avoid confusion, we distinguish two forms of reflexivity: an authentic and a narcotic reflexivity. The theory and practice of Bertold Brecht gives some insight into this. With authentic reflexivity, the spectator is actively involved. With many television programmes, by contrast, the consumer remains passive and is swamped with narcotic, culinary experiences. Brecht's goal was not to satisfy the audience expectations but to transform them, whereas the central impulse of commercial television is to transform only two things: the audience viewing habits and its buying habits. Brecht's goal was not to be popular in box-office terms but to become popular, that is, to create a new public for a new theatre linked to modes of social life, whereas commercial television's goal, at least from the point of view of its managers, is to be popular in the crudely quantitative

terms of „ratings". It is about the notion of becoming popular rather than being popular, transforming rather than satisfying desire.

(4) When you are after open systems which invite the user, are after becomings, how through habitation meaning can be established without a final conclusion, you opt for stammerings within a system. Stammerings reject a totalizing aesthetic where all "tracks" are enlisted in the service of a single, overwhelming feeling (as we know from so much design these days: Bilbao effect etc).

(5) You can create stammerings by certain kinds of alienating effects, or categories of the unknown, apply estrangement or foreign techniques which de-condition the use and make strange the lived social world, freeing socially conditioned phenomena from the stamp of familiarty, revealing them as other than natural.

(6) The dichotomy of entertainment versus education should be overcome. Entertainment or laughter (play) can be useful it is not only about consumption or educational – seen as difficult – Commodification and liberation go together, it is not a matter of either/or logics in space, the virtual versus the real, the near versus the far, the fictional versus the real, the object versus the subject, presence versus represnetation, dystopia versus utopia, but about being-in-space which is intrinsically impure, full of and conjunctions and relations, instead of the verb to be, it should be about what you can do in actuality. While you feel comfortable (at home) in the same instance you are challenged, through and by what is familiar. (kunsthal example).

(7) What I haven't mentioned so far – with so many words – is that an open work – as just discussed by the different criteria – should have a liberating (emancipating) directionality too, it cannot just be open because than it falls victim to the addiction of extreme reality (neoliberalism) as we have seen with the three projective practices I mentioned earlier. Certain societal issues should be addressed – who is the enemy, what is missing and for whom do we work?

As I have tried to sketch we should free the energies within the multitude within our contemporary society through both a curational practice (as seen in the projective practices after criticality) and develop a new science that researches new forms of parliament, how things can be public against a society of further privitization, the splintering of reality.

TO DEVELOP A DEMOCRACY OF THE MULTITUDE IS NOT AN EASY TASK, A WHOLE NEW SCIENCE AND PRACTICE NEEDS TO BE DEVELOPED, WITH MY PLEE FOR YET ANOTHER DEMOCRATIVE PROJECTIVE PRACTICE I HOPE I HAVE GIVEN YOU A BEGINNING TO THINK BEYOND FRESH CONSERVATISM AFTER CRITICALITY.

For a great deal of contemporary architecture the brief seems to represent a condition that is alien to architecture. It is seen as a framework that merely defines the field within which the architectural project unfolds - it is the mission to be fulfilled without questioning that mission too much. Yet by adopting this reactive relationship to the brief, architecture makes itself fatally dependent on the brief's quality. For if the brief is ill-defined, as so often is the case with competitions, then architecture's answer to the question posed cannot be a lot more intelligent. We therefore argue that in order to make a valid contribution to society, the architect has to treat the brief as an integral part of the project itself.

THE BRIEF IS NOT A GIVEN, BUT A MATERIAL TO BE PROCESSED, REFLECTED, TESTED, QUESTIONED, AND, IF NECESSARY, REDEFINED.

This act of reviewing the question can cause the architect to draw a variety of radical conclusions. One of them may be to reject the project altogether. It suffices to recall the famous anecdote about Cedric Price and the married couple whom had asked Price to build a house for them. As they started to explain the brief the house should fulfill, they got into an argument with each other, making evident their different desires and concepts about the house. Finally, Price interrupted them, saying that what they needed was not an architect, but a divorce lawyer - and rejected the commission. Even though Price did not do the project, he clearly did not do nothing. He made a very precise proposal by urging his clients to face the fact that their real project at this point was not to construct a house, but to reconstruct their relationship.

THUS A REFUSAL CAN IN FACT BE CONSTRUCTIVE.

This is even true when the project refuses to materialize as an oeuvre at all, like John Cage's famous composition entitled 4' 33" (1952), which consists of the pianist sitting at a piano and not playing for exactly four minutes and 33 seconds. This is obviously not nothing, and it becomes a very dense scenario. People start to wonder what's going on and why the musician don't start playing. To compensate for the unbearable silence they begin making furtive noises themselves – clearing their throats, moving nervously, causing the seat to squeak and so on. It's only when the musician eventually stands up from the piano and leaves the stage, that the audience finally realises that while they had been waiting for the performance to start, it had already ended. What may have appeared in the first instance to be an annihilation of music soon enough proved to be the contrary. By not letting the music play, Cage enabled the audience to listen to the sound of silence, and thus, in the same way that Beuys was enlarging the notion of the work of art, he radically enlarged the notion of music by eliminating the distinction between sound and noise. [1]

Therefore the suspension of an action which is expected can induce something very substantial to occur. We would like to think that architecture should reserve its right to take advantage of this form of inverted action as well.

Sometimes doing nothing is the only way to do the right thing. In their project for the Place Léon Aucoc in Bordeaux in 1996, Lacaton & Vassal pursued this architecture of omission to the ultimate degree. The city of Bordeaux had asked them to make proposals for the 'embellishment' of the square. Lacaton Vassal, however, already found it beautiful the way it was, and came to the conclusion that all the square needed was better maintenance and care. So they drew up a catalogue of suggested measures, but consciously refrained from physically altering the space.

With their 'negative' projects, both Lacaton Vassal and Cedric Price exposed how their briefs were posing the question incorrectly. Not only was the actual issue lying somewhere else, but it also could not be 'helped' by architecture. To find a way out, they tried to redefine the specificity of the intervention required - Price referred his clients to another expert able to deal with their situation more appropriately, while Lacaton Vassal tentatively acted in the role of that other expert for the sake of the project. That is to say, both architects used the intelligence of architecture to disengage it from a task ill-directed towards it.

Provided that a planned project has a minimum degree of legitimacy, architecture can launch a projective action by using a strategy of reprogramming. The brief is then no longer the administrative protocol that most architects have come to mistake it for, but the genuine matter of architecture.

THE BRIEF THEN BECOMES A PLASTIC MATERIAL OUT OF WHICH THE PROJECT WILL BE GENERATED.

To become operative, the brief has to be decomposed into its constituent elements; either in order to be recombined in a different order or to test their general suitability for the situation in question. If individual programs prove to be meaningless they can be eliminated, while missing programs considered to be crucial can be added. Whether it be the targeted user group or the project's proposed location, no element of the brief is safe from the trenchant

re-examination of reprogramming which transforms the brief from a prescriptive presumption into a dynamic scenario that stimulates, but does not anticipate, the course of the project.

Redefining the brief in this way has often proved crucial in endowing projects with space to maneuver.

NEVERTHELESS, IT REMAINS A REACTIVE STRATEGY.

Architecture can only intervene in situations which have already been defined as being worthy of intervention. Yet, to fully exploit its potential as a generator of reality, architecture has to position itself in a such a way that it is not bound to wait until a brief is presented (which it can then gratefully react to), but rather so that it can produce a brief in any given situation on its own. Architecture's ativistic habit of responding to a brief is then replaced by a practice of scanning reality for situations which have the potential to be acted upon by architecture itself. Escaping the reductive assignment of being the problem-solver, architecture assumes the capacity to pose problems, or rather, issues, that are relevant for an architectural intervention. In doing so architecture would ultimately escape the boundaries it has been living within for too long and start to self-confidently negotiate the limits of its action with every step it makes.
The projects we have selected to be presented hereafter refer to all three ways of positioning architecture to the brief that were mentioned above. The selection is not limited to architectural projects, but includes projects by artists as well, as the issue we are trying to address is more an issue of approach than of discipline.

[K] "Inspired by his experience in an anechoic chamber – where instead of experiencing total silence as he had anticipated, Cage heard both the pitched impulses of his nervous system and the low-pitched drone of his blood circulating – he decided to demonstrate that ‹silence› in music is actually composed of any number of 'incidental' sounds originating from sources other than the musicians and their instruments." Henry M. Sayre, The Object of Performance. The American Avant-garde since 1970, Chicago 1989, S. 105.

1. Lacaton Vassal Architectes, Place Léon Aucoc, Bordeaux, 1996.

In 1996 the city of Bordeaux launched a project for an 'embellishment of places', asking a number of architects to develop proposals for the aesthetic improvement of specific sites in the city. Lacaton & Vassal were given the Place Léon Aucoc, a little triangular square near the main railway station, a square as one can probably find in countless cities all over France - inconspicuous enough to allow an architect the illusion of being able to improve it by way of an architectural intervention. Yet for Lacaton & Vassal the square was already beautiful the way it was, and they did not see how and why they should intervene. They analyzed the architecture of the surrounding houses, the surface materials and urban furnishings of the square, and the organisation of traffic and interviewed the inhabitants. In the end they found only minor misfits, none of which would have been 'solved' by an architectural project.

INSTEAD OF REPRESSING THE EVIDENT USELESSNESS OF AN ARCHITECTURAL INTERVENTION WITH A SYMBOLIC PROJECT, THEY PROPOSED A SIMPLE CATALOGUE OF STRIKINGLY OBVIOUS MAINTENANCE MEASURES:

regularly cleaning the square of dog shit in order to make it possible to play the game of petanque on it once again; cleaning the leaves of the lime trees off the benches so that one could sit on them; rearranging the parking spaces; reorganizing the traffic in order to reduce through-traffic. Finally, they proposed the reintroduction of the St. John Fires, a customary public event which had previously been interdicted by city authorities in the name of security. After the city officials were presented this catalogue, they asked the architects what they would actually physically change in the square. The answer was: nothing. Startled by this response, the city politicians at first chose not realize the project. In the long run, however, it made them question the very conditions of their embellishment project and how a different way of looking at a given situation may effectively vaporize the 'problem' architecture was supposed to 'solve'.

2. Renata Stih + Frieder Schnock: Bus Stop, Berlin, 1996.

Among the many entries submitted to the competition for a central monument dedicated to the murdered Jews of Europe to be placed in the historic center of Berlin, the proposal by Renata Stih and Frieder Schnock was one of the few

TO QUESTION THE IDEOLOGICAL SYMBOLISM OF THE BRIEF.

Why concentrate the commemoration of a genocide which had happened all over the country in one central and representative place in the German Capital? Why build one pars-pro-toto-monument when there are about a hundred Holocaust memorial sites in Germany, among them the remains of the former concentration camps, most of which are under financial pressure and could well do with the money instead? Careful not to create a symbol designed to bear the nation's feeling of historical guilt, Stih and Schnock proposed a scenario where an individual practice of commemoration would generate the kind of historical memory which cannot be produced by a monument itself. The only physical manifestation of their "monument" would be a bus stop on the proposed site near Brandenburg Gate, which is a central hub of Berlin's sight-seeing tourism. Red London-type tourist double-decker buses would depart from that stop to various memorial sites commemorating the Holocaust in Germany and beyond (Poland, Czech Republic and beyond). They published a time table with all the destinations and their departure times. Consciously playing with the ambiguity of departing and deporting, the artists engage the tourist as an agent of memory. In the process, the monument as an object is replaced by a politicized form of sight-seeing, the physical and mental movement of society to the places of a suppressed past in an effort to face the shame, horror, and disgust it continues to ellicit. The bus-stop project could have lowered this threshold, addressing the passer-by with a kind of Benjaminian shock-effect as they strolled by Brandenburg Gate on their tour of historical Berlin, inviting them to explore the hidden layers of German history. Incidentally, the bus-stop project received a great deal of critical acclaim by those who visited the exhibition, who favoured it over of Eisenman's sculptural mise-en-scène of history, now executed.

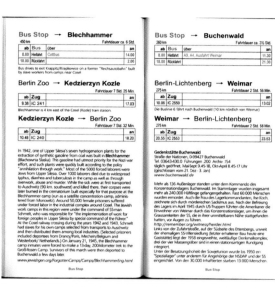

4

Renata Stih & Frieder Schnock; BUS STOP Fahrplan / Timetable; 1. Edition Berlin 1995, 2. Edition 2005 (in German + English, 128 p.) (c) Stih & Schnock, Berlin / VG BildKunst

Renata Stih & Frieder Schnock; BUS STOP, Berlin / Pariser Platz; Collage, 1995; (c) Stih & Schnock, Berlin / VG BildKunst

3. RELAX (Chiarenza & Hauser & Co): Secret Public, Biel (CH), 1993

A public square in the historic center of Biel had been given an urbanistic clean-up, including the elimination of all car traffic. Without the cars, the social life also disappeared. Suddenly the planners realised that the square was dead and sought for ways to enliven it again. Ultimately, they decided that a piece of public art placed on the square could fill the vacuity of the space. The artist group RELAX was invited to take part in the competition for the art work. However, as they did not want to make up for the shortcomings of the political planning process, the artists asked the client whether they would also be able to get the commission even if they did not make a visual intervention in the square. Surprisingly, the answer was yes.

SO THEY CREATED AN ACOUSTIC INTERVENTION

in which three loudspeakers turn on every day at 7 minutes before noon, with two voices calling people for lunch in French and Swiss-German (the two languages spoken in the city). The announcement of this private event in the public space creates a moment of irritation. In contradiction to the casual ritual of a family lunch, the loudspeakers spread an atmosphere of authority and order. In fact, they direct the attention to an important programmatic element of the square - a police station, which is so smoothly housed in one of the cute historic buildings of the square that you can only barely identify it as such when passing by. Surreptitiously, the innocent coziness of the post-card image of the square is blurred by an ambiance of control, the very element that public space is normally seen to be the counterpart of.

4. Roche, DSV & Sie: Folding, Soweto, South Africa, 1997.

Shortly after Apartheid in South Africa ended, the African National Congress (ANC) decided to build a memorial museum at the very place where the colored child, Hector Peterson, was killed by white South African policemen in a political demonstration in the 1970s. Roche, DSV & Sie got involved in the project, but found the idea of a museum dedicated to the history of Apartheid at this very place rather dubious. Despite the end of Apartheid, Soweto was still such a threatening place that the prospect of a normal museum audience visiting there was quite unlikely. It became clear that one would need to create a strong reason for people to actually come to the location and spend their time and money. Hence, the architects radically redefined the brief and the target group of the project by proposing to relocate the archives of the apartheid from the white universities of Johannesburg to this new museum. Researchers studying the history of the townships of Soweto would actually have to go to the very site where that history occurred.

THIS REPROGRAMMING WOULD ENTAIL A TRANSFORMATION

of the identity of the planned museum into an archive and become a device for active memory rather than abstract contemplation of history. In order not to compete with the serenity of the grave of Hector Peterson, the architects proposed to bury the building almost entirely in the ground, leaving no visible traces above ground except a gentle movement of the landscape.

This occupation of the ground was crucial for winning the support of the ANC, who could read it as a symbolic reappropriation of the gold-mines where the majority of Soweto's population had been working to excavate the country's wealth without duly benefiting from it. That the project was never realized is thanks to the French Ministry of Culture who took the self-empowerment of an architect who dared to launch such a project without being politically entitled to do so as an intolerable offence, and urged the ANC to stop working with Roche, DSV & Sie.

5. R&Sie...: Asphalt Spot, Tokamashi, Japan, 2003.

Situated several hours north of Tokyo, the region of Echigo-Tsumari has always been a landscape primarily characterized by agriculture. Yet with the accelerating modernization of post-war Japan, the role of agriculture has steadily diminished, causing abandonment of vast swaths of land and the critical depopulation of many local communities. To counter this development, six municipalities of this region launched the „Echigo-Tsumari Art Triennial" in 2000. It aimed

TO INTRODUCE PROJECTS OF ART AND ARCHITECTURE AS CULTURAL LANDMARKS

in the landscape in order to generate a new 'tourism' that granted the region fresh visibility and public attention. Artists and architects were asked to produce prototypes for a new kind of site-seeing in the landscape. The project by R&Sie... Architects adressed this task in an ambiguous manner by producing not a sight as such, but a stop: a parking lot. Underneath the project's folded surfaces, there is some usable space. However it is not enclosed, and so it is not possible to use it in a conventional way - in particular due to the region's extreme winter season where up to five meters of snow can submerge the architecture almost entirely. But even in the hot and sultry summer season, the project has a dubious presence.

NORMALLY YOU WOULD EXPECT A TOURIST ATTRACTION TO BE SERVED

by a parking space. Here you have a parking space, but no tourist attraction. You arrive by car and are greeted by nothingness. You have to define what the attraction could be: Is it is the landscape, despite all its uneventfulness? Or the parking spot itself where the inclined ground forces the driver to manage his or her own risk (of flipping over)? Or is it maybe just the very experience of coming to this spot in the first place - that journey with no cause other than to loose one's self in a dérive through the landscape?

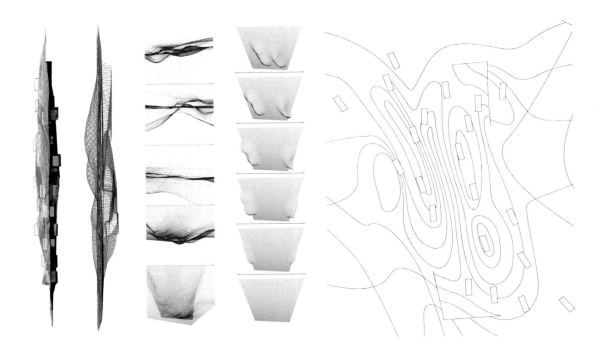

1

Asphalt Spot
Tokamashi, Japan; Architect: R&Sie… Paris; Creative team: François Roche, Stéphanie Lavaux, Jean Navarro, Pascal Bertholio; Key dimensions: 300 m²; Client: City of Tokamashi, Art Front Gallery; Cost: 0,7 million USD; Program: 20 parking places, 300 m² exhibition room, public facilities

Creation of an outdoor exhibition space inside a car park

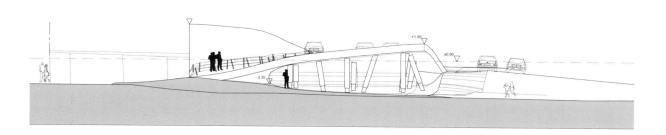

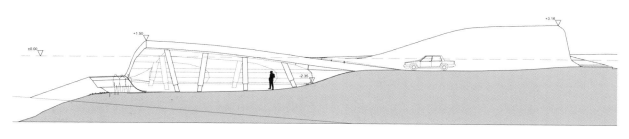

Folding
Soweto, 1997, South Africa; Architect: R&Sie... Paris; (name of the agency at this time : Roche, DSV & Sie);
Creative team and associates partner : François Roche, Stephanie Lavaux, Gilles Desévédavy, Gilles Clement;
Key dimensions: 2,200 m²; Client : African Institute of Contemporary Arts / Johannesburg and Frac Reunion.Cost : 4 M$

Design of a museum-memorial on the tomb of Hector Peterson, integrating the archives of the township (exhibition hall, archives, conference room, restaurant) and a landscaped area of 3 hectares.

6. 51N4E: Allotment Athletica, Oigem, Belgium, 1998.

The competition brief for a suburban development in Flanders had called for a community center and the development of a new private housing typology for 35 houses. However, 51N4E concluded that most people who move to a suburb have already made up their minds about the type of house they want to live in - the free-standing single-family house. Instead,

THE ARCHITECTS BELIEVED IT WOULD BE MORE WORTHWHILE TO REFLECT UPON PUBLIC SPACE

– not only because this space is used jointly by all, but also because it could lend an identity to this development and distinguish it from countless similar developments. To define a narrative for this identity, they focused on one of the few local features - a sports ground, and extrapolated it into a 'theme' for the settlement's public space. Extending the sports ground, the architects organized the entire circulation system like an athletics track. In contrast to usual street layouts, the size of the car lane was reduced in favor of more pedestrian 'tracks'. At the same time, car traffic and pedestrian lanes were not sectioned off by curbs. Moving on the same plane of action, both parties must be more considerate of each other. Drivers are likely to drive slower, not least due to a sense of displacement on this surface normally used by humans. While the car lanes were made of red tarmac, the pedestrian ones consisted of soft red rubber (like the one actually used in athletic stadiums) and hence encouraged a whole variety of active uses on this surface. As the residential houses line both the inside and outside of the track, they look onto the sportive public space like sports fans watching a sporting event. Suddenly public space becomes interesting again, a stage for the every-day activities enacted by the inhabitants who are both actors and spectators of the 'play' of the every-day.

7. 51N4E: LAMOT ™, Mechelen, Belgium, 2000-2005

After years of vacancy, the building complex of the former beer brewery Lamot in Mechelen was supposed to be reprogrammed into a museum cum congress center. A competition was held to determine the scenography of the museum part. As the sole architect in the competition (the other participators were genuine scenographers), 51N4E argued that the question of the museum should not be treated separately from the whole program of the building. At the same time, they questioned the very program of the museum. After studying the proposed content of the museum – a collection of modern art from local artists – and consulting museum experts, 51N4E concluded that the quality of the collection was not good enough to justify a museum. They noticed however, that a vibrant scene of cultural activities (such as theater, library, art, and concert programs) which already existed in the city, did not have a permanent space of their own. Why not use the content which is out there, asked the architects, and convinced their client, the town council of Mechelen, to host these local cultural initiatives of the city in the building.

IN RETURN, LAMOT™ WOULD BECOME A COMPRESSED FORM OF THE CITY IN ITSELF.

5

To allow urban life to occur inside the building, the architects proposed slitting open its entire first floor which cuts the building in three horizontal zones. The ground level would be filled with commercial uses like shops, restaurants, and a micro-brewery, which feeds the building with a steady flow of general public. The floor above, labeled 'Mechelen Centraal' in order to unmistakably announce its projected role in the city, would be a 1300 m^2 indoor plaza which would allow for various forms of informal cultural consumption (with but one fixed element: the reception desk). The upper floors take up a critical mass of project spaces (lounges, auditorium, banquet-hall, temporary art exhibition halls etc.). Whereas the client's intial scheme wanted to separate museum and congress hall, LAMOT™ consciously accomodated commercial and cultural programs side-by-side, fostering a mix of different audiences. The result of this reprogrammation is a new kind of cultural infrastructure: instead of a musem of the 20th century, i.e. the programmatically fixed permanent exhibition of a kind of culture primarily indebted to a 19th century notion of art, Mechelen is likely to soon feature a museum of the 21st century: a programmatically open space acting as a temporary exhibition of its changing urban culture.

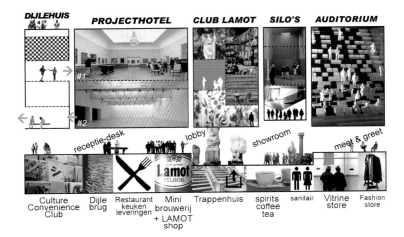

DIJLEHUIS   *PROJECTHOTEL*   *CLUB LAMOT*   *SILO'S*   *AUDITORIUM*

receptie-desk   lobby   showroom   meet & greet

Culture Convenience Club   Dijle brug   Restaurant keuken leveringen   Mini brouwerij + LAMOT shop   Trappenhuis   spirits coffee tea   sanitair   Vitrine store   Fashion store

8. b&k+, IfaU, Le: Flora_n; office park, Cologne, 1999.

Flora_n issued from a competition for an urban master plan of an office park. It tries to break the typological conventions of an office park by taking it apart into its nominal components (office, park) in order to recombine them again, but this time resulting in a park with offices instead of the stereotypical agglomeration of office buildings with green set-backs. To give the green space a generative role for the architecture, the architects proposed a formal amendment to the existing local building code which defines the quality of green space in relationship to the 'building mass index', by replacing it with a newly coined 'green mass index'. The latter indicates the amount of green space that has to be created in order to build a certain amount of building space. Building density is connected with vegetal density and vice versa. Green space, however, is not necessarily outdoors, it may also be brought indoors like in a winter garden. Furthermore it can be programmed and is therefore as much of a commodity as regular built space, following already existing examples like CenterParc's themed aquadomes or the cafeteria-equipped lobbies in garden markets. Thanks to this programming of green space, Flora_n does away with the usual dichotomy between functional buildings and green, but otherwise useless, set-back surfaces in favor of a highly-dense built landscape where built space and green space are continuously cross-referencing each other.

BY SUGGESTING NOT ONLY A SPECIFIC DESIGN PROPOSAL, BUT A RESEARCH PROTOTYPE FOR THE CONCEPTUAL UPGRADING OF AN OVERCOME TYPOLOGY, THE PROJECT OFFENDED THE COMPETITION JURORS WHO PREDICTABLY OPTED FOR A WELL-PROVEN SCHEME.

Possible arrangement of building and green space.

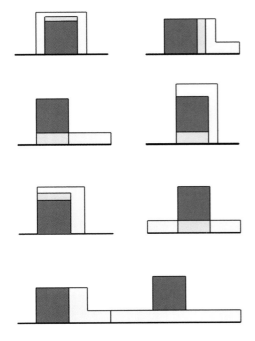

3

Structural elements

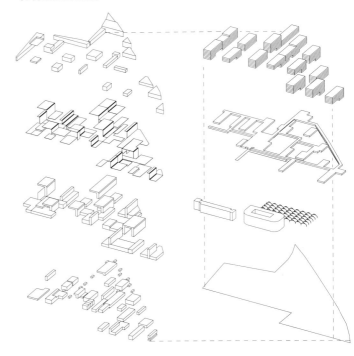

■ Construction volume
□ Green space
▨ Allotment of commercialised space

1. Exterior green space
2. Roof
3. Interior green space
4. Specialised use

5. Office
6. Development
7. Existing state of the building
8. Lot

Building and green space allocation guidelines

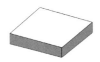 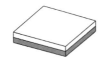  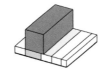

1. BMZ
2. $BMZ = BMZ\_n + GMZ\_n$
   $BMZ\_n = GMZ\_n$
3. $h = \dfrac{BM\_n}{l \times b}$
4. $GM\_n + BM\_n$

9. studio uc_klaus overmeyer/ kunst+herbert/ cet-0: Fischbek-Mississippi, Hamburg-Fischbek, 2002.

The brief of the competition launched by the city of Hamburg called for a housing development project of 1200 residential units at the periphery of Hamburg. To give the prospective inhabitants the "impression" of having natural surroundings, the participants were asked to integrate public neighbourhood parks into their design. This seemed an odd proposal for the architects, given the site's location in the middle of a traditional agricultural area. Why would one import urban green-space typologies like parks and replace agricultural land with suburban development if the dream of living in the green was the main reason that people chose to live in suburbia? The architects decided to take this dream seriously and developed a prototype for an agricultural housing settlement where the existing farmland could either be cultivated by residents themselves (as part-time farmers, hence the "Mississippi Ranger" metaphor) or by the actual farmers who were already using the fields. In this way, the character of the landscape was preserved and costs to the local community for maintaining public space were minimized (which is crucial due to the notoriously tight budgets of local communities in Germany). In administrative terms, the whole system was based on a residents' association, the 'Mississippi Club'. With a modest membership fee, the residents could lease, manage, and maintain over 50% of the area. These 'domesticated' fields could either be used as pastures for animals, play areas for all different ages, fruit and vegetable gardens, or multi-purpose experimentation/exhibition areas. Mississippi products, such as honey, fruit juice, fruit, and vegetables would be for sale in the local shops, with discounted prices for club members. The remaining areas were to be leased to local farmers who would cultivate it ecologically with crops or pasture. Local authorities would only have to maintain public walkways. Should this scenario prove to be too optimistic, the architects also devised a less ambitious scheme:

IF THERE WEREN'T ENOUGH RESIDENTS ENJOYING A LIFE AS MISSISSIPPI FARMERS, THE COMMON AREAS COULD BE MAINTAINED WITH MINIMAL OUTLAY BY A LOCAL FARMER CONTRACTED BY THE RESIDENTS.

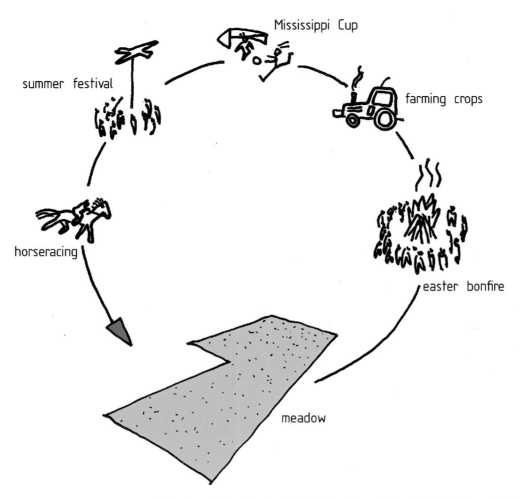

summer festival

Mississippi Cup

farming crops

easter bonfire

horseracing

meadow

The landscape follows the principle of multiple and repeated use. Mississippi rejuvenates itself daily.

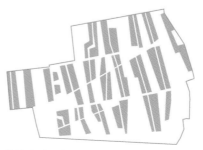

fields for housing

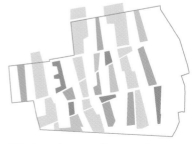

fields for agriculture and communal use

Strip C
Scattered orchard strip: facilities such as small playing fields, lawns, hedged cabinets and perennial gardens are embedded in the strip.

Strip A
a mosaic of small plots with high-density mixed use such as gardens, lawns, pony-runs, soccerfields, a lawnmowing club, active playgrounds, and barbecue areas.

1

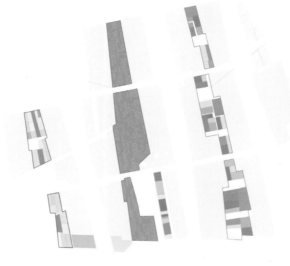

Strip E
A patchwork of fields, similar to Strip A.

Strip D
Agricultural fields: gardens, strawberry fields, flowers, or gardens leased and tended by the farmer in which small grassed and play-areas are integrated.

Strip B
Mississippi shop-window: central promenade from the train station to the clubhouse, flanked with display gardens, juice production, community services, markets and a fruit-tree nursery.

public space

Mississippi-Club Income

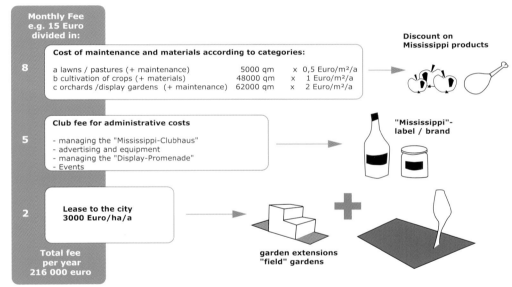

**Monthly Fee
e.g. 15 Euro
divided in:**

Cost of maintenance and materials according to categories:

8

a lawns / pastures (+ maintenance)   5000 qm   x 0,5 Euro/m²/a
b cultivation of crops (+ materials)   48000 qm   x 1 Euro/m²/a
c orchards /display gardens (+ maintenance) 62000 qm   x 2 Euro/m²/a

**Discount on
Mississippi products**

Club fee for administrative costs

5

- managing the "Mississippi-Clubhaus"
- advertising and equipment
- managing the "Display-Promenade"
- Events

**"Mississippi"-
label / brand**

2

**Lease to the city
3000 Euro/ha/a**

**garden extensions
"field" gardens**

**Total fee
per year
216 000 euro**

Mississippi finance

7.

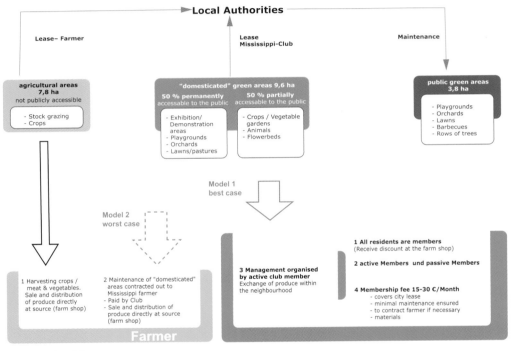

Local Authorities

Lease– Farmer

Lease
Mississippi-Club

Maintenance

**agricultural areas
7,8 ha**
not publicly accessible

- Stock grazing
- Crops

"domesticated" green areas 9,6 ha

50 % permanently
accessible to the public

- Exhibition/
  Demonstration
  areas
- Playgrounds
- Orchards
- Lawns/pastures

50 % partially
accessible to the public

- Crops / Vegetable
  gardens
- Animals
- Flowerbeds

**public green areas
3,8 ha**

- Playgrounds
- Orchards
- Lawns
- Barbecues
- Rows of trees

Model 1
best case

Model 2
worst case

1 Harvesting crops /
meat & vegetables.
Sale and distribution
of produce directly
at source (farm shop)

2 Maintenance of "domesticated"
areas contracted out to
Mississippi farmer
- Paid by Club
- Sale and distribution of
  produce directly at source
  (farm shop)

Farmer

3 Management organised
by active club member
Exchange of produce within
the neighbourhood

1 All residents are members
(Receive discount at the farm shop)

2 active Members und passive Members

4 Membership fee 15-30 €/Month
- covers city lease
- minimal maintenance ensured
- to contract farmer if necessary
- materials

management model

3

The residents determine and create their own environmental surroundings. Depending on interest and motivation, the common areas can either be used intensively according to the Mississippi ideology, or be maintained with minimal outlay.

10. Santiago Cirugeda: The mutant (and silent) architecture, Sevilla, 2000.

The work of urban activist Santiago Cirugeda invariably deals with the conflict between individuals' spatial interests and the rules defined by society to control them. Each of his urban installations

GIVE FORM TO A HUMAN DESIRE THAT IN ORDER TO FULFILL ITSELF NEEDS TO NEGOTIATE A SET OF LEGAL CONSTRAINTS.

Instead of opposing these constraints explicitly, Cirugeda carefully studies them in order to harness their potential. Between the lines of the legal code he sniffs out unforeseen residual possibilities of action and grants them (il)legal asylum in his architectural interventions in public space. In order to add a balcony to his apartment (which was not permitted), he vandalized the facade of his building with graffiti. To clean a façade, one is entitled to erect scaffolding for a period of three months – during which time he appropriated the scaffolding as his balcony. In another project he applied for a permit to install a construction waste container in order to make a play area for children in the street. Once he had the permit, he closed the container with a platform and then mounted a seesaw on the platform. In yet another project he realized a (forbidden) apartment roof-top addition by making the shape and material of the illegal habitat such that it would be invisible to the administration officers who regularly surveyed the roof-scapes from helicopters. In Cirugeda's urban interventions the very instruments of control intended to streamline every-day life in the name of the law uncanningly mutate into tools which help to overcome these restrictions and open up spaces for potential action.

DIVINA
PASTORA

11. Benjamin Foerster-Baldenius, Schreber's Delight, Berlin, 2000

A couple in Berlin wanted to give up their old 120 square meter apartment in a representative 19th century building in favor of a domestic life in the green on their private garden plot. They hired architect Benjamin Foerster-Baldenius, a member of the Berlin-based architecture network Raumlabor,

TO THINK ABOUT HOW THEY COULD LIVE ON A SITE WHERE NO HOUSE COULD BE BUILT

without risking an overtly illegal situation. While local rules of garden allotments outlaw the construction of any building suitable for permanent living, they allow their users to place arbors, green houses, or sculptures without a building permit. The arbor can only be one story high, without a basement, and must not exceed 24 m^2 in usable surface and 3.60 m in ridge height - clearly an area too small to live in. However, and this was the strategy of the architect, if you combine it with a green house and a sculpture, you may end up with a livable house. The construction began by cutting the existing arbor with a chainsaw - à la Gordon-Matta Clark - in two parts. One part, the 'Matta-Clark-Module', was kept and serves today as wardrobe and storage space. The other surviving parts of the old arbor were worked into the 'scultpture', which marks the entry-way of the new house and contains a corridor and bathrom with a compost toilet. At the top of the sculpture is the 'van-Lieshout-Module', quoting Dutch Artist Joep van Lieshout with its capsule-like shape and rounded corners, it contains a small bedroom for two people. Attached to the sculpture is the arbor-part of the construction which uses the applicable measurements to the max. This space contains a living room and kitchen on the ground floor, and a ladder leads to the bedroom and a mezzanine gallery with the study. The final part is a 'greenhouse' of 7 m^2, which contains sanitary equipment and effectively serves as the bathroom. Taken together, all three elements give 47.3 m^2 of usable surface and 150 m^3 of usable volume. It's less then CIAM's Existenzminimum, but has a bigger garden. And its clients have been living there now for 4 years, using it as a primary residence.

12. EM2N, Schreberkicken, Zürich, 2003

A new training center for the Zurich soccer team GCZ
sparked a fierce discussion in the city and its media,
because to give way for its allotment gardens would need to
be relocated. EM2N took this public polemic as an occasion
to intervene as architects without commission. They started
analyzing the relation between soccer fields and allotment
gardens in Zurich. Both programmes have a high surface-
area consumption, both are often located directly side-by-
side within the urban fringe, both are under the pressure of
the real estate market, and both allow their users to escape
temporarily from the routines of everyday life – a crucial
factor in a perfectly organized city like Zurich. But while the
demand for allotment gardens is steadily decreasing, the
need for soccer pitches is growing continuously. To mediate
between these two social tendencies EM2N proposed
adapting the outdated typology of the allotment garden
colony to meet the needs of the current users. Whereas the
existing regulations still viewed the allotment gardens as a
means of achieving self-sufficiency by growing vegetables
and raising small domestic livestock, for current users
they were simply places for relaxation and individual self-
fulfilment. EM2N responded to this trend by repealing the
traditional regulations that restricted the use and layout
of the sites (e.g. it was forbidden to spend the night there,
the area of lawn could not exceed 50% of the garden and
there was an obligation to grow plants), calling instead for
tolerant anarchy with a minimum of regulations - where use
and configuration of the plots would be left to the tenants
and living there on a permanent basis would be allowed.

AT THE SAME TIME, THEY PROPOSED REDUCING THE SIZES OF INDIVIDUAL GARDEN PLOTS IN ORDER TO INCREASE THE COMMUNAL AREAS.

This was achieved by creating a higher vertical density:
the gardens were arranged in several levels above each
other (terracing ensured sufficient direct sunlight and rain
for each site) so that the area gained could be programmed
with intensive uses of land such as half-pipes, playgrounds,
restaurants, and – soccer fields.

24-hours time frame: use / intensity

eating

gardening

amusing

tinkering

eating sleeping eating animals

gardening

gardening tinkering

tinkering

amusing

animals

animals

sleeping

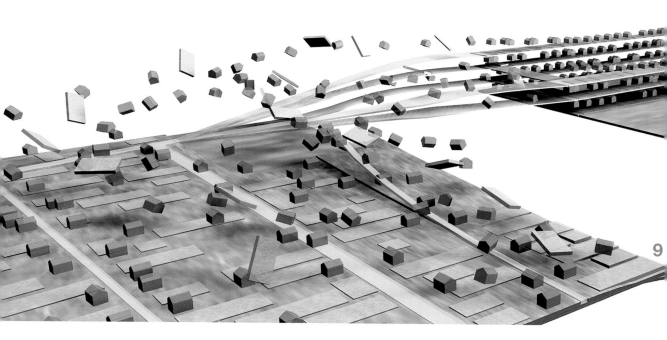

9

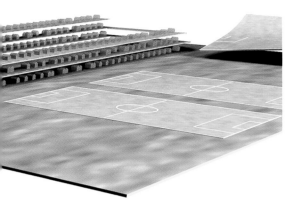

5

13. realities united: stereo transformer, Berlin, 2002-03

Invented in the early nineties as a political demonstration, the Berlin Love Parade started as a bottom-up movement bringing the techno scene from the clubs into the public space of the city to share the experience of music and dancing on the street with the general public. This approach was extremely successful and the event soon became a model for mega-sized urban pop music events. But with the event's success a problem also appeared: the more people that joined the parade, the less they became active members of the event, rather, they became a passive audience looking up at some dancers and listening to music installed on top of heavy trucks driving by.

Locating the event's problem not in its size, but in its conventional set-up, Jan and Tim Edler of realities:united developed a new vehicle system, which for the first time dealt consequently with the need for appropriate design, technology, and sound at such open air events. To achieve the simple vision of providing excellent sound and adequate space to dance for large numbers of people, realities: united split vehicles into two parts with separate speaker systems on each part. This set-up provided the structural precondition for putting the people in the center and surrounding them with the sound system – not the other way around.

IT TAKES THE LEAP FROM MONO TO STEREO.

Everyone who loves music understands the difference. With stereotransformer realities:united revolutionized the experience of music and dancing on the street. The system defined a new scale for performing at street parades and will ultimately reach an audience of millions. This is because the system will not only participate in a cultural event scene but the spectacular gig will also collect a maximum of media attention, which is an important issue for an event that is dependent on commercial sponsors. So far the stereo transformer has not been implemented by the Love Parade organizers, who have not been too keen on developing the event further. Because of this, sponsors have been steadily loosing interest in the event, resulting in the cancelling of the Love Parade both in 2004 and 2005.

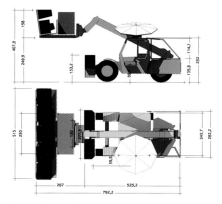

Project "Stereo Transformer", 2002-03; ©realities:united, Berlin, http://www.realu.de/stereo_transformer/

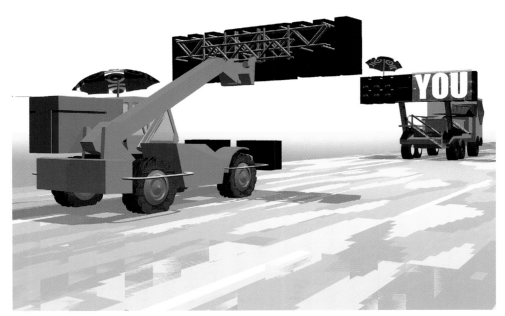

Project "Stereo Transformer", 2002-03; ©realities:united, Berlin, http://www.realu.de/stereo_transformer/

14. realities:united: Flussbad Museumsinsel, Berlin, 1998-dato

1. dam
2. changing facilities
3. swimming pool
4. sand bed water treatment basin
5. reed bed water treatment basin

The area of the Museumisland in the historic center of Berlin presents a strikingly mono-functional profile. Over-equipped with museum culture and federal agencies, the area caters predominantly to the needs of tourism and national representation while lacking facilities for the every-day life of local inhabitants. With their studio space located during the 1990s on the Spree river banks facing the Museum Island, Jan and Tim Edler of realities:united could study the effects of this sterilisation of public life from up close: a thriving urban place with all kinds of unique spaces but unfortunately struck by a lack of corresponding richness of use. Their Flussbad proposal tapped right into this gap by transforming a river arm of the Spree, originally created for shipping but now completely out of use, into a public swimming pool. It provided badly-needed recreational facilities around the center and brought authentic life back into the functional waste-land of the museum island.
To enable the project, only a minimum of action was necessary: the upper course is used as a reed bed filter of about 1.8 hectar which naturally purifies the inflowing water. At the end, a barrage prevents the unpurified water from the main river from flowing back into the swimming area. A quay wall generously transformed into a large stair provided access. Some limited necessities like locker rooms and footbridges completed the system. In addition to its social impact, the project also accomodates ecological and economical development. By focusing on making natural water accessible and usable, Flussbad becomes more of a beach than a conventional swimming pool.

THUS IT NOT ONLY REDUCES MAINTENANCE EXPENSES, BUT ALSO ADDRESSES THE ECOLOGICAL INTERESTS OF AN URBAN PUBLIC IN TIMES WHERE POLLUTION OF AIR AND WATER MAKE CITIES INCREASINGLY UNATTRACTIVE PLACES TO LIVE IN.

ect "Flussbad – a river becomes swimming pool", 1998-dato; ©realities:united, Berlin, http://www.realu.de/flussbad/

Project "Flussbad – a river becomes swimming pool", 1998-2020; ©realities:united, Berlin, http://www.realu.de/flussbad/

1

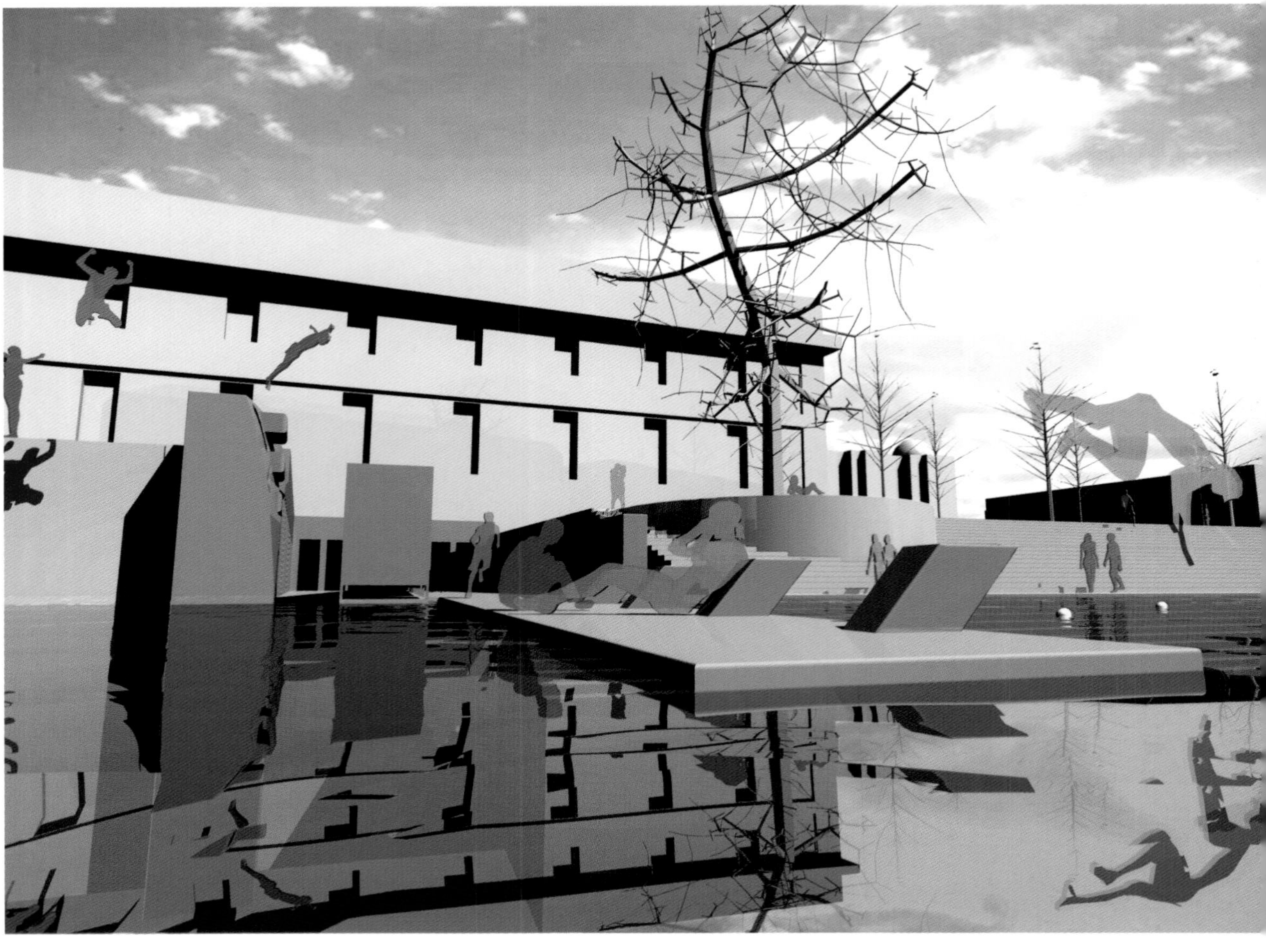

3

In advanced societies, change is the last remaining constant. We have come to expect that anything can happen, and all that surprises us anymore is when things remain the same. Heraclitis' pronouncement that you cannot step into the same river twice, a distressing truism that completely contradicts our everyday experience, has become a subjective certainty that conditions our actions.

WE HAVE LEARNED TO PERCEIVE SEEMINGLY STABLE CIRCUMSTANCES AS STEADY-STATES OF TEMPORARY EQUILIBRIUM THAT MIGHT ABRUPTLY BECOME TURBULENT OR SUDDENLY COLLAPSE.

To investigate the impact of this development on architecture,

IT IS HELPFUL TO DISTINGUISH BETWEEN ARCHITECTURE AS A BUILDING AND ARCHITECTURE AS A PROCESS. ARCHITECTURE AS A BUILDING

is characterized by attributes like its form, its function and its performance, the latter comprising such measurable aspects as thermal insulation as well as the subtle articulation of power structures by means of a floor plan. Architecture as a process, on the other hand, can be defined as a sequence of actions and decisions – from the initiation of a project through its planning and execution, the resulting structure's utilization and eventual re-adaptation, all the way to its ultimate demolition.

In considering architecture as a building, the demands lodged by society and the individual come last and are only loosely connected with the structure itself via the concept of performance. In the case of architecture considered as a process, it is just the opposite: the agenda is headed by social forces that lead to particular – and sometimes contradictory – demands being placed on the constructed environment. The focal point of interest is occupied by various protagonists and ideas, the history of their impact and their side-effects. The edifice that gets built is regarded as only a single consequence among others.

THESE TWO CONCEPTS OF ARCHITECTURE COMPLEMENT EACH OTHER, WHEREBY THEY ORGANIZE THEIR CONTENTS IN ONE CASE ALONG A SPATIAL AXIS AND IN THE OTHER ALONG A TEMPORAL ONE.

Obviously, there can be no architecture as a building without a corresponding process. Conversely, though, it is indeed possible to initiate an architectural process that never leads to an actual building but that has momentous consequences nevertheless.

Here, I am not only referring to the influential but never realized projects we are familiar with from our study of architectural history. Every project leaves behind traces and experiences on the part of protagonists and observers, and these endure even if the project is ultimately shelved. Dispensing with implementation cannot necessarily be equated with failure.

Often enough, the architectural process brings out new priorities and alternatives that make not going ahead with construction seem like the best solution for everyone involved. From the perspective of the process, a building that has been completed and celebrated at its dedication ceremony constitutes only a single point on a time axis, a temporary state situated between valuable experiences in the past and in the future.

NEVERTHELESS, THE ARCHITECTURAL DISCOURSE TENDS TO ASCRIBE MUCH HIGHER VALUE TO THE BUILDING THAN TO THE PROCESS.

Thus, the reactions of those participating in this discourse in addressing the question of how architecture should respond to the demands placed upon it by a turbulent, unstable world are correspondingly building-oriented. We can cite as an example of an extreme response those tendencies that attempt to position architecture as the final bulwark of stable worldly wisdom based upon anthropological constants.

The architect garbed in the clerical vestments of His Eminence the Master Builder who draws upon stores of accumulated archetypes and promises thereby to create what Leibniz called "pre-stabilized harmony" obviously – as attested to by the New Urbanism in the USA and the success of Krier and Kohl in the Netherlands – has bright prospects for success on the market in advanced societies, or at least in places where willing submission to a hierarchy is regarded as an alternative to the unrelenting pressure of self-determination. Likewise building-focused are those attempts rooted in the 1960s to create a reactive architecture that responds mechanically to the turbulence of its environment. The architectural visions of ARCHIGRAM such as "Walking City" are tantamount to architecture's general mobilization, the martial origins of

which are to be found in the war machinery that the Allied armies of World War II deployed off the Normandy coast as part of the effort to break through the massive defensive fortifications of the Germans' Atlantic Wall.

WHATEVER THIS ARCHITECTURE GAINS IN THE FORM OF MOBILITY, IT NEVERTHELESS LOSES FLEXIBILITY DUE TO ITS MACHINELIKE CHARACTER.

Even Cedric Price's Fun Palace for Joan Littlewood ultimately remains arrested in this machine paradigm. Conceived as a temporary construction in a continual state of transformation, it turns users into machinists who spend their time operating the apparatus. The Pompidou Center as realization of Cedric Price's vision owes its success not to a real gain in flexibility, but rather to its inspired metaphorical imagery of a reactive architecture. Extravagantly conceived as a machine, the structure that was put into use ultimately became a monument to itself.

In architecture, we much more frequently encounter examples of buildings that were conceived from the very outset as purely sculptural representations of the dynamism of the Machine Age. Their origins lie in early-20th-century Futurism. In the Futurist Manifesto of 1909, Filippo Tomaso Marinetti made it patently clear which standards the art of the future would have to live up to:

A "ROARING CAR" WAS SAID TO BE "MORE BEAUTIFUL THAN THE WINGED VICTORY OF SAMOTHRACE."

"Unique Forms of Continuity in Space," Umberto Boccioni's 1913 sculpture that was inspired by Marinetti's manifesto, blends man and machine into a "metallized body" and is, in turn, the standard of reference for later artistic attempts to commingle the organic and the mechanical.

Over the last few decades, most world-class architectural sculptors-on-a-grand scale – first and foremost Frank

O. Gehry, but Coop Himmelb(l)au and Zaha Hadid as well – draw their inspirations from this formal repertoire. They thus implicitly adopt this practice of venerating the "metallized body" of the machine that Marinetti glorified in the Futurist Manifesto: "gluttonous railway stations swallowing smoky serpents … bridges leaping like athletes hurled over the diabolical cutlery of sunny rivers … adventurous steamers that sniff the horizon."

FRANK O. GEHRY'S STATA CENTER THAT OPENED IN 2004 ON THE CAMPUS OF MIT IN BOSTON IS AN EXAMPLE OF SUCH AN ADVENTURE-SEEKING "METALLIZED BODY."

Every single component of the $285 million signature building seems to be sniffing at the horizon, ready and willing to set off to new shores. The edifice is a monumental statement of MIT's claim to being one of the world's foremost universities as well as a testament to the financial potency of its sponsors, for whom the individual wings of the building are named. For instance, there's a Gates Tower and a Gates Entry, whose W-shaped glass roof provides no conclusive answer as to whether it's meant to honor William or Windows. The building's interior features an almost endless profusion of ideas for engendering a creative atmosphere, full of nooks and crannies as situations for informal meetings and vertical views culminating in exterior vistas.

The Stata Center was erected on a parcel that had previously been the site of the most beloved research facility on the MIT campus, the legendary Building 20. Designed in 1943 as a new facility for radiation research, the building was an artifact of wartime haste. Designed in an afternoon by MIT grad Don Whinston, it was ready for occupation six months later:

A COMPLETELY UTILITARIAN STRUCTURE, FRAMED WITH HEAVY WOOD TIMBERS

Ray and Maria Stata Center, model

Umberto Boccioni,
Unique Forms of
Continuity in Space, 1913

Frank O. Gehry, Ray and
Maria Stata Center, MIT
Boston, 2004
Photo: Wikimedia,
(Marc Pellegrini)

1990 - Author Fred Hapgood wrote in 1993 of Building 20, "The edifice is so ugly that it is impossible not to admire it, if that makes sense; it has ten times the righteous nerdly swagger of any other building on campus." (*Up the Infinite Corridor*, New York: Addison-Wesley)

MIT Boston, "Building 20," 1943, (Photos: MIT Museum)

since steel was unavailable because of the war. The building was exempted from the fire code on the condition that it was a temporary structure. It was one of the strongest buildings on campus, bearing 700 kg per square meter. In spite of being conceived as a temporary structure, the building remained in use for almost 50 years. With its dark central corridors and a completely repetitive plan and façade,

THE BUILDING LACKED ANY ARCHITECTURAL AMBITIONS.

In spite of its appearance, Building 20 had the highest reputation of all buildings on the campus when it celebrated its 25th birthday in 1978. This was partly due to its legendary history of housing important breakthroughs in research. But the building was revered by its users mainly for a lot of practical reasons that made it appear "the best research building ever designed," as one of its users put it. [1] In his book "How Buildings Learn," Stewart Brand quotes some of the reasons users gave for this assessment. They value the "possibility to design your own space.

IF YOU DON'T LIKE A WALL, YOU JUST PUT YOUR ELBOW THROUGH IT. [...] THE USERS SEE THEMSELVES AS THE CREATORS OF THE BUILDING: 'IF YOU MAKE A HOLE INTO THE FLOOR TO GET MORE VERTICAL SPACE, YOU JUST DO IT WITHOUT ASKING [...]

This is really our place. We have designed it, we run it. The building is full of micro-environments, each one a creative space of its own. It has so much personality.'" [2] Building 20 is the prototype of an architecture in which the building itself takes a backseat to the process. The building's appropriation by the users, the permanent process of reconstruction and the micro-environments that resulted from it were the key features of this architecture.

The planners of the Stata Center were most certainly aware that they might long be haunted by the ghost of Building 20. By implementing moveable wall systems in certain

lab areas, they sought to impart at least a modicum of flexibility to the new edifice's higgledy-piggledy floor plans. Nevertheless, it is an unlikely proposition that in 25 years, there will be users maintaining that a building designed by Frank O. Gehry that they walk into every day through a Gates Entry is "really their place" and that "they designed it, and they run it.
" The Stata Center will remain a monument, a walk-through memorial to the power of those who commissioned it and the mastery of its architect.

THE OVERALL STRATEGIC OBJECTIVE BEING PURSUED BY THE MIT ADMINISTRATION IN ERECTING THE STATA CENTER AND A NUMBER OF OTHER NEW BUILDINGS ON CAMPUS IS TO CREATE VERY HIGH-PROFILE SETTINGS AS A MEANS OF ENDOWING THE INSTITUTION WITH A DISTINCTIVE IMAGE THAT SETS IT APART FROM OTHER UNIVERSITIES.

In order to build its own brand, MIT commissioned the major brand names of the architectural profession – in addition to Gehry, the roll of honor includes Steven Holl, Fumihiko Maki and Charles Correa – to deliver the appropriate goods. Indeed, architecture certainly does play a role in the university's process of transformation, but the decision in favor of a spectacular signature building was made at the very outset so that latitude for innovation was limited in several respects.

The architects had nary a chance to develop projects beyond the confines of their signature style, to say nothing of the question of whether the signature building was even the most suitable solution for the university's actual needs. Building 20 suggested a completely different tack: Though it most certainly did not lodge ambitious claims to formal excellence, its neutral structure that was a permanent source of stimulus to making productive changes obviously did contribute to that very culture of scientific innovation that has made MIT one of the world's leading universities.

IT WOULD BE NAÏVE TO CONCLUDE FROM THIS EXAMPLE THAT ONLY COMPLETELY NEUTRAL STRUCTURES ARE ABLE TO PROVIDE USERS WITH THE POSSIBILITY OF SATISFYING THEIR "TRUE" NEEDS.

The idea of explicit renunciation of design ambitions might be useful as a polemic thought experiment, [3] but once this is declared to be an official strategy, the resulting vacuum will quickly be filled by planning experts from a wide array of fields ranging from management consultants to Feng Shui gurus. The outstanding quality of Building 20 was not its neutral, open plan; rather, this was inherent in the specific culture of change that established itself there over the years as a practice of open planning.

IF WE IN THE ARCHITECTURAL PROFESSION WISH TO CONTRIBUTE TO SUCH A CULTURE, IT WOULD BE ADVISABLE TO ABANDON THE CONCEPT OF ARCHITECTURE AS A BUILDING AND INSTEAD CONSIDER IT AS A MEDIUM OF CHANGE IN WHOSE IMAGINED AND REAL SPACES SOCIETY'S INTERESTS AND NEEDS ARE ARTICULATED AND NEGOTIATED.

[1] Stewart Brand, How Buildings Learn, Penguin Books, 1995
[2] Ibid.
[3] As Cedric Price and Reyner Banham, among others, did in the 1960s; see: Reyner Banham, Paul Barker, Cedric Price and Peter Hall, " Non-plan: An Experiment in Freedom," in New Society, March 20, 1969, no. 338

Thus, instead of a one-sided relationship between process and building in which the process is nothing more than a means to an end, there emerges mutually advantageous reciprocal feedback between process and medium.

THIS CONCEPT OF ARCHITECTURE AS A MEDIUM TO EFFECTUATE CHANGE SHOULD NOT BE CONFUSED WITH THE CLAIMS OF CLASSIC MODERNISM TO IMPROVE THE WORLD THROUGH ARCHITECTURE – FOR INSTANCE, LE CORBUSIER IN "TOWARDS A NEW ARCHITECTURE" CALLING FOR "ARCHITECTURE OR REVOLUTION!"

A medium is not a tool that can be applied to modify something external to it. It's just the opposite: A medium provides external forces with a certain bandwidth of articulation possibilities that the medium is in a position to propagate. According to Marshall McLuhan's classification of media as hot and cool, architecture is one of the coolest. In contrast to hot media like books, films and radio broadcasts that focus on particular senses and display high information density, architecture permits a great deal of latitude for the interpretation of content, whereby, in this context, architecture's content is meant to be understood as its performance. Architecture is a cool medium because most architectural forms permit a wide range of performance – for example, a structure built to serve as a stadium can also be used as a high-occupancy prison or refugee camp; after all, functionally speaking, it is nothing but a machine to control the movements of human masses.

IT WOULD BE EASY TO USE THIS DETOUR AS A WAY OF REINTRODUCING THROUGH THE BACKDOOR AS IT WERE THE IDEA OF AN "AUTONOMOUS ARCHITECTURE."

If architecture is the medium and the performance is its message, then McLuhan's assertion that the medium is

the message would have to apply here too. But nothing would be gained from this line of argumentation. McLuhan's importance does not stem from an attempt to postulate media's autonomy but rather from having pointed out that their characteristics often have a stronger impact on society than the content these media transport. Media without messages – as "post-humanist" and "post-functionalist" tendencies in architecture are not to be labeled – are not autonomous. They're dead.

Among the most important tasks confronting architecture today, therefore, is to credibly get across its potential as a medium of social change. This cannot be accomplished solely by the turn to projective architecture as is currently being discussed by architectural theorists (above all in the USA). [4] Their enthusiasm for collaboration with anything that moves energetically enough is insufficient to come to terms with the contradictions of our advanced societies.

TO DO SO, ARCHITECTURE MUST ALSO BE EFFECTIVE AS A MEDIUM OF THINGS QUOTIDIAN AND QUIET, AND OCCASIONALLY PERHAPS EVEN WORK AS A CRITICAL BACKGROUND THAT POINTS OUT ALTERNATIVES TO PREVAILING CONDITIONS WITHOUT BEING PUSHY AND MAKING A SPECTACLE OF ITSELF.

1

[4] Cf. Ole Fischer, "Critical, Post-Critical, Projectice? Szenen einer Debatte" in: Archplus 174, p. 92

3

CAN ARCHITECTURE INITIATE CHANGE, AS THE MODERNISTS ALWAYS PROMISED?

Back in 1985, Rem Koolhaas explained that "architecture is monstrous in the way in which each choice leads to the reduction of possibility," whence the once popular slogan, "where there is nothing, everything is possible. Where there is architecture, nothing (else) is possible." [1] For Koolhaas, then, architecture is a regime of discipline, a limitation to freedom, a crossing out of possibilities.

1❬ Koolhaas, Rem, „Typical Plan",S,M,L,XL. Ed. Rem Koolhaas and Bruce Mau. Köln, Benedikt Taschen Verlag, 1997, 344; Koolhaas, Rem, „Imagining Nothingness," S,M,L,XL, 199; originally published as Koolhaas, Rem, "To imagine nothingness", in: L'architecture d'aujourd'hui, no. 238, april 1985, p. LXVII.

This idea could probably be traced back to Michel Foucault's discussion of Jeremy Bentham's Panopticon. Foucault explains that in the modern, panoptical society, "the man described for us whom we are invited to free, is already himself the effection of a subjection much more profound than himself.

A 'SOUL' INHABITS HIM AND BRINGS HIM TO EXISTENCE, WHICH IS ITSELF A FACTOR IN THE MASTERY THAT POWER EXERCISES OVER THE BODY.

The soul is the effect and instrument of a political anatomy; the soul is the prison of the body." [2] Not only did Koolhaas deal with Bentham's ideas directly, as OMA renovated a panoptical prison in Arnhem, but he has repeatedly come to the idea of architecture as a form of social control. As early as his diploma at the AA in 1971, he proposed rewriting the history of architecture from the premise that the paradigmatic building would not be the Urhütte of Laugier but the Berlin wall. If architecture is identified with police measures in this way, it does seem reasonable to conclude that in order to carve out a little piece of freedom, one needs to reduce architecture to zero degree, and this seems to have been a central concern for Koolhaas. Responding to "traditional criticisms" inability to grasp what Koolhaas is all about, Jeffrey Kipnis explains that "one and only one cultural aim drives the work, from the writings to the projects and buildings, coloring each decision at every scale, from domestic to urban, from diagram to detail. That aim focusses the work into such an acute convergence that as a body, it begins to constitute a treatise on the topic. That aim, so brazen that almost no one but Koolhaas ever mentions it in other than occult terms, is simply this:

TO DISCOVER WHAT REAL, INSTRUMENTAL COLLABORATION CAN BE EFFECTED BETWEEN ARCHITECTURE AND FREEDOM." [3]

At the time when Kipnis made his statement, the architect had formulated two crucial concepts that promised to negotiate this collaboration: the Typical Plan and the Generic City.

Typical and generic

Koolhaas opens his 1993 essay on the typical plan by asserting that it is "an American invention. It is zero-degree architecture stripped of all traces of uniqueness and specificity. It belongs to the New World." [4] As is evident, Koolhaas likes to use quotations without quotation marks. For example, the concept of "zero-degree architecture" echoes the Barthesian concept of "writing zero-degree." While Roland Barthes defined writing as "a compromise between freedom and a memory," Koolhaas is on the side of freedom, and places little hope in memory. [5]

5   THUS, ALSO THE TYPICAL PLAN IS AN INVENTION, AND IT SIGNIFIES THE NEW WORLD.

This rhetoric is taken up again and again in what follows: "Typical Plan is a segment of an unacknowledged utopia, the promise of a post-architectural future." [6] It represents "the discovery ... of a new architecture." [7] It creates "new territories for the smooth unfolding of new processes." [8] Moreover, its only function is said to be "to let its occupants exist." It is the ideal accommodation for business, the most formless of programs, for "business makes no demands," or so Koolhaas claims. [9]
The generic city is comparable to the typical plan as another regime of freedom; Koolhaas calls it „the apotheosis of the multiple-choice concept: all boxes crossed." [10] Both the typical plan and the generic city promote freedom because they have no character or identity.

FOR KOOLHAAS, THE LACK OF IDENTITY IS A GOOD THING, FOR "THE STRONGER THE IDENTITY, THE MORE IT IMPRISONS, THE MORE IT RESISTS EXPANSION, INTERPRETATION, RENEWAL, CONTRADICTION."

In contrast to a generic city, "Paris can only become more Parisian – it is already on its way to becoming hyper-Paris, a polished caricature." Another European example mentioned by Koolhaas is Barcelona, a city that in recent decades has invested a lot in improving its urban and architectural

qualities. Despite these efforts that have been praised all over the world, Koolhaas' judgment is harsh: "Sometimes an old, singular city, like Barcelona, by oversimplifying its identity, turns Generic. It becomes transparent, like a logo." [11] Given the praise he lavishes on the typical plan and the generic city, it is strange that Koolhaas also complains, for example, about the city of Brussels having "no authenticity" and always commissioning the same offices to build anonymous office buildings for the EU. [12]

[2] Foucault, Michel, Discipline and Punish. The Birth of the Prison. Tr. Alan Sheridan. New York: Pantheon, 1977, P. 30. [3] Kipnis, Jeffrey, "Recent Koolhaas." El Croquis # 79, 1996, pp. 26-37, here p. 27.
[4] Koolhaas, „Typical Plan", p. 335. [5] It is a compromise because even though the writer initially might have chosen a particular writing freely, he gradually becomes a prisoner of the words of others and his own words as automatic reflexes replace free choice and the writer becomes an imitator of his own style. History will defuse even the most self-conscious and determined attempts to find a neutral voice, a zero-degree writing, that would be "free of any servitude to a marked order of language. For Barthes, Albert Camus came closest to this kind of writing without rhetoric in his novel the Outsider. For Barthes, Albert Camus came closest to this kind of writing without rhetoric in his novel the Outsider. Barthes, Roland, Writing Degree Zero. 55. Even more important than the echoes to Roland Barthes are the two references to America. The deliberately quaint expression "New World" is of course an old European projection, bringing to mind Goethe's lines on the United States: „Amerika, du hast es besser als unser Kontinent, das alte, hast keine verfallene Schlösser und keine Basalte. dich stört nicht im Innern zu lebendiger Zeit unnützes Erinnern und vergeblicher Streit." Goethe, Johann Wolfgang von, "Der Vereinigten Staaten," Verweile Doch. III Gedichte mit Interpretationen. Hrsg. Marcel Rauch-Ranicki. Frankfurt/Main: 1997.
[6] Koolhaas, „Typical Plan", p. 336. [7] Ibid., p. 336. [8] Ibid., p. 337. [9] Ibid., p. 337. [10] Koolhaas, Rem, "Generic Cities",S,M,L,XL, p. 1253. [11] Ibid., pp. 1248, 1250. [12] Koolhaas, Rem, „€-conography," in Content, ed. by Rem Koolhaas and Brendan McGetrick, Cologne: Taschen, 2004, p. 381.

The Chicago School

Koolhaas' discussions of cities resonate with ideas introduced by the earliest urban sociologists, including Georg Simmel and the Chicago School. [13] In the twenties, Robert Park developed spatial theories of the city based on Chicago as a giant laboratory that represented "the norm in North American urbanization." [14] In 1929, referring to Von Ogden Vogt, Park distinguished between communities that are descript and those that are nondescript. Exemplified by Oberammergau, Bangkok and Oxford, descript communities are places of unity and charm where the common view is set forth in "laws, customs and the arts of life." In contrast, nondescript communities, such as the Lower North Side of Chicago in the twenties, lack on overriding sense of common purpose, mutual understanding or organized public opinion. Nine years later, Park further articulated the problem of nondescript cities, linking their emergence to globalization. In 1938, he talked about "a great ocean highway" that connects London, New York and San Francisco with Yokohama, Shanghai, Hongkong, Calcutta, Bombay, as well as the Mediterranean with great ocean liners. "A trip around the world in one of the seagoing hotels now in vogue is now as much of an adventure as a bus trip up Fifth Avenue in New York or taking a stroll on Michigan Avenue in Chicago." [15] Similar repetition of the generic metropolis must characterize also Koolhaas' experience as he flies from city to city around the world. Although Koolhaas finds it surprising that

"THE TRIUMPH OF THE GENERIC CITY HAS NOT COINCIDED WITH THE TRIUMPH OF SOCIOLOGY"

for "the Generic City is sociology," there is no evidence that Koolhaas would have been familiar with Park's work. [16] However, another precursor of the generic city would certainly have been familiar to Koolhaas: Reyner Banham who put forward the concept of a Non-Plan to describe Los Angeles. Together with Cedric Price, Peter Hall, and Paul Barker, Reyner Banham issued the manifesto "Non-Plan: An Experiment in Freedom" in New Society in 1969. All four were enthusiastic about Los Angeles, and applied Banham's lessons of Los Angeles to Britain, asking: "What would happen if there were no plan?" Reyner Banham attacked planning because it meant "the imposition of

certain physical arrangements, based on value judgements or prejudices … judgements about how they think of other people – not of their acquaintance or class – should live." [17] The manifesto further promised that spontaneity and vitality would inform "the living architecture of our age", as in Californian Non-Plan developments. Planning should be an expression of vital culture, but in Britain, as the authors commented, "we seem so afraid of freedom." [18] What Banham particularly appreciated in the urban structure of Los Angeles was the loose grid system, "with its infrastructure of roads and services" in which all the enclosed circles were "equal in importance and potential," and the lack of a grand design. Anticipating the repeated references to autopoiesis in Koolhaas's Mutations, Banham applauded Los Angeles planners for attempting "to create the conditions in which it could design itself, changing organically according to need" and claimed that the Angelene "freedom of movement" would result in a

"BROWNIAN MOTION OVER THE WHOLE AREA." [19]

In his book Los Angeles: The Architecture of Four Ecologies, Banham described the metropolis as uniform in structure and function: "all its parts are equal and equally accessible from all other parts at once." [20] Koolhaas' description of the generic city is similar. Liberated from the straitjacket of identity, the generic city is " city without history. It is big enough for everybody. … It is equally exciting – or unexciting – everywhere." [21] "The Generic City is fractal, an endless repetition of the same simple structural module; it is possible to reconstruct it from its smallest entity, a desktop computer, maybe even a diskette." [22] The idea of reconstructing the whole from a partis of course an old and popular one. Adolf Loos declared that if nothing were left of an extinct race but a single button, he would be able to infer, from the shape of that button, how these people lived, dressed, built their houses; what was their religion, their art, their mentality. [23] He got this idea via Eugène-Emmanuel Viollet-le-Duc from Georges Cuvier's promise to reconstruct an extinct animal from one bone, which in turn echoes Plutarch's claim that a competent sculptor should be able to reconstruct a lion from its claw, ex ungue leonem. [24] It is odd that Koolhaas should follow such an old conception of an organic whole, as the notions of generic cities and later junk space do not seem to imply such a cohesiveness.

12❬ Koolhaas, Rem, „€-conography," in Content, ed. by Rem Koolhaas and Brendan McGetrick, Cologne: Taschen, 2004, p. 381.

13❬ It is particularly instructive to compare Koolhaas' „Generic Cities" or „Junkspace" with Simmel's „Metropolis and Mental Life," required reading in almost every architecture school.

14❬ Ley, David, A Social Geography of the City. New York: Harper and Row, 1983, p.22.

15❬ Park, Robert, „Introduction," in Zorbaugh, H. M., The Gold Coast and the Slum. Chicago: Chicago University Press, 1929; Park, Robert, „Introduction," in Lind, A. W., An Island Community: Ecological Succession in Hawaii. Chicago: Chicago University Press, 1938. As quoted in Hannigan, John, Fantasy City. Pleasure and Profit in the Postmodern Metropolis. London: Routledge, 1998, p. 199.

16❬ Koolhaas, "Generic Cities", p. 1255.

17❬ Whiteley, Nigel, Reyner Banham. Historian of the Immediate Future. Cambridge, Mass.: MIT Press, 2002, p. 241.

18❬ Ibid., p. 242.

19❬ Inid., p. 243.

20❬ Ibid., p. 236

21❬ Koolhaas, "Generic Cities", p. 1250.

22❬ Ibid. p. 1251.

23❬ Loos, Adolf, "Antworten auf Fragen aus dem Publikum." Sämtliche Schriften. Ins Leere Gesprochen. Trotzdem. Wien: Verlag Herold, 1962, p, 372.

24❬ The phrase comes from a Latin translation of Plutarch's De defectu oraculorum, 3 or " The Obsolescence of Oracles," 3, in Plutarch's Moralia with an English translation by Frank Cole Babbitt. Vol. 5. London: William Heinemann Ltd./Cambridge, Mass.: Harvard University Press, 1957, 409-410. Plutarch attributes the notion to Alcaeus while Lucian writes: "At least, they say some sculptor (Phidias, I think) saw only the claw of a lion and from it estimated the size of the whole animal on the assumption that it was modelled on the same scale as the claw." Lucian, "Hermotimus or Concerning the Sects," The Works of Lucian with an English translation by K. Kilburn. Vol. VI. Cambridge, Mass.: Harvard University Press / London: William Heinemann Ltd., 1954, 360-363. Eugène-Emmanuel Viollet-le-Duc wrote: "Just as when seeing the leaf of a plant, one deduces from it the whole plant; from the bone of an animal, the whole animal; so from seeing a cross-section one deduces the architectural members; and from the members, the whole monument." Viollet-le-Duc, Emmanuel, Dictionnaire Raisonné de l'Architecture Francaise du XIe au XVIe Siècle.Paris, 1854-68, Vol. 8, 482. In Recherches sur les Ossemens Fossiles Georges Cuvier makes the following celebrated statement: "In short, the shape and structure of the teeth regulate the forms of the condyle, of the shoulder-blade and of the claws, in the same manner as the equation of a curve regulates all its other properties; and, as in regard to any particular curve, all its properties may be ascertained by assuming each separate property as the foundation of a particular equation; in the same manner, a claw, a shoulder-blade, a condyle, a leg or arm bone, or any other bone, separately considered, enables us to discover the description of teeth to which they have belonged, and so also reciprocally we may determine the forms of the other bones form the teeth. Thus, commencing our investigation by a careful survey of any one bone by itself, a person who is sufficiently master of the laws of organic structure, may, as it were, reconstruct the whole animal to which that bone had belonged." As quoted in Steadman, Philip, The Evolution of Designs. Cambridge: Cambridge University Press, 1979, p. 40.

Freedom and determinism

For both Banham and Koolhaas, neutrality equals flexibility that is further understood as freedom. This idea goes back at least to a legendary dispute between Mies van der Rohe and Hugo Häring who shared an office in the twenties.

HÄRING ATTEMPTED TO PERFECT THE THEORY OF FUNCTIONALISM BY PROPOSING THE CONCEPT OF LEISTUNGSFORM OR PERFORMANCE FORM, AS EXEMPLIFIED BY THE COWSHED AT THE GUT GARKAU.

The unusual oval shape of the shed is derived from an exact analysis of the spatial parameters of each function, and calculated to maximize the speed and efficiency of the cows' movements. Mies, however, rejected such attempts to optimize shape and told his colleague: "Hugo, just make your rooms big, then you can do everything in them." Although Mies is obviously right to a degree, it is clear that any room which is equally good for every function is not particularly good for any of them, nor it is exactly economical. Mies' Crown Hall in Chicago or the National Gallery in Berlin make the point clearly. Koolhaas recognizes the fact that the open plan is not optimal for any function, writing about the Centre Pompidou:"In 1972, Beaubourg – Platonic Loft – had proposed spaces where 'everything' was possible. The resulting flexibility was unmasked as the imposition of a theoretical average at the expense of both character and precision – entity at the price of identity." [25] However, he does not seem to think that this recognition challenges his notion of the typical plan as the regime of freedom since he, echoing modernist ideas of authenticity, insists that the Pompidou was a "demonstration" while the American skyscraper realized "genuine neutrality ... without effort." [26] Yet it could be argued that neither a free plan nor standardization liberate the user of a building even though it might empower, for example, the owner by maximizing rentability. [27] Insofar as a plan organization can produce events at all, one might expect that it is not the typical and the normal that liberates

but rather the anomalous and the monstrous, something that can be neither ignored nor categorized. But Koolhaas insists that the "Typical Plan is to the office population what graph paper is to a mathematical curve. ... Typical Plan is relentlessly enabling, ennobling background." [28] What does the typical plan enable so relentlessly?In his essay, Koolhaas complains about the European resistance to the typical office plan and says that "for offices, Europe multiplies a plan known since the Renaissance: a corridor with rooms on both sides. (Is there a connection between the notorious absenteeism of the Western European office population and its sacred cow, the private cell?)" [29] One might point out that the double-loaded corridor has existed since Egypt but the parenthetical remark is more interesting:

KOOLHAAS RECOGNIZES THAT THE PRIVATE CELL LETS THE INHABITANT MAKE HIS OR HER OWN DECISIONS, UNLIKE THE OPEN PLAN WHERE EVERYONE EXERCISES CONTROL OVER EVERYONE ELSE.

Briefly, Koolhaas takes issue with some criticism of the typical plan: "An environment that demanded nothing and gave everything was suddenly seen as an infernal machine for stripping identity." Despite his many declarations to the effect that the typical plan, bigness or the generic city can fundamentally affect the lives of people, he now wants to ridicule such environmental determinism. Referring to attempts to personalize the neutral office environment, he laments that most offices today are "ghastly repositories of individual trophies" and other personal debris, such as family photographs and ferns, and quips: "Nietzsche lost out to Sociology 101." [30]

25《 Koolhaas, „Bigness", S,M,L,XL, p. 505. **26**《 Ibid., p. 505. **27**《 Ibid., p. 511. **28**《 Koolhaas, „Typical Plan", p. 341. Its neutrality records performance, event, flow, change, accumulation, deduction, disappearance, mutation, fluctuation, failure, oscillation, deformation. **29**《 Koolhaas, „Typical Plan", p. 349 **30**《 Ibid., p. 346.

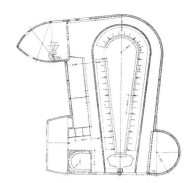

Still, neither the generic city nor the typical plan are Koolhaas' most extreme models of free architecture. If every architectural element is a limitation of freedom, then obviously full freedom is only achievable when there is nothing there, except for a void.

Discussing "Hilberseimer's 'Mid West' with its vast plains of zero-degree architecture", Koolhaas explains that "emptiness in the metropolis is not empty, … each void can be used for programs whose insertion into the existing texture is a procrustean effort leading to mutilation of both activity and texture. [31]

IN A SIMILAR VEIN, KOOLHAAS DESCRIBES BERLIN AS "A COLLECTION OF CENTERS, SOME OF WHICH ARE VOIDS" AND ROTTERDAM HAVING HAD ITS VOIDED CENTER "REPLACED BY AN ARTIFICIAL HEART THAT IS EMPTY AT THE CORE." [32]

He goes on to criticize Rotterdam planners from the seventies who wanted to intensify "the headquarters of emptiness," charging that "they were blind to the mysterious qualities of this alleged void, especially to its unlimited freedom. Blind to the fact that the toddlers who in the fifties played in the wading pools at the foot of the slabs … had grown up to form a mutant herd, perfectly equipped to fill and exploit this postmodern plane … where everything was possible and not a single social trope was suppressed by architecture. … Through the shift in urban ideology, they became a new kind of dispossessed: those chased from their modern habitat." [33] This implies that the absence of architecture does not mean the absence of functions that take place in the spaces. In a sense, there are actually no voids, since the absence of city planning or architecture invites or generates new functions. Later, Koolhaas promised to do "his best to avoid the Japanese word void." [34]

HE MAY NOT HAVE SPOKEN THE "JAPANESE" WORD 'VOID' BUT FOR THE MELUN-SÉNART PROJECT (1987) HE DREW A QUASI-CHINESE IDEOGRAM OF VOID SPACES,

surrendering the rest to "chaos".[35] This method Koolhaas characterized as "a deliberate surrender – tactical maneuver to reverse a defensive position." [36] Seven years later, he admitted that "in our more permissive moments, we have surrendered to the aesthetics of chaos – 'our' chaos. But in the technical sense chaos is what happens when nothing happens, not something that can

be engineered or embraced; it is something that infiltrates; it cannot be fabricated." [37] Logically, then, Koolhaas proclaims planning dead, explaining that the Generic City's "most dangerous and most exhilarating discovery is that planning makes no difference whatsoever." [38]

RELEASED FROM THE DEMIURGICAL ILLUSION, THE PLANNER BECOMES NIETZSCHE'S BLOND BEAST:

"Since we are not responsible, we have to become irresponsible. In a landscape of increasing expediency and impermanence, urbanism no longer is or has to be the most solemn of our decisions; urbanism can lighten up, become a Gay Science – Lite Urbanism." [39] This condition is for Koolhaas "a pretext for Nietzschean frivolity. We have to imagine 1,001 other concepts of city; we have to take insane risks; we have to dare to be utterly uncritical; we have to swallow deeply and bestow forgiveness left and right." [40] Koolhaas wasn't the first writer to advise architects to take risks. At the CIAM meeting at La Sarraz in 1928, Le Corbusier formulated his motto as follows: "lebet gefährlich, meine brüder! (zarathustra)." Originally, this advice indeed comes from Nietzsche, not from the Zarathustra but rather from The Gay Science where the author urges us to "live dangerously! Build your cities on the slopes of the Vesuvius!" [41]

DESPITE ALL OF HIS BELLIGERENT NIETZSCHEANISM, KOOLHAAS ARRIVES AT A SERENE LEIBNIZIAN POSITION:

"redefined, urbanism will not only, or mostly, be a profession, but a way of thinking, an ideology: to accept what exists." [42] This credo of Koolhaasian Realpolitik may not sound progressive in the traditional sense but the architect claims this position is the foundation of true freedom, explaining: "I think it's very important to say that we live without complaint, fear or trust under the following regime that you see here: the major currencies of the world, the Yen, the Euro and the Dollar. They describe a regime under which we are all active and willing [¥€$]. On the one hand, it is a regime that sets our parameters, and those parameters are fairly immutable. But on the other hand, it is also a regime that gives us an almost unbelievable amount of freedom to establish our own trajectories within it, and also to establish whatever connections within it, including connections between not only people but between different enterprises." [43]

Such a neoconservative understanding of freedom is based on a particular idea of the city and the community. Marketing himself as a global architect, Koolhaas is not interested in supporting community values or the

spatial structures that make society possible. For him, the only difference between architecture – say, a private house – and the city is that the latter is bigger and more complex. [44] This reductivist position is typical of European neomodernist architects. Massimiliano Fuksas, for example, justified his Twin Towers in Vienna with the following argument: "Transition, connection and transparency. For the city is energy and tension." In the polis of Koolhaas or Fuksas, there is no politics and, of course, no public space either: "The exterior of the city is no longer a collective theater where 'it' happens; there's no collective 'it' left. The street has become residue, organizational device, mere segment of the continuous metropolitan plane where the remnants of the past face the equipments of the new in an uneasy standoff." [45]

1

31 Koolhaas, „Imagining Nothingness," S,M,L,XL, p. 202.
32 Koolhaas, Rem, "The Terrifying Beauty of the Twentieth Century," S, M,L,XL, p. 206.
33 Ibid., p. 208.
34 Koolhaas, Rem, S,M,L,XL, p. xxxii.
35 Koolhaas, Rem, „Deliberate Surrender," S,M,L,XL, pp. 977, 981.
36 Ibid., p, 974.
37 Ibid., p, 969.
38 Koolhaas, "Generic Cities," p. 1255.
39 Koolhaas, Rem, "What Ever Happened to Urbanism", S,M,L,XL, p. 971.
40 Ibid., p. 971. In one of his letters, Nietzsche explains that „it is almost a formula for my philosophy that the deepest mind must also be the most frivolous." Sämtliche Briefe, vol. 8, 516f. As quoted by Safranski, Rüdiger, Nietzsche. A Philosophical Biography. London: Granta, 2003, p. 314.
41 For Le Corbusier, see G. E. Magnat's report as reprinted in Willett, John, The New Sobriety 1917-1933. Art and Politics in the Weimar Period. London: Thames and Hudson, 1978, p. 131; for Nietzsche, see Nietzsche, Friedrich, Die fröhliche Wissenschaft. Sämtliche Werke, Band V. Stuttgart: Alfred Kröner Verlag, 1965, §283, p. 186. English translation from The Gay Science. Tr. Walter Kauffmann. New York: Vintage, 1974, p. 228.
42 Koolhaas, "What Ever Happened to Urbanism," pp. 969-971.
43 Koolhaas, Rem, "Earning Trust." Lecture at a conference on Superhumanism in London in 2001. <http://www.dandad.org/content/super/pdf/koolhaas.pdf> p.1.
44 Thus, Koolhaas explains, for example, that "in the quantity and complexity of the facilities it offers, it [Bigness] is itself urban." Koolhaas, "Bigness," p. 514.
45 Ibid., p. 513.

The virtual and the actual

In 1996, with echoes of Neville Chamberlain, Kipnis praised Koolhaas for mounting "the most liberating, optimistic practice of our times." [46] Soon, however, Koolhaas' optimism about the typical plan and the generic city wore out. In his essay "Junk Space" of 2000, he preaches the omnipresence of junkspace and says that "its anarchy is one of the last tangible ways in which we experience freedom." [47] In trying to understand Koolhaas' pronouncements about freedom, we could distinguish between 'freedom from' (constraints or social and political ills) and 'freedom to' (actually do something, liberty), as Isaiah Berlin used to do. In Koolhaas' mind, the only function of the typical plan is "to let its occupants exist" for "Business makes no demands." [48] This plan will not offer much support for anything.

DEFINING THE PROPER FUNCTION OF A BUILDING AND DRAWING A PLAN TO SUPPORT IT MEANS TO EXERCISE A FORM OF CONTROL AND POWER.

However, the opposite of this kind of power is not freedom if power, as Foucault would see it, is not only restrictive but also constitutive. Koolhaas' position could only be meaningful if the desires of a person would be completely independent of any social context, a very problematic proposition.

So how can architecture then initiate change? How can an architect release positive freedom, the opportunity to do something? To take up this challenge, Koolhaas and many other architects usually part company with Foucault and rather side with Gilles Deleuze. The issue of freedom relates in part to his dual concepts of virtual/actual and possible/real. For Deleuze, following Henri Bergson and the Scholastics, the possible is exactly like the real except that it lacks real existence. Hence, even if a possibility would be realized, the process would not be creative: nothing new and no difference would emerge. The movement from the possible to the real is then characterized by preformation, resemblance and limitation: the realization of one possibility means that other possibilities will not be realized. In

contrast, the movement from the virtual to the actual is creative, for "while the real is the image and likeness of the possible that it realizes, the actual ... does not resemble the virtuality that it embodies. With no preformed order to dictate the form, the actualization of virtual being is a creative evolution, an original differentiation of organization." [49]

WHAT IS THEN VIRTUAL IN ARCHITECTURE?

Negative theology

For John Rajchman, "the virtual house is the one which, through its plan, space, construction and intelligence, generates the most new connections, the one so arranged or disposed as to permit the greatest power for unforeseen relations." [50] His characterization of the virtual is negative, like the descriptions of God by negative theologists or Spinoza: the virtual is that which takes place outside the "given identities of form, function and place," so that "the virtual looks like nothing we already know or can see." Hence a description of the virtual house, for example, is a priori impossible, and the only way left is "to try to formulate some questions implicated in the idea of the virtual house." [51]
Rajchman asserts that the multiplication of possibilities, although implying the negation of any fixed order, does not happen via abstraction, i.e. by providing a large, generic space, but on the contrary by a complex specification, by a maximum of singular points. "

THE VIRTUAL FUNCTIONS BY MULTIPLYING, BY THROWING TOGETHER SINGULAR POINTS AND SEEING WHAT THEY CAN DO.

Thus it inserts chance where there was only probability." [52]
In this essay, his example of this multiplication was Peter Eisenman's plan for Rebstock in Frankfurt.
The virtual is: "multiplying, complexifying, introducing the fresh air of other ... futures." [53] The desired fusion of indeterminacy and complexity admittedly poses a problem: "as the virtual is introduced into the life of a medium" – i.e. architecture or film or painting – "it becomes less determinate and more complex. Thus we reach a philosophical problem of complexity: we are complex in the precise sense that peculiar to each of us is a life that is at once indefinite and singular, composed of 'virtualities' of which the body and the mind are expressions."

THIS VERY PRECISE DEFINITION PROVOKES ANOTHER QUESTION ABOUT "HOW TO INTRODUCE SUCH VITAL COMPLEXITY INTO THE SPACES OF OUR HABITUS, OUR ETHOS, OUR MANNERS OF BEING AND BEING TOGETHER." [54]

[46] Kipnis, p. 36.
[47] Koolhaas, Rem, „Junkspace," Content, p. 165.
[48] Koolhaas, „Typical Plan", 337.
[49] Deleuze, Gilles, Bergsonism. Tr. Hugh Tomlinson and Barbara Habberjam. New York: Zone Books, 1994, p. 97; Cf. Bergson, Henri, Creative Evolution. Tr. Arthur Mitchell. New York: Henry Holt, 1911, See also Hardt, Michael, Gilles Deleuze. An Apprenticeship in Philosophy. Minneapolis: University of Minnesota Press, 1993, p. 18-19.
[50] Rajchman, John, "The Virtual House," in: Constructions. Cambridge MA, MIT Press, 1998, p. 115. See also „What's New in Architecture", in: Journal of Philosophy & the Visual Arts, 1990, pp. 32-37, in which Rajchman compares Foucault's concept of heterotopia with Deleuze's concept of the virtual.
[51] Rajchman, "The Virtual House," p. 115.
[52] Ibid., p. 120.
[53] Rajchman, „Artifice in an Ers@tz World", in: Any 19 (1997), The Virtual House, p. 19.5/4.
[54] Ibid., p. 19.4/3.

3

Technotricks

Rajchman's descriptions of virtual architecture are curiously imprecise, evasive and negative. Apparently, philosophers do not really like to issue positive norms. However, another follower of Deleuze, Brian Massumi has attempted to concretize the issue by taking 'onto-topological architecture' as an example.

IN 1993, MASSUMI RECORDED "THE FREQUENT COMPLAINT THAT THE ARCHITECTURE OPERATING IN THE TOPOLOGICAL FIELD IS FORMALLY INDISTINGUISHABLE FROM MODERNISM: THAT THERE IS NOTHING SO 'ORIGINAL' ABOUT IT, NOTHING TO IT BUT A LOT OF TECHNO-TRICKS IN THE DESIGN PROCESS THAT LEAVE NO VISIBLE TRACE IN THE BUILT FORM..."

First, Massumi stresses that there is a basic difference between high modernism, as exemplified by Le Corbusier, and the new, topological design approach. In the latter, "the impurities of the everyday – personal taste, dirty function, preference enforced in part by social convention, and most vulgar of all, cost – enter the process..." To be able to integrate such factors into the design, the architect needs, according to Massumi, intuition and a certain 'feel' for virtuality. The problem here is that Massumi's description of architectural design is virtually indistinguishable from how modernists always presented themselves. [55] Indeed, Massumi acknowledges that there is no way of effectively responding to the accusation that there is nothing in contemporary architecture that was not there in modernism"as long as there is no serious attention given to the afterlife of the design process in the life of the building." With the authority of Deleuze, he states that "the virtual itself cannot be seen or felt... [nor can it] not be seen or felt, as other than itself." In Massumi's interpretation, this means that "in addition to residue in static form, the formative process leaves traces still bearing the sign of its transitional nature ... [which] more fully implicate changeability and the potential for further emergence

than self-enclosed forms or ordered agglomerations of forms realising a rigid combinatory logic to produce ... formal compositions following the laws of perspective and resemblance designed to awaken habitual patterns of recognition and response." [56] In other words, the onto-topological architecture functions as a virtuality in the sense that it lets the radically new emerge.

Where does Massumi, then, expect to find the virtual in architecture? By his quotation of Deleuze, he is probably not suggesting that houses designed by topological architects would differ from those designed by traditionalists in a way that cannot be seen or felt. What he means instead is that there is a difference between the design processes applied by the new and the old architects, even though the design process as a whole cannot be viewed in the finished building but can only be reconstructed on the basis of some traces. This trivial point is, however, no answer to the charge that there is nothing new in the onto-topological architecture "but a lot of techno-tricks in the design process that leave no visible trace in the built form". On this issue, Massumi maintains that there is a difference in the design processes but then, contrary to the initial assumption, flatly states that the processes do leave visible traces of the formative process in the built form. In other words, he counters the critics who claim that the new architecture resembles the old not by presenting an argument but by simply saying that it actually looks different. Even though Massumi suggests that the critics misunderstand the new because they pay too little serious attention to the afterlife of the design process in the building, the afterlife is not the issue at all:

WERE THERE NO EMPIRICALLY OBSERVABLE DIFFERENCES BETWEEN THE TWO ARCHITECTURES, THERE WOULD BE NO DIFFERENCES IN THEIR AFTERLIVES EITHER.

It must be that the critics have not noticed the real and visible differences. According to Massumi, then, there is a material difference between buildings designed with different processes and this difference has important consequences. He suggests that when an architect draws

a house using a particular topological design strategy, with a built-in element of indeterminacy and chance, a moment of indeterminacy and chance is also opened up to the inhabitant: "

IT IS AN ECHO OF THE EXPERIMENTATIONS OF THE ARCHITECT.

But it does not resemble or in any way conform to them." [57]
If this notion of freedom is supposed to distinguish the new architecture from traditional, non-onto-topological architecture we would have to make the improbably assuption that in the latter, there are no details, points of view, or situations that the architect has not imagined and controlled with an iron hand, and thus the inhabitant has no chance of ever seeing or using anything differently from what the architect originally envisaged.

55 Letting the impurities of the everyday, including financial matters, enter the design process, was of course the core program of functionalism, but also the importance of intuition and the "feel" was always stressed. Three examples should suffice: Le Corbusier insisted that "architecture begins where calculation ends (L'architecture commence là où le calcul finit)"; as the touchstone of the architect he named the modenature or contour, remarking that modenature is "a pure creation of the mind" which excludes "the practical man, the bold man, the inventive man and calls for a plastic artist." Le Corbusier, L'art décoratif d'aujourd'hui. Paris: Les Éditions Arthaud, 1980, p. 86n2; Le Corbusier, Vers une architecture. Paris: Les Éditions Crés et Cie, 1924, p. 179. Hugo Häring also felt that "the work [of the architect] begins where the engineer, the technologist leaves off; it begins when the work is given life"; in other places he spoke of "the secret of the origin of form." Häring, Hugo, Schriften, Entwurfe, Bauten. Herausgegeben von Heinrich Lauterbach und Jürgen Joedicke. Stuttgart: Karl Krämer Verlag, 1965, p. 31. Uno Åhren recapitulated the idea in emphasizing that a prerequisite for successful design is "a secret understanding of the forms own logic." Cited in Råberg, Per G.,Funktionalistiskt genombrott. Stockholm: P A. Norstedt & Söner, 1972, p. 50.
56 Massumi, Brian, „Sensing the Virtual, Building the Insensible", in: Architectural Design, Vol. 5/6, No. 68: Hypersurface Architecture, p. 20.
57 Ibid., p. 22

The golden and the cool

Despite the necessary difficulties in characterizing what kinds of new things the new virtual architecture should produce, Massumi is not alone in repeating Deleuzean notions. More recently, Robert Somol and Sarah Whiting came to a similar idea of virtuality in their apology for shape, as opposed to form. They maintain that architecture that is obsessed with highly articulate form, such as Eisenman's designs, is hot, representational and narrative in promoting the index as the trace of the real, while the diagrammatic and non-specific shape of Koolhaas' projects is cool and projective in setting into motion the possibility of multiple engagements and providing room for maneuver and alternative realities, and significantly, the virtual. [58] For them, "the diagram is a tool of the virtual to the same degree that the index is the trace of the real." [59] As is typical of postmodern rhetorics, they also introduce a scientific metaphor and speak of the virtual in projective practice as "the Doppler effect."

The projective is said not to rely on "the oppositional strategy of critical dialectics" but the two authors are obsessively dialectical and oppositional. With a binary model similar to those used be art historians from Heinrich Wölfflin to Jacques Barzun to contrast the classic with the romantic, Somol and Whiting drive each other to a dizzying Pythagorean frenzy, piling one dichotomy upon another:

Critical practice	Projective practice
Peter Eisenman	Rem Koolhaas
difficult	easy
autonomy	instrumentality
representation	performativity
signification	pragmatics
index	diagram
dialectic	atmosphere
hot media	cool media
Robert De Niro	Robert Mitchum [60]

Thus, for example, Somol and Whiting compare the architecture of fom to Marshall McLuhan's hot media and that of shape to cool media. According to McLuhan, "a hot medium is one that extends a single sense in 'high definition'. … hot media does not leave so much to be filled in or completed by the audience.

HOT MEDIA ARE, THEREFORE, LOW IN PARTICIPATION…"

Conversely, a cool medium is one of low definition, it gives little information and demands high participation or completion by the audience. "Naturally, therefore, a hot medium like the radio has very different effects on the user from a cool medium like the telephone." [61] With its low-resolution images, television is a cool medium while film is a hot medium, and their effects are opposite. Thus, because it is shown on TV, the soap opera "One Life to Live" challenges your mind and initiates change, while "My Life to Live," if shown in a movie theater, has the opposite effect. [62] Exactly in the same way, shape electrifies you and activates the virtual while form drains your energy and only duplicates the possible. [63]

What can we expect projective practice to produce? If it is a virtuality, what emerges when it is actualized? Somol and Whiting close by saying that "within architecture, a project of delivering performance, or soliciting a surprising plausibility, suggests

MOVING AWAY FROM A CRITICAL ARCHITECTURAL PRACTICE – ONE WHICH IS REFLECTIVE, REPRESENTATIONAL, AND NARRATIVE – TO A PROJECTIVE PRACTICE.

Setting out this projective program does not necessarily entail a capitulation to market forces, but actually respects or reorganizes multiple economies, ecologies, information systems, and social groups." [64] Unfortunately, they fail to give any examples of such cases.

58 Somol, Robert and Whiting, Sarah, "Notes around the Doppler Effect and other Moods of Modernism." The Yale Architectural Journal Perspecta 33. Mining Autonomy. Cambridge, MA: MIT Press, 2003, pp. 72-78.
59 Ibid., p.
60 This is an incomplete list. The authors also suggest that critical practice is oriented against reification while projective practice is directed towards emergence, and the former is looking backwards and the latter forwards. See Roemer van Toorn, "No More Dreams?" Harvard Design Magazine, Fall/Winter 2004, p. 22.
61 McLuhan, Marshall, Understanding Media: The Extensions of Man. New York: McGraw Hill, 1966, pp. 22-23; for the effects, see also pp. 30-31, 311-312, 317, 319. The speculations of McLuhan have little basis in psychology. There seems to be no reason to suppose that the mind would habitually fill in the missing detail in a low-resolution image, such as a TV picture or a cartoon, as long as the image is recognizable. Rather, it would appear that the perceptual mechanism has to be more active in recognizing patterns in images full of information.
62 "My Life to Live" is the English title for Jean-Luc Godard's Vivre sa vie, 1962. McLuhan refutes the commonplace claim that TV presents an experience for passive viewers with the following argument: "TV is above all a medium that demands a creatively participant response. The guards who failed to protect Lee Oswald were not passive. They were so invooved by the mere sight of the TV cameras that they lost their sense of their merely practical and specialist task." McLuhan, p. 336.
63 Although the authors to do mention it, McLuhan's discussion anticipates some of the issues brought up by the post-decon generation. In his 1964 book McLuhan explains, for example, that "concern with effect than meaning" is characteristic of "our electric time." P. 26. He also talks about „field conditions" as a another characteristic our new electromagnetism.
64 Somol-Whiting, p. 77.
65 Surely, this oversight was not a conscious strategy of ambiguity and abstraction but rather something that could not be avoided. It is more important to point out that the theory Somol and Whiting propose does not really fit very well. Among others, George Baird has pointed out that neither Koolhaas nor Dave Hickey are as uncritical as Somol and Whiting suggest. See Baird, George, „Criticality and Its Discontents," Harvard Design Magazine. Fall/Winter 2004, pp. 20-21.

War and freedom

Rajchman, Massumi and Somol/Whiting have attempted to theoretically extend Deleuze's ideas about the virtual to architecture, and have ended up promoting very different kinds of architecture as the correct translation. Practising architects have also tried to design the virtual and create architecture that would promote new events and new freedoms.

One example is provided by Lebbeus Woods who promotes the concept of free-zones and freespaces by which he means "an architecture of indeterminacy" and "the matrix of unpredictable possibilities for culture, social and political transformation latent in human knowledge and invention." [66] These spaces are incomplete and therefore tolerant of self-contradiction, self-paradox, self-reference.

"HETEROS IS THE ESSENCE OF THE FREE-ZONE AND FREE-SPACE PROJECTS, HENCE ALSO OF DIALOGUE AND THE POLITICS THAT SPRING FROM IT.

… It is not possible to name any individual or group as the designated inhabitants of the freespace structures and the free-zone network, without compromising its open nature and structure. At the same time, if inhabitation of the structure and the network is left open to whoever can 'seize' them, by whatever means, then the freedom of this aggressive elite could become a tyranny for others. … It is inherent in the inhabitation of freespaces and free-zones, unbounded [sic] as they are by any logic imposed by existing conventions." [67] Woods believes that his architecture produces freedom because it is not limited by traditional typologies but unlike Koolhaas he sees this as a way of criticizing capitalism:

"FREESPACE … DOES NOT BELONG TO ANY EXISTING BUILDING TYPE, WHICH EXCLUDES IT FROM THE MARKETPLACE." [68]

Instead of using diagrams to escape typological fixation, Woods wants to achieve this by involving the user: "it is constructed by an individual or small working group who see it in its inception as an instrument of transformation of 'self' and of 'world', by the very fact of its presence as a new, alien, indeterminate condition."

Despite the different ways of producing the space of freedom in Koolhaas and in Woods, the results are said to be similar.

Woods explains that "Freespaces have no preconceived way of inhabitation. … architecture must initiate events, even very aggressively foment them. The architect is not, in this case, a detached professional, upholding timeless values, but an instigator, an agitator, an active participant." [69] Woods' brand of critical architecture culminates in his notorious conclusion that "war is architecture, and architecture is war;" consequently, he proposed adding steel structures that resemble parts of American bomber airplanes and helicopters to the partially destroyed buildings in Zagreb, bombed by American troops serving under the UN flag. [70]

Nuclear reactions

While he used to advocate the reduction of architecture to zero as the royal road to freedom, Koolhaas has also recommended its opposite, the maximal inclusion of everything, although these two approaches are hardly the same. This inclusive solution used to be known as Bigness. It can be simply defined by opposition:

"BIGNESS = URBANISM VS. ARCHITECTURE." [71]

Koolhaas argues carefully that "Bigness recognizes that architecture as we know it is in difficulty, but it does not overcompensate through regurgitations of even more architecture. It proposes a new economy in which no longer 'all is architecture' but in which a strategic position is regained through retreat and concentration, yielding the rest of a contested territory to enemy forces." [72] The retreat that he is talking about means giving up "the twin fantasies of order and omnipotence" and accepting what exists; the enemy is presumably "power" [73] – but what is the strategic position that is thereby gained? Caricaturing French prophets of doom, Koolhaas

9

66❬ Woods, Lebbeus, „Crucial Question". http://members.tripod.
com/~septimus7/ibea/gall10.html
67❬ Ibid. **68**❬ Ibid. **69**❬ Ibid.
70❬ Woods, Lebbeus, „Manifesto (1993)," in Jencks, Charles, Theories
and Manifestoes of Contemporary Architecture. London: Academy
Editions, 1997, p. 304.
71❬ Koolhaas, „Bigness," p. 515
72❬ Ibid., pp. 510-511.
73❬ Koolhaas, Rem, "Whatever Happened to Urbanism?" S, M, L, XL,
pp. 969-971: "A profession persists in its fantasies, its ideology, its
pretension, its illusions of involvement and control, and is therefore
incapable of conceiving new modesties, partial interventions,
strategic realignments, compromised positions that might influence,
redirect, succeed in limited terms, regroup, begin from scratch even,
but will never reestablish control." P. 965 "Through our hypocritical
relationship with power – contemptuous yet covetous ¬we dismantled
an entire discipline, cut ourselves off from the operational, and
condemned whole populations to the impossibility of encoding
civilizations on their territory – the subject of urbanism." P. 967.

summarizes: "according to Derrida we cannot be Whole, according to Baudrillard we cannot be Real, according to Virilio we cannot be There." [74] As against such postmodern pronouncements, Koolhaas promises that Bigness will reconstruct the Whole and resurrect the Real. [75]

MOREOVER, BIGNESS LIBERATES LIFE FROM ARCHITECTURAL DETERMINATION: "ITS VASTNESS EXHAUSTS ARCHITECTURE'S COMPULSIVE NEED TO DECIDE AND DETERMINE.

Zones will be left out, free from architecture." [76] In so doing, "Bigness transforms the city from a summation of certainties into an accumulation of mysteries." [77] In a rare passage, Koolhaas even identifies an architectural precursor to his thought, explaining that "Yona Friedman's urbanisme spatiale (1958) was emblematic: Bigness floats over Paris like a metallic blanket of clouds, promising unlimited but unfocused potential renewal of 'everything'." [78] This accumulation of everything is true freedom, and thus "Bigness depends on regimes of freedoms, the assembly of maximum difference." [79] This is the Hegelian Aufhebung, the completion and negation, of architecture: "

ONLY BIGNESS INSTIGATES THE REGIME OF COMPLEXITY THAT MOBILIZES THE FULL INTELLIGENCE OF ARCHITECTURE." [80]

Given all the things Bigness would produce, it is surprising that it also had its critics, but apparently "there are many 'needs' too unfocused, too weak, too unrespectable, too defiant, too secret, too subversive, too weak, too 'nothing' to be part of the constellations of Bigness." [81] In this sentence, Koolhaas lists "too weak" twice; apparently, there are many people out there who are not strong enough to survive the freedoms provided by Bigness, and who will sheepishly run to the arms of architecture. But Nietzsche is not going to let Sociology 101 take the field that easily. Anyhow, Bigness does not need to prove itself: "it is, finally, its own raison d' etre." [82]

Undaunted, Koolhaas insists that the "programmatic alchemy" of Bigness reinvents the collective, reclaims maximum possibility, engineers the unpredictable, creates freedom, provides serenity and excites perpetual intensity; enthusiastically, he even promises that big buildings will start a nuclear reaction in the social world: "Like plutonium rods that, more or less immersed, dampen or promote nuclear reaction, Bigness regulates the intensities of programmatic coexistence." [83]

THIS IS THE COMPLETION OF KOOLHAAS' MANHATTAN PROJECT, STARTED ALREADY IN THE SEVENTIES WITH DELIRIOUS NEW YORK WHERE THE SKYSCRAPER DIAGRAM IS SAID TO RELEASE UNEXPECTED EVENTS THROUGH ITS DISCONTINUOUS ASSEMBLAGE OF FUNCTIONS. [84]

74[Koolhaas, "Whatever Happened to Urbanism?" p. 967.
75[Koolhaas, „Bigness," 510, cf. 503, 508.
76[Ibid., p. 513. 77[Ibid., p. 501. 78[Ibid., p. 504. 79[Ibid., p. 511.
80[Ibid., p. 497. 81[Ibid., p. 516. 82[Ibid., pp. 495, 514, 515. 83[Ibid., 511-512. 84[Koolhaas, Rem, Delirious New York: A Retroactive Manifesto for Manhattan. New York: The Monacelli Press, 1997, pp., 85, 153-155, 197, et passim.

Silence, please

Talking about the Miami Music Complex project, Koolhaas also applied the nuclear reactor metaphor, reminding us that "in physics, the notion of critical mass indicates the point where by accumulating mass, it passes from one condition to another, more dynamic one." [85] Kipnis finds here a deeper, disguised motive:

"A CRITICAL MASS IS NOT JUST THE POINT WHERE RADIOACTIVE MATTER BECOMES MORE DYNAMIC, IT IS THE POINT WHERE ITS INTERNAL INTERACTIONS SOAR BEYOND CONTROL.

An apt metaphor, for Koolhaas would like to amplify the event-structure of the performance complex to the point where it, too, risks spiraling out of control." [86]
With 'event-structure' Kipnis referred "all of the social activities and chance events, desirable or not, that an architectural setting stages and conditions. These include, but are not limited to the expressed activities of the program. An event-structure is congruent with the program when no significant events in a setting are encouraged by the architecture other than those pre-written in the program, though, of course, absolute congruence can never be achieved. An architect may reasonably strive for a congruent event-structure in a prison or a hospital, but such an extreme congruence would be intolerable in a house." [87]

AS EXAMPLES OF THE EVENT-STRUCTURE FAR EXCEEDING THE PROGRAM KIPNIS MENTIONS EARLY SHOPPING MALLS AND A BUSY STREET.

One assumes that the World Trade Center towers, because of their height or symbolism, engendered the terrorist attacks and can thus be taken for another successful example of an event-structure exceeding the program, but of course almost any construction would exceed the program by enabling also those activities that were not written in the original design brief. Ultimately, this definition

of congruence hinges on what is understood by 'significant' events, but no precise definition is provided. Instead, Kipnis suggests that freedom can be engendered by architecture when the event-structure is not only incongruent with a building's program, but exceeds it to the point of interference. He explains: "In political terms, intensifying the event-structure amounts to unaligned activism, to a profligate operation that does not selectively enfranchise so much as it diminishes restriction. When achieved, it muffles a badgering program and distracts the visitor with frissons of danger and excitement as it magnifies the possibility of the unexpected. It should, in principle, stage a richer range of all events – including none." [88]

DOES KOOLHAAS' ARCHITECTURE ENGENDER POLITICAL ACTIVISM AND FREEDOM?

Admitting that his architecture offers little resistance to consumerism, Kipnis exculpates the architect by suggesting that he deliberately avoids "any a priori, universal definition of Freedom. For Koolhaas, architecture is able, but only able, to engender provisional freedoms in a definite situation, freedoms as the experiences, as the sensations, as the effects – pleasurable, threatening, and otherwise – of undermining select patterns of regulation and authority." [89] Kipnis describes how the architect cuts into the brief more like a sadist than a surgeon, hacking away the residues of "unwarranted authority, unnecessary governance and tired convention." This kind of "reductive disestablishment provides the crucial stratagem in each of Koolhaas' recent projects, the intellectual modus operandi by which the architect begins to transform the design into an instrument of freedom." [90]
Kipnis further analyzes one (perhaps the only one or the main) disestablishing mechanism that represents

"A PROFOUND THREAT TO THE DISCIPLINE OF ARCHITECTURE AS WE KNOW IT." [91]

He calls this mechanism of engendering freedom the "Infrastructural Tenet" and pits it against the "Garden Principle." According to the former, what really

matters in architecture is how the building performs in full use, while the latter principle asserts that architecture is at its best when a buidling is empty; what really matters are things like the "fineness of material and joinery, brilliance of structure and construction, elegance of shape and proportion, drama of light and shadow, intricacy of formal relationships, sensitivity to context, profundity of space." [92] Kipnis admits that programmatic concerns often enter into architectural discussions but claims that "prescripting activity … limits use and moves people quickly," reducing distraction. [93]

IN ACCORDANCE TO THE INFRASTRUCTURAL TENET, KOOLHAAS SAYS ABOUT THE JUSSIEU PROJECT THAT "THE ARCHITECTURE REPRESENTS A SERENE BACKGROUND AGAINST WHICH 'LIFE' UNFOLDS IN THE FOREGROUND."

85[As quoted by Kipnis, p. 31.
86[Kipnis, p. 31.
87[Ibid., p. 30. The author goes on to explain that „The event-structure of a sidewalk on a busy street far exceeds its program – sometimes dangerously. An unexpectedly high level of event-structure incongruity occurred in early shopping malls, particularly in the U. S. and Japan. Though the program of the mall was confined to circulation and shoppoing, the event-structure in these buildings so burgeoned that they became the public spaces of choice, particularly for adolescents and young adults." The street and the mall will then also be realms of freedom.
88[Kipnis, p. 31.
89[Ibid.,, p. 27. Kipnis also argues that while "Koolhaas' work never resists authority," it nonetheless "sabotages authority from within" (p. 27). Unfortunately, for some reason Kipnis fails to explain how the Congrexpo building or any other realized Koolhaas design sabotages authority.
90[Kipnis, p. 30, 91[Ibid., p. 37.. 92[Ibid., p. 36. 93[Ibid., p. 36.

94⟨ However, immediately before this sentence, he also maintains that "vis-à-vis the monumental scale of the architecture – the average distance between floor and ceiling is seven meters – the 2.5-meter crust of human occupancy is insignificant." 95⟨ This description seems to agree with the Garden Principle. Koolhaas may be disestablishing the Infrastructural Tenet as well. As an example of reductive disestablishment, Kipnis describes how

KOOLHAAS OFTEN VIOLATES THE PROGRAM BRIEF

of a competition. In the case of the Jussieu libraries, for example, the requirement was to provide space for two separate libraries (one for science, the other for humanities) but Koolhaas chose to make just one, as his concept of one continuous ramp was not flexible enough to accommodate two entities. 96⟨ The critic elaborates: "In Jussieu, the architect stacks the libraries in a unified structure formed by using a ramping system typical of parking structures to connect the isolated floor plates of Domino into a single-surface concourse. ... The disestablishing design of Jussieu severs the Library from a history in which the institution has sedimented into an unyielding building type. ... Liberty is staged at Jussieu as a permissiveness attained by lifting the burdens of convention – institutional, historic, even moral." 97⟨ As for the moral freedom engendered by the project, Kipnis explains that the warping ramp allows "visitors to gaze surreptitiously at others above and below. The effect shatters the ideal horizon line of Domino and folds the fragments back into the space as a [sic] eroticized web of partial-horizons." 98⟨ This is entirely appropriate, as Kipnis claims that

FREEDOM FOR KOOLHAAS IS A MATTER OF EROTICS:

"Though Koolhaas' architectural notion of freedom never strays far from the realm of politics, its emphasis on experience and its preference for demonstrable instrumental effect over abstract ideality situates it as much in the realm of erotics. ... In his project for the University Libraries at Jussieu, the architect revisits

Corbusian themes to generate a social setting organized less by the program than by the erotic fantasies of the voyeur." 99⟨ To illustrate the freedom engendered by the Jussieu design, Kipnis explains that "a 'Quiet, Please' sign would seem merely comic as one searched in vain for a proper place to hang it." 100⟨
The sign would no doubt be comical in its superfluity for the library has been conceived as a panoptical space where each visitor is always already controlled by other visitors and the staff at each and every point along the ramp, making sure that the events could never spiral out of control.

BUT THEN AGAIN, MAYBE WE SHOULD ACCEPT KIPNIS' READING OF THE PANOPTICON AS NOT THE DIABOLICAL MACHINE OF UBIQUITOUS SURVEILLANCE THAT FOUCAULT OBSESSES ABOUT, BUT RATHER AN INSTRUMENT OF POLITICAL AND MORAL FREEDOM.

1

94⟨ Koolhaas, Rem, „Unraveling," S,M,L,XL, p. 1328.
95⟨ Ibid., pp. 1327-1328.
96⟨ One wonders what would have happened to the concept (to the continuous open space in particular) if the project had ever been develop to meet the fire code.
97⟨ Kipnis, p. 30.
98⟨ Ibid., 30.
99⟨ Ibid., p. 29. Staying with erotic metaphors, Kipnis goes on to describe how "at Jussieu, Koolhaas invaginates Domino, mobilizing it from a static diagram of infinite, equalizing solitude to a finite, fluid field of interactions, benign and otherwise." Ibid.
100⟨ Kipnis, p. 30.

An inventory of effects

Given the ambiguities in Kipnis' exegesis, let us simply accept what Koolhaas says about architecture releasing the virtual and engendering freedom, new functions and events. But remembering that the virtual cannot be predetermined, we can only recognize in retrospect that which has emerged out of Koolhaasian diagrams: the mushroom cloud, the Doppler effect, the erotic pleasures of a science library. Talking about bigness, one example might be the Congrexpo in Lille. The building is a large oval-shaped shed, containing an exposition hall, a congress center and a concert hall. Still having no tall buildings to his credit, Koolhaas likes to describe the Congrexpo as a horizontal skyscraper. Typologically and urbanistically, however, the building could be put in the same category where Koolhaas places the Guggenheim in Bilbao and the Getty Center in Los Angeles: all of them are shopping malls without the shops.[101] Whatever the Congrexpo really is, it is definitely not a nuclear reactor of events. Perhaps it is too small.

Then let's take a look at the largest shopping mall in the world (until Dubai opens its Mall of Arabia in 2006), the West Edmonton Mall. With 22 million visits per year, it is the number one tourist attraction for the province of Alberta. More than 23,500 employees work in over 800 stores and services, including 110 eating establishments.

There are six anchor stores, an amusement park, a dolphin lagoon, a waterpark, adventure golf, an ice palace, movie theaters, bingo as well as a fantasy hotel. The mall also boasts the world's largest parking lot with more than 20,000 parking spaces. This is all very exciting, but the mall can hardly be described as a virtuality that engineers the unpredictable, as Koolhaas says in his nuclear reactor metaphor. In fact, it is a curious metaphor in that mere bigness or dense packing of heterogeneous stuff is usually not enough to start a nuclear reaction. One would need radioactive material, such as uranium or plutonium, which can start fission naturally, although in a nuclear reactor fission is induced artificially by making some atoms absorb a slow-moving free neutron which releases energy and leads to a self-sustaining chain reaction.

LOOKING FOR SOME KIND OF A CHAIN REACTION IN THE SOCIAL WORLD, WE MAY ASK WHAT KIND OF CONDITIONS WOULD BE REQUIRED TO RELEASE NEW EVENTS.

A situation similar to what Koolhaas is describing has happened often, but not really at the level of buildings, even big buildings, but at the level of cities. I am thinking of the birth of the Medieval towns in Europe.
Starting at about the eleventh century, cities started to grow into centers of trade, of refined craft production, manufacture; cities also became centers of administration and education. This eruption of new functions was the result of changes in the relative power positions of the church, the kings and the nobility, and it was supported by legal structures. A German medieval saying goes: "Stadtluft macht frei" – city air makes you free. It refers to the special law applying to German cities. Every inhabitant of the city was a free man, as opposed to serfs living on the countryside. A serf who succeeded in running away from his farm and living in a city without his owner claiming him for one year and one day was given full freedom. If noblemen moved into the city, they equally lost their status as noblemen. Robert Park comments: " Law, of itself, could not, however, have made the craftsman free. An open market in which he might sell the products of his labor was a necessary incident of his freedom, and it was the application of the money economy to the relations of master and man that completed the emancipation of the serf." [102] The urban revolution released a programmatic alchemy that not only made the economy bloom, but also encouraged inventions and technological advances, founded universities, relaxed religious restrictions and enabled nonconformist, innovative as well as deviant activities. [103] Growing denser and more diversified, the industrial city came to resemble, in Louis Wirth's famous words, "a mosaic of social worlds in which the transition from one to the other is abrupt." [104] According to Koolhaas, a similar condition is characteristic of skyscrapers and in other cases of Bigness, but in a radically smaller scale. Le Corbusier, who developed his own Theory of Bigness six decades before Koolhaas, famously declared that the American skyscrapers were not

big enough. [105]

The same could be said of Koolhaasian Bigness. To have any of the effects that Koolhaas promises,

ONE NEEDS A UNIT WITH THE SIZE AND COMPLEXITY OF A CITY – AS WELL AS A HOST OF OTHER FACTORS – OTHERWISE WE WILL NOT WITNESS THE PROGRAMMATIC ALCHEMY OF A NUCLEAR REACTOR.

The architect's judgment about modernism applies equally well to Bigness: "modernism's alchemic promise – to transform quantity into quality through abstraction and repetition – has been a failure, a hoax: magic that didn't work." [106]

101 Koolhaas, Rem, "Junkspace," Domus #833, January 2001, p. 39: "The Bilbao Guggenheim, even the Getty, for all its ostensible primness: what are they, if not, in the final analysis, malls?"
102 Park, Robert, "The City." In Sennett, Richard (ed.), Classic Essays on the Culture of Cities. Englewood Cliffs, N.J.: Prentice-Hall, 1969, p. 101.
103 Richard Sennett points out the difference in the concepts of freedom proposed by Park and his teacher Simmel. „The freedom Park envisioned was behavioral, and involved the capacity of men to express themselves through acts unlike, and unrestrained by, the community as a whole. The liberty Simmel envisioned does not suppose this condition of social deviance; it was instead a transcendental, inner activity of searching out a sense of selfhood beyond petty routine, routine Simmel took to be an ineradicable condition of metropolitan life. Where Park's free urban man is an innovator, a deviant, Simmel's free urban man is more like a monk." Sennett, Richard, „An Introduction," in Sennett, op. cit., p. 16.
104 Wirth, Louis, „Urbanism as a Way of Life." In Sennett, op. cit., p. 155.
105 Le Corbusier, „Bolshoi... or the Notion of Bigness," The Radiant City. New York: The Orion Press, 1964, pp. 182-184. The original book, La Ville Radieuse, was published in 1934.
106 Koolhaas, "Whatever Happened to Urbanism?" p. 961. On p. 27 of his article, Kipnis also talks about "the failure of Modern Architecture to fulfil its promise as a tool able to implement democratic political form or egalitarian social theory" which to him would seem to cast doubts over similar ambitions on the part of Koolhaas, "as would the reflection by some 20th century thinkers such as Bataille on a fundamental conflict between architecture and liberty." However, he does not reflect longer on the topic.

Utopias

Another link that could be forged between Koolhaas and medievalism is the concern with shopping. Commerce as the origin of the city in the Middle Ages, and according to Koolhaas, shopping is the city's end: he declares that

SHOPPING IS "THE LAST REMAINING FORM OF PUBLIC ACTIVITY." [107]

According to Markus Schäfer, one of the writers of Koolhaas' Harvard Design School Guide to Shopping and OMA/AMO architect, a revolution is taking place in commercial architecture. Instead of Bigness or such juggernaut malls as the West Edmonton Mall, small convenience stores are on the rise, apparently delivering the same revenues per floor area as large department stores. Schäfer continues: "While the department stores were the retail microcosms of the emerging consuming middle class that showcased everything the world had to offer in one large building, the convenience stores specialize in providing daily necessities in close proximity to the consumer. ... While the department stores rely on architecture to contain goods and people, the convenience stores achieve a coherent organization by means of the data networks for logistics and business intelligence that connects them. Brand and data replace typology. The convenience stores are like the brightly glowing ends of a network infrastructure of fiber optic cables permeating the city, a Metabolist's wet dream, yet invisible to his conscious professional eye." [108] Emulating the veritable city of metaphors that Koolhaas erects in every one of his texts, Schäfter goes on to predict that "the ethereality of content, the metabolism of digital data and interactions and the relative solidity of architecture at best combine like the laminar flows around the wings of an airplane resulting in maximum lift." [109]
Koolhaas himself might well join Schäfer in eulogizing the convenience store as the next revolution. One of the favorite strategies of the avant-garde in the twentieth century was the revaluation of things, in particular the glorification of something that was generally seen to have no value. Thus, modern architects tried to convince

their rich clients to build houses that were modeled after factories or North African casbahs, as for example Haus Scheu by Adolf Loos. Applying the same strategy, Koolhaas likes to stress the value of things that for others are worthless banalities, such as the typical plan or the generic city. If he is right, it is precisely because of their banal invisibility that they harbor transformative potential, a promise of Utopia, even. In recent times, Koolhaas has occasionally spoken of utopias, as for example when he declared that at the LACMA (Los Angeles County Museum of Art) is almost a Utopian condition. [110] We cannot determine what Koolhaas' utopia is – the Medieval city, the corner drugstore or something completely different – but its ethical necessity can no longer be called in doubt. [111] As the architect explains: "Utopia ... is the dirty secret of all architecture, even the most debased: deep down all architecture, no matter how naïve and implausible, claims to make the world a better place.

... WITHOUT REFERENCE TO UTOPIA, HIS [AN ARCHITECT'S] WORK CANNOT HAVE REAL VALUE..." [112]

All images archive Kari Jormakka

107 Chuihua Judy Chung, Jeffrey Inaba, Rem Koolhaas, Sze Tsung Leong, eds., Harvard Design School Guide to Shopping. Cologne: Taschen, 2001, quote on inside of front cover.
108 Schäfer, Markus, "From Form to Performance." A+U, #406, p. 119. Thinking of such examples of Metabolism as Kenzo Tange's old Tokyo Bay project, it seems, pace Schäfer, a tad unconvincing to call the convenience store the wet dream of a Metabolist. To get excited by a convenience store one may have to be Dutch, at least if we accept what Max Weber argued about the connections between protestant ethics, the spirit of capitalism, and the Netherlands.
109 Schäfer, p. 119.
110 Koolhaas, „LACMA," Content, p. 126.
111 See also Gropius, Walter, The New Architecture and the Bauhaus. Translated by Morton Shand. With an Introduction by Frank Pick. Great Britain: Charles T. Branford Co. 1935, p. 112.
112 Koolhaas, Rem, „Utopia Station," Content, p. 393.

THOMAS DUSCHLBAUER ‹
MICHAEL SHAMIYEH ‹ After Architecture: Comfort or Challenge?

A study recently released by the American Institute of Architects indicates that only about 30% of all students enrolled in accredited architecture programs end up becoming architects although approximately 60% ultimately complete their studies (compared to 98% of those attending med school and 95% of those studying law).[1] Moreover, according to a survey conducted in July 2003 by the Harvard University Graduate School of Design, only 44% of its graduates were even working in the field of architecture per se, whereas 39% were employed in architecture- or design-related fields and 17% were pursuing careers totally unrelated to architecture. [2] A poll taken in March 2003 at the Swiss Federal Institute of Technology in Zurich yielded similar results: approximately 50% of all currently employed graduates were working in an unrelated field! [3]

THUS, IT ALREADY SEEMS TO BE HIGHLY PROBLEMATIC TO EVEN SPEAK OF AN ARCHITECTURAL PROFESSION IN CONNECTION WITH UNIVERSITY-TRAINED ARCHITECTS.

[1] See The American Institute of Architects (Ed.), 2002, AIA Compensation Report, A Survey of U.S Architecture Firms (Washington, DC, 2002).
[2] Information based on the Harvard Alumni/ae Databank as of July 29, 2003; obtained from Career Services of the Harvard University Graduate School of Design.
[3] Study conducted by Paul Meyer, Professor of Architecture and Building Realization, spring 2002 test session, January 20, 2002; also, survey of departing graduates, March 11, 2003.

It is paradoxical to be forced to conclude that just as the architect's status is in the process of crumbling and his knowledge is being relativized by various and sundry "institutions of higher learning," [4] our modern language has upgraded the term "architecture" to the rank of metaphor signifying fundamental structures – for instance, in neologisms like processor architecture and European security architecture.

WHILE WE CARRY ON IN OUR HERMIT-LIKE EXISTENCE PREOCCUPIED WITH THE DESIGN AND MANIPULATION OF FORMS, THE REST OF THE WORLD SPEAKS OF ARCHITECTURE AS IF IT WERE THE MEDIUM THROUGH WHICH THE ESSENCE OF ORGANIZATION AND STRUCTURE IS REVEALED.

Here, it would be appropriate to recall Hans Hollein's programmatic statement that "Everything is architecture" – 30 years ago, he was already expressing doubt about the validity of limited conceptual specifications and traditional definitions of architecture as well as the means at the discipline's disposal, and was calling for our efforts to be focused on the "environment as a whole [...] and all the media that determine it." [5] In this connection, we also see revealed before us the whole dilemma that we have brought upon ourselves and whose origins are attributable solely to architects' schizophrenia. Accordingly, the follow remarks will take a closer look at the behavior of architects and provide a sort of productive diagnosis.

Forgetfullness of things past

Norbert Bolz's pithy remark that "Nothing is older than something whose time has just passed" is characteristic of not only the general media-hype-induced cluelessness about recent history but also the way in which architecture comes up with the themes it chooses to focus on nowadays. To propagate this forgetfulness of things past, media outlets' economic considerations dictate that the term Phenomena that actually would be better described as short-lived fads are, accordingly, more and more often referred to as trends. It is evidently no longer sufficient to be stylish today; one has to follow a trend. Not only does stylishness thereby become a trend – which should actually be an expression summarizing a longer-term social development – but also the trend itself becomes style. For many years now, the media, as a result of having declared the changes undergone by change to be their guiding principles, have been telling us about a time of sudden upheaval and, in doing so, have spared only themselves from coming across as being old hats. This is the only possible explanation for the fact that to this very day, the Internet and even TV are still being referred to as "new" media. Naturally, even if the messages that they disseminate have essentially remained unchanged, at least the media themselves have to be "new," since, after all, it certainly does make a difference to some people if they no longer have to read their horoscope, sports report or other superfluous information in the newspaper but can instead access the latest updates online or even receive them directly via SMS. The media are dependent on propagating what's "new" and thereby furthering the past's slide into oblivion.

From this perspective,

PHENOMENA LIKE SHOPPING, BRANDING AND ENTERTAINMENT AREN'T REALLY NEW EITHER. NOR ARE THEY NEW IN CONNECTION WITH ARCHITECTURE,

in spite of the media repeatedly suggesting otherwise (although this might well be yet another attempt to dredge up grounds for a crisis). Rem Koolhaas, for example, holds the opinion that it was still possible in the '60s and '70s to maintain a critical distance to the phenomenon of shopping; today, this distance is becoming increasingly difficult if not impossible since shopping is simply overwhelming us. [6] It is a widely forgotten fact, though one recognized even by Victor Gruen, a man much discussed in the Harvard Guide to Shopping, that a commercially-based architecture has been brought forth by every advanced civilization, which is, after all, by definition something that defines itself through, among other factors, trade and the process of exchange with other cultures. [7]

A STROLL THROUGH THE EXCAVATIONS OF POMPEII OR THE SHOPPING MALL FROM THE MIDDLE AGES DISCOVERED IN LONDON MAKES THIS PATENTLY CLEAR.

Leafing through the history books also reminds us that city life in the late 19th century in the USA as well as in Europe was completely pervaded by commerce, which was not only present on a massive scale in the cityscape itself (due to the glut of billboards and signage) but also in the graphic arts. [8] The phenomenon of entertainment is likewise nothing new, since specific realms to which visitors came to be fascinated by novel experiences existed in the past as well. For instance, the 1873 World's Fair in Vienna featured a miniature mock-up of Venice, an idea that was recently resurrected to great acclaim in Las Vegas. [9] But as we are reminded by, among others, Rem Koolhaas in his book "Delirious New York," such spectacles in the late 19th century were not restricted solely to dedicated, discrete

domains; even back then, they spread throughout the metropolis on the synthetic platforms of specifically themed skyscrapers. [10] And we tend to forget that it is precisely society's urge to consume and to be entertained that led to the culture of congestion. The essence of what is today a highly praised architectural strategy is the simultaneity and spatial overlaying of a broad spectrum of programs, functions, concepts and ideologies, and the use of state-of-the-art technologies to stage artificial worlds.

THE OMNIPRESENT ANGST AND FEELING OF BEING THREATENED BY THE MODERN MEDIATIZATION OF OLD THEMES LIKE SHOPPING AND FUN IS THEREFORE NOT REALLY UNDERSTANDABLE.

Nor is it made any more comprehensible when we consider that the main driving forces behind the development of cities are commercial forces, and architects have never constructed more than 5% – and usually even less than 1% – of a nation's building volume. [11]

5

4 Michael Shamiyeh, Thomas Duschlbauer, "Pop," in: Architektur & Bauforum, no. 219 (Vienna, 2002), pp. 74-77.
5 Hans Hollein, "Alles ist Architektur," in: BAU, no. 1/2 (Vienna, 1968), p. 2.
6 Rem Koolhaas, unpublished text of a speech delivered at the "Learning From the Mall of America" conference held on November 22, 1997 at the University of Minnesota at Minneapolis, p. 16.
7 Victor Gruen, Larry Smith, Shopping Towns USA, The Planning of Shopping Centers (New York: Reinhold Publishing Corporation, 1960), prologue, pp. 17-24.
8 See, among others, Rachel Bowly, Carried Away, The Invention of Modern Shopping (New York: Columbia University Press, 2001).
9 See Norbert Rubey, Peter Schoenwald, Venedig in Wien, Theater- und Vergnügungsstadt der Jahrhundertwende (Vienna: Ueberreuter, 1996).
10 See Rem Koolhaas, Delirious New York (New York: 1978).
11 Charles Jenks, "What is Critic Modernism?", in: UmBau, no. 18 (Vienna, 2001), p. 82.

New York, 1909

Venice in Vienna, 1873

Artist/Scientist

A schizoid nature has always been characteristic of the architect. This allows him the option, depending on the situation and the client, of assuming the stance of an artist or a scientist (even though he never has complete artistic freedom and isn't really a scientist).

VIEWING HIMSELF AS A SORT OF RENAISSANCE MAN POSSESSING UNIVERSAL KNOWLEDGE, HE GADS ABOUT THROUGH THE PROFESSIONS LIKE A TOURIST WHO IS CONSTANTLY BEING CONFRONTED BY THE EMBARRASSING FACT OF HIS UNFAMILIARITY WITH THE TERRITORY,

and ultimately – in stark contrast to the artist – being damned to bring the banalities of everyday life into a structural form. This is obviously a lapidary attempt to adroitly elevate architecture to a special status within society, an effort that has been going on since the early 20th century and, as we can see from our present vantage point, has yet to succeed. The strategy that Modernist architects have derived from this – to develop an efficient building production process in order to proceed hand-in-hand with the governing of the population on a grand scale and to make available optimal, hygienic living conditions – was, indeed, very successful at first but subsequently did a turnabout to its very opposite. The institutions that mediated between the populace and the architects successively took over some of the profession's major areas of responsibility. From then on, there were few remaining domains – except for the artistic sphere – in which architects could make a significant contribution. [12]

TO THIS DAY, THE ARCHITECTS HAVE STILL NOT SUCCEEDED IN REACQUIRING THEIR ANTICIPATED RECOGNITION AS AUTHORITIES IN THE FIELD OF SCIENCE.

Only a handful of highly specialized major architectural firms with in-house experts are in a position to offer full-service solutions. Smaller practices – 76% of firms in the USA have nine or fewer staff members, 53% have four or fewer, and only 7% of all staffers of American architectural firms are engineers – are increasingly forced to commission outside firms to perform non-design-related tasks such as producing construction and installation plans, writing calls for the submission of job bids and cost estimates, and construction supervision and control. [13] All that was left for architects (in their schizoid manner) to do was to attempt

to reassert their former artistic monopoly and – with the support of those public institutions, no less – to incessantly issue calls for "architectural quality." But, by the end of the 20th century as an upshot of the euphoria over the recently achieved freedoms operational in our pluralistic society, even this claim morphed into an effort to assert unrestricted arbitrariness. Architecture, a profession now proud of its ability to manipulate images and forms in an accepted canon – the weakest justification for credit, confidence and esteem in the eyes of society – is thus relegated to the role of tolerated bystander on the margins of a market dominated by official and institutional bodies.

Specific/Generic

Since the mid-'90s, a touchy subject that had long constituted a latent dilemma on architecture's back burner has once again taken the spotlight of attention: the question of the specific versus the general and featureless. The history of this issue perhaps goes even further back than the 18th century, but, in any case, that was when it was the subject of a discussion that was momentous for architecture's future and that we would now do well to briefly recall.

FOR RENAISSANCE ARCHITECTS, THE SEARCH FOR ARCHITECTURE'S ORIGINS HAD A SIGNIFICANCE THAT WAS EQUIVALENT TO THAT OF NEWTON'S DISCOVERIES IN PHYSICS, LOCKE'S IN EPISTEMOLOGY AND ROUSSEAU'S IN PHILOSOPHY.

In contrast, perhaps, to the other disciplines, the investigations of the architect-philosophers yielded no clear results. On one hand, there stood the Vitruvian-Laugierian model of the primeval hut that was assumed to have originated on the basis of natural laws; on the other hand, there was what both Jesuits and Freemasons accepted as the origins of all architecture and assumed to be the God-given model of Solomon's Temple in which a special symbolic significance was attributed to each measurement and every element. [14] Thus, the generic model of the House of Adam was juxtaposed to the specific model of the House of God, a constellation that split 18th-century architecture into two camps, and this, in turn, is possibly one of the reasons for the development of the schizoid traits that the profession continues to exhibit today.
Rem Koolhaas recently diagnosed the merits of the city without qualities and thereby triggered a heated discussion of the dichotomy between the specific and that which lacks definitive characteristics. In his essay "The Generic City," Koolhaas expresses his profound distrust of the

conventions of the specific – what has been generally accepted up to the present as "good" architecture – and, in doing so, elaborated on a position that had existed in latent form in some of his previous theoretical works (e.g. "Delirious New York" and "Typical Plan"). His call was heeded by a whole generation of architects, who from then on pointedly demanded that buildings have generic features, sought to reform the design process from this perspective, and likewise developed a predilection for investigating the contemporary city with its characterless traits.

WHAT THE INDIVIDUALS OVERCOME BY THIS EUPHORIA TOTALLY FAILED TO NOTICE WAS HOW RADICALLY BIFURCATED – OR, ACTUALLY, SCHIZOID – THE ARCHITECTURAL CROWD'S BEHAVIOR WAS.

While the "Project on (what used to be) the City" that Rem Koolhaas had initiated at Harvard was still attracting enthusiastic imitators at numerous American and European institutions determined to carry on research on a global basis into architecture that lacked specific qualities, everyone else was celebrating and glorifying the specific designs of architecture's superstars – Rem Koolhaas among them. He, for example, reacted in the context of Stimmann's Berlin – a city seeking to reconstitute itself with an exclusively generic set of regulations – with a specific intervention for the Dutch Embassy. The generic excrescences of shopping were studied in preparation for delivering obviously specific designs for Prada. In an interview with Ole Bouman, Rem Koolhaas said: "My work itself is ambiguous. But this schizophrenia doesn't bother me a lot so long as I can live intensely." [15] What manifests itself here is a schizoid mode of behavior that holds true not only for a few stars of the profession; rather, this is generally valid for architects who, driven by an economy of attention, try to produce masterpieces only.

12 In the late '60s in Great Britain, half of all architects were employed in the public sector, and the half working in the private sector lived from jobs commissioned by the public sector; see Martin Pawley, Terminal Architecture (London: Reaction Books, 1998), p. 124.
13 See The American Institute of Architects (Ed.), AIA Firm Survey 2000-2002 (Washington/DC, 2002)
14 See, among others, Anthony Vidler, "The Idea of Type: The Transformation of the Academic Ideal, 1750-1830" in: Oppositions Reader, with a foreword by K. Michael Hays (Ed.), (Princeton: Princeton Architectural Press, 1998), pp. 438-457.
15 Ole Bouman, "Stay on alert! An interview with Rem Koolhaas" in: Archis, no. 12 (Utrecht, 1998), p. 64.

Temple of Salomon, 1740

Abbé Marc-Antoine Laugier, Primitive Hut, 1753

Stability/Instability

Rem Koolhaas' fascination with the city without qualities can be traced back to the fact that it possesses no identity liable to be abused, compromised or toned down. This means that the great quality of the "Generic City" inheres in its genuine potential to skillfully undermine the omnipresent mechanisms of the market economy that would buy and sell anything and everything. Therefore, it is for him – similarly to what Delirious New York had previously been – the very epitome of freedom and form of resistance, since it is, of course, also resistant to all other blanket impositions of ideologies or value systems, a quality that could be potentially significant for the future development of societies. Meanwhile, in the wake of Rem Koolhaas having left Western societies behind him to devote his attention to the countries and cities just entering the stage of economic take-off, the new generation of architects was rashly accepting the market economy as the final phase of human history, having apparently forgotten that the last half century had already put forth a whole series of notable ideological variations (including fascism, communism, Islamic theocracy and Western democracy).

HERE, THE SCHIZOID ATTITUDE OF OUR PROFESSION MANIFESTS ITSELF ONCE AGAIN.

On one hand, it uncritically accepts the market economy while, on the other hand, ignoring its manic lifecycles that are transforming our environment in ever-shorter intervals and ruining all of our initiatives for betterment. Thus, we see ourselves constantly confronted with the problem that the stability of our architecture is diametrically opposed to the instability of the events dictated by economic interests that are going on all around us.

Fashionable/Timeless

Like no event before it, 9/11 made is crystal clear how the media is capable not only of focusing tremendous attention on architecture but also of ascribing to it a particular meaning, a symbolic character. This terrorist attack didn't target just any skyscraper; ground zero was the World Trade Center, a symbol of globalized capital. But at the same moment, it also dawned on the media to reduce architecture to a fad, to a fleeting lifestyle accessory or to the "stuff that surrounds you" [16] whose value is based on the lowest common denominator – namely, the taste of the general public. Architecture – or rather everything we subsume under that heading and regard as such – thus exists in a relationship of extraordinary dependency upon the media, and this situation sure hasn't done anything to redirect into a positive direction architects' schizoid strivings for attention.

COMMUNICATION IN THE MASS MEDIA HAS LONG SINCE CEASED FUNCTIONING AS A SOURCE OF IMPORTANT INFORMATION – FOR INSTANCE, TO FACILITATE ORIENTATION IN AN EVER-MORE-COMPLEX WORLD.

Instead, communication itself has become a transcendent magnitude, mostly self-referential. The more the mass media draw from their own reality, the more attractive they become and the better they are able to appropriate reality in its sublime entirety. "Extra-medial" reality is increasingly left out of the picture and a new medial reality is created. As out-of-touch as this may sound, it is in fact thoroughly realistic since even those outlets that, through their mediation of secondary experience, dispose over an apparent monopoly on shaping their audience's image of reality have long been pursuing this strategy. On one hand, they deal more and more in the thematic merchandise on hand in their own inventory; on the other hand, they have developed a gift for putting any topics that strike their fancy onto the agenda as long as we find them interesting or at least new. Amateurish programming and even "bad" taste thus suddenly attract a cult following. In contrast to the way things used to be, it's no longer about ratings alone in the media. Now, there's something that guarantees even higher revenues: forming a community that, strictly speaking, can also be regarded as a staged gathering of people with similar tastes and convictions for the purpose of increasing profit derived from the economy of attention. In order to temporarily prop up the illusion of this reality, any

recollection in the community's consciousness of a prior presence of any sort of similar reality has to be expunged. In contrast to Machiavelli's prescription, the old stuff isn't just razed in order to erase it from our memory; instead, it's staged as something totally new, as hype.

THE HISTORY OF ARCHITECTURE AND ITS INSTITUTIONAL BEGINNINGS ALSO BEAR THE MARKS OF A MEDIAL REALITY.

Since its very inception, architecture has been determined by an ongoing search for generally accepted, universal rules beyond the realm of fleeting fashion and personal taste. Indeed, this was the very reason why architecture in the 19th century – thus, at the very time it found itself in the deepest "abyss" of its history – began to be taught as a field of study in its own right on the university level. This was a time when the growing influence of architectural publications disseminating diverse and contradictory theories about the arts gave rise to a prevailing climate of stylistic chaos and confusion. [17] As a result, there was widespread support for instituting institutional control over formal instruction (and, of course, media as well) as a means of subordinating architecture to what was purported to be a universal system. This development was typical of the 19th century and, as Michel Foucault has pointed out, had an impact on other disciplines as well: "From the 19th century on, every scholar becomes a professor or the director of a laboratory. This means that the 'freelance' scholar (who performs no other function than to speak the truth or to dispense counsel) disappeared and was replaced by those whose knowledge is immediately authenticated by the power they wield." [18] The practitioners of Modernism,

[17] Mark Wigley, "Prosthetic Theory, The Disciplining of Architecture" in: Assemblage, no. 15 (Cambridge, MA, 1991), p. 11.
[18] Michel Foucault, Mikrophysik der Macht, Über Strafjustiz, Psychiatrie und Medizin (Berlin: Merve, 1976), p. 120.

although they rejected the teachings of their predecessors – as exemplified by Walter Gropius' line about destroying the library at the Harvard Graduate School of Design – were also convinced that there existed a universal system in which the true and timeless essence of architecture was to be found. Accordingly, whole generations of architects complied with the precepts of their Masters by wrapping their structures in white uniforms whose shapes were

DERIVED FROM BASIC GEOMETRIC FORMS IN THE BELIEF THAT THIS WAS THE WAY TO REJECT TRENDINESS IN FAVOR OF THE RIGOR OF FUNCTION.

And even at a time when gurus like Le Corbusier, whose published remarks were disseminated far beyond the borders of Europe, had long since taken leave of fashion's catwalks full of white uniforms, there were still those who believed in the white surfaces' resistance to the processions of short-lived fashions and were unwilling to recognize that this architecture was nothing but a seemingly anti-modern fad adroitly staged and propagated by the media. High on Modernism's agenda was satisfying the needs of the masses, whereas nowadays the point is to continually arouse new needs, and this is what has simultaneous given rise to the economy of attention.

ATTENTION ATTRACTS PURCHASING POWER AND IS DECISIVE IN TODAY'S DOG-EAT-DOG COMPETITION FOR MARKET SHARE.

This explains why shopping and entertainment have embraced one another in an even more intimate symbiosis. Retailing needs the right staging, which, in turn, is dependent on the consumer's attention.
The merchandise itself is available in great abundance but attention is always in short supply, which is why attention has become a life-or-death resource in Late Capitalist Society. For instance, the media might latch on to a building by Herzog & deMeuron (Vinery) or Peter Zumthor (Bad Vals) promptly after its completion in order to promote some

contemporary lifestyle or a particular take on fashion in a feature one day, only to dismiss it as "out" the very next, [19] whereby the architect as well is at the mercy of the fickle finger of fashion.

ACTUALLY, ANYONE UNABLE TO DRAW ATTENTION TO HIMSELF NOWADAYS DOESN'T EVEN EXIST ANYMORE.

After all, the merciless laws of the economy of attention apply equally to the architects and to the objects they create, and this paves the way for incessant publicity-seeking and the media's search for what is new and original and anything that has news value.

Architecture as a discipline has traditionally strived for the timeless and has sought universal-autonomous rules as a means of achieving it; today, however, architects are schizophrenically obsessed with attracting attention, which dictates that they submit to the zeitgeist and toss to the wind the warning that "Speed Kills!" They thereby uncritically call into question their own time-honored aims while still claiming to posses the universal-autonomous knowledge that justifies their status as guardians of the public interest.

Staging/De-Staging

Naturally, architects have recognized this unbearable lightness of seeming and are now going all out on the dramatic staging of their productions.

CLEAVING TO THE BELIEF THAT THE GENERAL PUBLIC NO LONGER PAYS ATTENTION TO ARCHITECTURE'S ORIGINAL MESSAGE ANYWAY, THEY FIRST TRIED ADORNING IT UP WITH IMPRESSIVE-SOUNDING PRONOUNCEMENTS FROM BIOLOGISTS, COMPUTER SCIENTISTS, DROMOLOGISTS (TACHOLOGISTS TO BE PRECISE), LITERARY CRITICS, ETC.

But as solemn as they sounded, these communiqués from the other ivory towers nevertheless failed to yield any added value in the economy of attention since, just like in the art world, it turned out that the epistemes of science don't follow any internal logic either. In art, nobody's taste is infallible; but now, it's becoming increasingly clear that the findings of science as well are subject to arbitrariness from the very outset and, as Foucault realized, Francis Bacon's dictum that "Knowledge is power" actually got it reversed, since power always brings forth its own knowledge. [20]

IN THIS RESPECT, ARCHITECTS, IN PURSUING THIS STRATEGY OF APPARENTLY OPENING UP TO OTHER DISCIPLINES, HAVE PUT THEIR MONEY ON THE WRONG HORSE.

But this wasn't really a case of a profound interdisciplinary encounter anyway since, in this regard, the profession is rather more tempted to react reflexively – and not reflectively – to the zeitgeist in order to enwrap itself in a certain popular (scientific) image. Moreover, many of the authors that it has been so fashionable to cite in this context – the likes of Baudrillard, Deleuze and Virilio – have difficulties of their own even understanding theories derived from the natural sciences, as Alan Sokal and Jean Bricmont pointedly demonstrated in their book "Fashionable Nonsense. Postmodern Intellectuals' Abuse of Science." [21]

17[Mark Wigley, "Prosthetic Theory, The Disciplining of Architecture" in: Assemblage, no. 15 (Cambridge, MA, 1991), p. 11.
18[Michel Foucault, Mikrophysik der Macht, Über Strafjustiz, Psychiatrie und Medizin (Berlin: Merve, 1976), p. 120.
19[On this subject, also see The New York Times Magazine, September 20, 1998, Part 2; and Wallpaper (London, January/ February 1998).
20[Thomas Duschlbauer, Medien und Kultur im Zeitalter der X-Kommunikation (Vienna: Braunmüller, 2001), p. 32.
21[Alan Sokal, Jean Bricmont, Eleganter Unsinn, Wie die Denker der Postmoderne die Wissenschaften mißbrauchen (Munich: Beck, 1999), p. 22.

5

Another strategy and form of staging of the schizo-architects is the internalized form of self-de-staging that can simultaneously be interpreted as seeking refuge in the meta-message.

Authors have been leading a similar chant for years. For example, they complain in every TV interview they give that the good old book is being displaced by television, the computer and video games, that the poet in his simple, unpretentious garb is a mere relic, and that their relatives, fellow authors and the publisher are the only ones who show up at their readings.

The message of this self-de-staging, which is also being masterfully disseminated by architects at present, is: "Look at us. We're no longer extant. Therefore, we still exist only for ourselves." This is why the architect has actually himself become the monument of architecture.

IN PRINCIPLE, THIS STRATEGY FOLLOWS THE LOGIC OF THE PERVERSION OF THE ECONOMY OF ATTENTION –

If I am no longer perceived from outside, and am no longer extant for this external world, then I simply declare the external world to no longer exist.

Architecture

More and more architects have come to cherish the belief that what they do is legitimate because there's a demand for it. They produce a completely safe architecture, something arbitrary, just space that people can more or less walk in and out of. Modernism brought forth a bold and fertile architecture, but what's being turned out today – at least since the '90s – is what society absorbs or, in the most favorable case, simply consumes.

THERE'S NO MYTHOLOGY LEFT SURROUNDING ARCHITECTURE – EXCEPT FOR THE MYTH OF NORMALITY, OF COURSE.

What can we do to get things moving in the right direction: towards professional renewal and raising practitioners'

ambitions, which is irrevocably interconnected with the development of self-criticism and even with the danger of failure. We think that liberation from the comfortable, risk-free dream-world of social acceptance that we are currently enjoying is indispensable. But to achieve this, it is necessary to rethink our techniques, instruments, skills and (schizoid) claims after not having hesitated in the least to expose them to the intensive processes of the outside world.

THUS, WHAT IS CALLED FOR FIRST AND FOREMOST IS AN ASPIRATION TO REALITY,

followed by concentration on our own expertise and coupled with a culture of cooperation on stable positions. In this regard, we think that architects ought to stop constantly groping about in the dark in other disciplines. We would be better off solidifying our own capabilities. Practicing architecture implies that the practitioner possesses some very specific knowledge and skills that continue to be undervalued in the current context of new technologies, the transience of all types of processes, and interdisciplinary exchange.Therefore, the problem is not to acquire new capabilities but rather to apply our own expertise more effectively.